In Praise of *Year of No Garbage*

"It's about time someone looked carefully at this part of everyone's life—and thank heaven it was someone with a sense of humor and grace. You will learn a lot!"

—Bill McKibben

"What starts out as a humorous search for Zero Waste turns into a profound investigation into the limits of personal responsibility in a culture thoroughly entrenched in toxic plastic. *Year of No Garbage* is both a delightful memoir and the wakeup call we need to start seriously addressing the Plastic Crisis today."

—Judith Enck, Former EPA regional administrator and founder of Beyond Plastics

"*Year of No Garbage* is an utterly delightful read! Schaub is relatable, informative, and non-judgmental. Her book encapsulates the many ups and downs of trying to reduce one's waste, and most importantly shining the light on one of the biggest problems—manufacturing and policy."

—Kathryn Kellogg, author of *101 Ways to Go Zero Waste*

"This year gave me *emotional damage!* I couldn't believe how much disposable plastic we all use every day and how harmful it really is. Read this book and you will never look at garbage the same way again."

—Steven He, YouTuber, creator of the "emotional damage" meme, 14 million followers

Dedicated to the Beyond Plastics community
And the optimists, activists, and true believers everywhere

YEAR OF NO GARBAGE

Recycling Lies, Plastic Problems,
and One Woman's Trashy
Journey to Zero Waste

A Memoir

EVE O. SCHAUB

Skyhorse Publishing

Skyhorse Publishing books may be purchased in bulk at special discounts for sales promotion, corporate gifts, fund-raising, or educational purposes. Special editions can also be created to specifications. For details, contact the Special Sales Department, Skyhorse Publishing, 307 West 36th Street, 11th Floor, New York, NY 10018 or info@skyhorsepublishing.com.

Skyhorse® and Skyhorse Publishing® are registered trademarks of Skyhorse Publishing, Inc.®, a Delaware corporation.

Visit our website at www.skyhorsepublishing.com.

10 9 8 7 6 5 4 3 2

Library of Congress Cataloging-in-Publication Data is available on file.

Cover design by Erin Seaward-Hiatt

Print ISBN: 978-1-5107-7463-6
Ebook ISBN: 978-1-5107-7540-4

Printed in the United States of America

SUSTAINABLE FORESTRY INITIATIVE
Certified Chain of Custody
Promoting Sustainable Forestry
www.forests.org
SFI-01268
SFI label applies to the text stock

CONTENTS

TEN STATISTICS
TO BE HORRIFIED BY

1. Trash is America's number one export.[1]
2. The average American singlehandedly produces enough trash in their lifetime to build a Statue of Liberty: over one hundred tons of garbage.[2]
3. Ocean garbage patches now occupy 40 percent of our oceans. [3]
4. By 2050 there will be more plastic in the ocean than fish.[4]
5. If plastic were a country, it would be the fifth-largest producer of carbon emissions.[5]
6. In its history, eight billion metric tons of plastic have been produced.[6] That's the mass equivalent of 100 Moons.[7]
7. Between now and 2060, global producers are on track to triple plastic production.[8]
8. Microplastics have been found in the ocean, the soil, and the air of the most remote places on earth.
9. Microplastics have been found in human blood, lungs, breast milk, placenta, and poop.
10. No one yet knows exactly what the health effects of microplastics in the human body will be.

To do your best is no longer good enough.
We must all do the seemingly impossible.
—Greta Thunberg

INTRODUCTION

A TRULY TERRIBLE IDEA

When I was a little kid in the 1970s watching *Sesame Street*, I loved Oscar the Grouch. Probably for the same reason so many kids loved him; Oscar was everything kids weren't supposed to be: Mean. Dirty. Grouchy.

And he kept things that were supposed to be thrown away.

At our house we even had the record that featured Oscar singing his signature song "I Love Trash." In it, he gleefully lists his favorite trashy belongings: A holey sneaker. Rotten fish wrapped in newspaper. A broken clock, umbrella, and telephone. Old trombone parts.

What I never noticed back then about Oscar's trashy treasures is that they looked nothing like my family's actual trash. Instead, they were what we'd all like to *think* trash is: objects that have gone bad or been used up, presumably after a long and useful life. But even in the 1970s that's not what most trash was. Most trash then, and even more so today, was disposables: items whose whole purpose was to be used once and then discarded.

Tin cans. Glass bottles. Aluminum foil. Plastic bags.

Back then, most people didn't see any problem with that. In television commercials we sang along with Woodsy the Owl about keeping America "looking good," and understood that the Native

American with a tear in his eye would stop crying if we just stopped littering. Everyone knew that trash was fine as long as it ended up in its proper place: the garbage can. What happened after that, few people concerned themselves with. I wouldn't encounter an actual recycling bin until I went to college. Like everybody else we knew, my parents threw pretty much everything into one big garbage can: tin cans, plastic containers, cereal boxes, glass bottles, and food scraps.

I clearly recall gazing into the black plastic bag under the sink and thinking to myself: *Huh. That doesn't seem quite right.*

Garbage. Trash. Rubbish. Waste.

Whatever you want to call it, we *love* it.

Americans love garbage so much that we lead the world in creating it. If there were a Trash Olympics, we would bring home all the gold: the average American creates over one ton of garbage per year.[1]

In our lifetimes, each one of us will leave behind an average of 102 tons of trash.[2] A blue whale's worth of garbage.

Or a Boeing 747.

But, in the grand scheme of things, is this important? After all, it's a big planet. What does it really matter how much we all throw away?

It matters. It matters because when we say "garbage" what we're really saying is climate change. What we really mean is discrimination. What we really mean is cancer. Garbage is at the root of so many things that are going wrong in the world today—from global warming and environmental racism to cancer: the number two killer of Americans—and it's getting worse all the time.

It can be hard to understand the extent of the problem, though, because trash is a thing we're used to hiding. Of course, its invisibility is part of the allure of trash. We love it because we don't have to look at it; we love it because it's a problem that goes away. And throughout all of human history, it has.

Today, however, we live in a unique moment. Because humans are producing waste on an unprecedented scale, much of it plastic, the system that has long made garbage disappear is starting to break down. Our trash is no longer invisible; it's everywhere, and it's not going away:

- Ocean garbage patches now collectively occupy 40 percent of our oceans, a larger square mile area than all the land on earth combined.[3]
- Landfills have become mausoleums of trash so airless that nothing degrades, not even organic material.[4]
- Trash is America's number one export, dumped on the landscapes of impoverished nations around the world all in the name of a fictitious system of "recycling."[5]
- It's not just in our environment—the trash is ending up in our bodies as well. Recent studies prove that we all ingest about a credit card's worth of plastic per week.[6] The toxic body burden of plastic has been correlated with endocrine disruption, neurodegenerative disorders, cardiovascular disease, and cancer.[7]

It's much harder to ignore trash when it just keeps showing up: at your local beach, in your backyard, in your food, and in your body.

Fast-forward to me as a young adult, married and living in Vermont. We were doing construction at our house that involved moving an old barn, and in the process a lot of dirt got stirred up. One day my husband, Steve, came to tell me that they had discovered the "old garbage dump" of the house. Because our late 1800s house predates the invention of the garbage truck, apparently people used to just toddle across the dirt road and pour their trash down the hillside. Voilà!

But most of the trash that was being uncovered was actually pretty recent. Tin cans, some glass bottles . . . from the looks of them it was only in the 1940s or 1950s that people had started to toss things that had no intention of degrading anytime soon.

I was amazed by this. That moment—the one in which some-one decided it was okay to discard perfectly good materials—has stuck with me ever since. I guess because it is representative for me of what came before it: living *without* disposability. Although archaeologists can attest to the fact that "garbage" has been with humankind for a very long time, the idea of going to the trouble of making an object only for it to be briefly used and then discarded is extremely modern.

"Trash is new," Rivka Galchen wrote in an article for the *New Yorker*. "During the nineteenth century, New York was dirty but much of its garbage consisted of leftovers and scraps and other items to reuse. Sunday's roast became Monday's hash; Monday's bread became Wednesday's bread pudding. Pigs roamed the streets, eating old lettuce and radish tops. 'Swill children' went from house to house, collecting food scraps that they sold to farmers as fertilizer and animal feed. Bones became glue. Old grease was turned into tallow candles, or mixed with ashes to make soap. Disposable packaging was almost nonexistent."[8]

Something about trash just kept fluttering at the edges of my consciousness, leaving me feeling bothered in a vague, unspecific way. At some point the term *Great Pacific Garbage Patch* entered my vocabulary, and like many folks for a long time I imagined an actual island of trash that a person could literally get out and walk along, perhaps bobbing up and down with the currents flowing underneath. A while after that I became aware of the ladies on social media holding up mason jars to represent their trash for the year. *What was one to make of that?* I wondered.

At one point I was asked to help sell cards at a local bingo fundraiser, an event that the folks running it clearly had down to a science. At the end, as the bingo-ers lucky and unlucky alike began to file out, the ladies sprang into action like a well-oiled machine: rolling up plastic tablecloths from each long row of tables, gathering along the way anything and everything that happened to have been left behind on them. Plates, cups, returnable cans, bingo cards, discarded food. It seemed to me that a wad of hundred-dollar bills and a baby zebra wouldn't have deterred them from the path they pursued with the efficiency of a genial bulldozer. One colossal armful after another was carted across the driveway outside until the entire hall had been emptied of everything save the tables and chairs, and the dumpster outside was full to the point of overflowing. In a few days, I knew, they'd do it all over again.

Huh. I thought. *That doesn't seem quite right.*

Over time, an idea began to form. The more I thought about trash, its newness, the wastefulness of it, the more I thought: what if we *didn't* throw things away? People had lived without disposability before, once upon a time. Today there was a small but deeply dedicated movement of folks who espoused the virtues of "zero waste" living.

But, us, our family, in today's world . . . could *we* do it?

Could we live without garbage?

New Year's Eve was coming, and I was getting excited.

As of January first, our family would finally begin the experiment I'd been dreaming about for a few years now: trying to live for an entire year without garbage.

It was definitely a terrible idea, but not without precedent. I'd convinced my family to try living for a year without eating any added sugar in our food and we all lived to tell the tale. Because of that I'd written a book entitled *Year of No Sugar* that ended up becoming part of a burgeoning conversation about the negative impacts of the sugar-saturated American diet that is at the root of pretty much every Western disease you can think of. Film crews came from all over the world to talk to us about it. My kids got to be on television.

Then I decided to do a more personal project. As the self-confessed polar opposite of Marie Kondo, I spent a year confronting my inner hoarder and wrote a book called *Year of No Clutter*. While that project surely affected the family, it didn't hold a candle to the disruption that had been caused by the enterprise of avoiding sugar all day, every day, for an entire year.

But my curiosity still lingered on one last question, and three always seems to me like a nice, neat number. How would my family react to one last project? I had checked in with Steve, who responded with some very sensible hesitation.

"I just don't know if it's possible," he said, cautiously. "It could shut down our ability to function. I mean, you're fighting *society*." He wasn't wrong, but I was persistent.

Ultimately, he left it up to me to get the kids on board. If I could do that, all systems would be go. In fact, I was counting on Ilsa, our youngest daughter, to be my greatest ally because of her burgeoning interest in environmentalism. She was in the Environmental Club at school! This was right up her alley! We were taking a walk to the end of our road and back when I told her my idea and I waited for her enthusiastic response.

"Um," she said. "Can't you wait till I go to college?"

What?

"I mean, this will be like, *five times* harder than Year of No Sugar."

Ilsa was fourteen and about to start her freshman year of high school. She was, I realized, decidedly *not* keen on beginning at a new school, a school whose students didn't necessarily think of her as The No Sugar Girl, only to have a brand-new project thrust upon her identity. And one that had to do with garbage, for Pete's sake.

"I mean, I'm a teenager. I just want to live my life, and not have to be a guinea pig," she said. "It's tiring being the family who does everything first. And then everyone *asks* you about it." She made an exasperated face. "And the TV people come and ask you all the same questions every time: *What was it like? Were you mad at your mom?*"

Meanwhile, our older daughter, Greta, was nineteen and studying acting in New York City. When I broached the subject with her, I knew, there'd definitely be resistance. Since she spent most of her time at school, she'd be doing it alone, without us there to commiserate with when things got difficult or confusing. Surely a college-age kid would have more pressing concerns on her mind than her mom's kooky projects. I braced myself for another "Please, *no*."

"I'm in." Greta said immediately.

Wait. What?

"Even if I'm away, I'll still do the family project. I'll just come home and tell you about it."

Was she really sure?

"Mom, it's like a roller coaster. Sometimes it's fun, but once in a while you feel sick. But mostly it's fun. Let's do it."

Ever since high school had ended Greta had been showing signs of ambivalence about this whole growing-up business, which was surely not all it was cracked up to be. But all at once in that moment I saw her: young, but confident, sure of herself in a way I hadn't seen before.

And just like that I knew I was talking to my daughter, the young adult.

With both Greta and Steve on board, and Mom's solemn assurance that this was I-Swear-The-Very-Last-Family-Project-So-Help-Me-God, we managed to convince Ilsa that the topic of trash would not come to define the rest of her childhood existence. Probably.

And then everyone was ready. Everyone was set.

Who knew? It seemed that 2020 might be an auspicious year after all.

"We're going to live for a whole year without throwing anything away!"

So far, I had only told a handful of folks. Despite my enthusiasm all of them were highly skeptical. When I told our friend Bob that the family was going to do without garbage for a year his response was: "*Well*. Are you going to do without oxygen too?"

But almost always the reaction went something like this: There'd be a pause, a thoughtful "hmm" look, followed by a smile and then: "What about (*insert random trash item here*)?"

What about *milk containers*? What about *old clothing*? What about the *plastic cellophane wrap at the top of a water bottle*?

And as the new year loomed ever closer on the family calendar, in our house we'd all stopped countless times to look up and suddenly ask a variant of this question to each other.

What about Band-Aids? What about the paper they wrap our sandwiches in at the local deli? How about chips? Are those bags recyclable? What about toothpaste? Or plastic pull-tabs?

So many questions. Which, of course, is one of the reasons I loved the idea of this project. As the last week of December unfolded, it was as if every time I went to throw something into the trash I'd go into slow motion, pausing to consider: what was I really throwing away, anyway? And, as if for the first time ever, I really *looked* at our trash. Sure, there were things I realized on second thought probably were recyclable after all, and which were then rerouted to another bin. But many things were just "hmmm" things—things I had never been given a real reason to stop and consider before.

There were yarn bits from a knitting project. The wax coating from a block of cheese. Plastic netting from a bag of lemons. Foam packaging from a new piece of technology. The waxy wrapper from a stick of butter.

Oh my, yes, this would be a very interesting year.

We'd need some rules of course—a few general parameters we'd already decided and others that we haven't even realized we needed to consider. The main gist we arrived at was this: we could recycle. We could compost. We could donate, give away and sell. But *no* trash, *no* garbage, and *no* landfill. After one big final sweep of the house on December 31st, all the trash cans in our house would be removed.

And there would be a few important exceptions. If one of my kids needed a Band-Aid, or medicine with a made-for-the-landfill wrapper? They'd get it. Period. In each of our two bathrooms I installed a small wastebasket with a handwritten sign taped to it reading: HEALTH AND SAFETY. Also, my husband's photography business would need to continue to function, so his studio would still be able to throw away actual trash, with the understanding that he would work to minimize it as much as possible.

Given that Greta was now living in Brooklyn, a location that surely would present different challenges than those of a tiny town in southern Vermont, her experiences promised an entirely different vantage point on the project.

We would, of course, make mistakes. There would be dead ends. There would be a box to contain the items that represented all those moments, which I named the Whoops Box.

Steve renamed it the WTF Box.

On December 31, the very last day before beginning our family's Year of No Garbage, we made a video of ourselves emptying all the different garbages in the house—the wastepaper baskets, the container in the bathroom, the kitchen bin, and office garbages. *Who knew we had this many garbage receptacles?* Everything went into the bin outside. It felt weirdly celebratory, like smoking a last pack of cigarettes before going cold turkey.

Our garbage pickup service allotted us one ninety-six-gallon container worth of trash removal a week, and I'd been paying attention: we filled it every week. That meant our household alone was contributing nearly five thousand gallons a year to a landfill somewhere. This usually took the form of five or six or seven kitchen-size trash bags filled with everything from kitty litter and ripped pantyhose to food containers that were too moldy to bear opening again. Sure, we also had a ninety-six-gallon container devoted to "single-stream" recycling, and I thought we were pretty good about getting all the things were understood to be recyclable into it: cardboard, paper, glass jars, tin cans, plastics #1–7, and so on. Surely, if I looked into it, I could up my recycling game, bravely confront the moldy containers and wash them for recycling, discover what things could go in that bin that I hadn't known, or find alternative venues for recycling. Anything we couldn't recycle would have to be sold, repurposed, or given away.

I imagined I was at least somewhat ahead of the curve, though, because I considered myself already waste conscious. I mean, I brought my own bags to the store, I made my own yogurt to avoid buying commercial in plastic tubs, and I'd even installed a device on my washing machine that eliminated the need for laundry detergent (more on this later). I composted my food waste and had a small vegetable garden. We had a few backyard chickens, which meant I only had to buy eggs in cartons in their "off-season." And yet somehow we filled that ninety-six-gallon curbside container every single week. Easily.

This year? Our goal was to reduce that five-thousand-gallon contribution to *none*. And I have to admit, as the beginning of the new year loomed, I was feeling pretty good about our chances.

I mean, really. How hard could it be?

CHAPTER ONE

....

THIS SUCKS AND
EVERYONE HATES ME

W ell, *THIS* is going to be *fun*. I don't get to eat *crackers* for a
whole year?"

Greta was fuming. Crabbiness was coming off her like vapor off
a steam engine as we plodded back to her Brooklyn apartment in the
slush. We were returning from our first visit to her local grocery store
of the new year—our brand-spanking-new Year of No Garbage—
and I think it would be fair to categorize it as an unmitigated disaster.

"I'm just saying. Carr's Crackers are my *childhood*. They're part
of my *ritual* when I come home from classes. I mean—*I've finally
figured out all the things here that have no sugar!*"

I felt terrible. Everything I said to try to console her just turned
into another argument. We can make crackers! *Yeah, but they won't
be as good.* They might be even better! *Probably not.* The Greta who
had breezily characterized this last family endeavor as "fun" only a
few months ago had been replaced by Greta the Supremely Pissed.

Of course, it wasn't just about crackers. The first five things we
had picked up in the store had *all* been returned to the shelves in
despair: clementines? Came in plastic netting. Bacon? Was in vacuum-sealed plastic. Battalions of dried pasta peered out at us from
behind cellophane windows, cheeses of all shapes and sizes snuggled
into their plastic shrink-wrap, and of course, the infamous, last-straw

1

Carr's Crackers, which our family well knows contains a crinkly plastic bag inside the paperboard box.

Ilsa, meanwhile, was just as indignant. Her eye had been on a package of smoked salmon and cream cheese pinwheels that had been wrapped in approximately fourteen different kinds of plastic, all of which shrieked *landfill!* to anyone who would listen.

So in between sparring with Greta on the hopelessness of our situation, Ilsa jumped in with her own helpful commentary. (Me:) What if we make our own pinwheels? We could buy smoked salmon and cream cheese. *Smoked salmon* comes *in plastic.* We can get it at the fish store! *I don't like that kind as much. Besides they won't sell it to you without a plastic bag either.*

Despair, despair, despair.

In desperation, I even pulled out the Big Picture Talk: "You know guys, this year . . . it's going to be a *process.* It isn't going to just be easy. And a lot of things we'll have to research and learn, and that's the value of doing this whole thing, right?"

They just looked at me with blank faces. Well known to parents of young people, it's the look that says: "Yeah. *Right.*"

By the time we were walking in the door of Greta's basement apartment, I'd about had it: "Look. Guys. It's day *two.* Are we ready to give up? Is that it? And Greta, you *volunteered* to do this in the city. If you don't want to do this then you don't have to."

Yes I do! No you don't! *Yes I do!*

There was an aggravated silence, broken at last by Steve. "So! How was the store?"

"It was awesome. *Everybody's mad at me,*" I responded.

"I'm not mad." Greta said, growing quiet. "I guess I'm just . . . scared." I was stopped dead by the abrupt shift in her demeanor.

"I'm sorry, Mama. I just feel like, if I don't do this project, I won't be a part of this *family* anymore." She paused. "And, I also feel like you've forgotten how hard Year of No Sugar really was."

She had me there. "First of all, you are *always* a part of this family, no matter what." I said firmly. "And second . . . you're right. Sometimes I think I remember, but I also think I forget, too." After a pause, I added, "Plus, you guys are older. You fight back *much* harder now." This made the girls smile. And just like that, the First Big Argument was over. We were on the same team again.

The fact is, I had forgotten how hard it is to do a big against-the-societal-grain-project like this. It's like swimming upstream, all day long, every day. How could I have possibly forgotten that? And how could I fail to take into account the amount of strain that puts on our family? Of course, I knew the answer to my own question: it was because I get so mesmerized by the power of the Big Life-Changing Idea, and I wanted so badly to do it. Was it wrong for me to ask that of my family? I don't always know the answer to that question.

But I was heartened by Greta's ability to identify her fear and her ready willingness to express it. If only, I thought, *if only* we can all manage to work together as a team, and not take our frustrations out on each other, that would be essential to getting us through this year in one piece. That, and a little luck. With that thought, I put the last few groceries away in the cupboard—a meager assortment consisting of bananas, bread in a paper-only bag, and a few cans of beans—and breathed a sigh of relief.

Then we went outside to find that our car had been towed.

Back in Vermont a few days later, the struggle continued. I felt like I was leading an expedition to the North Pole blindfolded. How could I tell my family to live in this new way, when I had no idea myself? Every turn presented fresh *I don't know*s, and the grocery store was the biggest minefield by far. Over and over, I was finding myself in the position of needing to buy food, yet being confronted by aisles and aisles of That Which Is Forbidden. Where before I had been amazed at the omnipresence of various forms of sugar in virtually every product on the store shelf, now I was dumbstruck by the shocking overabundance of unrecyclable packaging. And when I say "unrecyclable packaging," of course, I'm talking about *plastic*.

Crinkly plastic. Stretchy plastic. Molded plastic.

Whereas previously I had kinda sorta had the impression most plastics were numbered and mostly fell within the range of types that was accepted by our garbage service's single-stream recycling, I was now wholly disabused of that notion. What about bags with foil on the inside? Or produce stickers? Did those contain plastic too? What about the thin plastic tab that peeled off to open the milk? Or the clear plastic rings that encircled the lids and caps of nearly *everything*?

The learning curve was so steep I was getting a nosebleed.

Three foods had immediately surfaced as being the most troublesome in terms of avoiding disposable packaging, but the good news was that they were just incidental things, like meat, bread, and cheese. I know what you're thinking: well, duh. *Of course* meat, what with all the concerns about contamination. Heck, we can't seem to keep our meat disease-free as it is, even though we wrap it in enough single-use packaging to kill a goat.

But *bread*? I'm not even talking about sandwich bread, which for some reason comes wrapped for protection from the apocalypse, but even the "let's pretend we have a real bakery in the supermarket!" bread that comes in the homey brown paper bag, because those bags all too often have *shiny little windows*, presumably so the consumer can *see* the lovely bread without having to touch it with their dirty consumer hands.

Don't get me wrong. For the health advances made possible by modern packaging science I am grateful—*truly*. In fact, when I posted on social media a picture of my favorite peanut butter jar with a heretofore unnoticed-by-me plastic ribbon around the lid, a friend rightly commented that those plastic bands are *there to keep people from putting poison in my peanut butter*.

I mean, really. How dare the peanut butter people try to save my life? The *nerve*.

But, I'm aware that the problem of how to exist in a less-damaging way upon the earth, while deeply important, is nevertheless a first world problem. If you are facing starvation or fleeing oppression, you aren't going to care about whether your rice comes in a dolphin-friendly bag. You're just not.

Trying to figure out how to live with less or zero garbage, while a legitimate endeavor, is a challenge we are lucky to be able to prioritize.

So if I was whining about the annoying plastic wrap on my favorite peanut butter, I just want to be clear that I realize how fortunate I am that, on any given day, this was the biggest of my problems. There are an overwhelming number of people in the world struggling with food insecurity and ecological disaster. Do I think my frustrations with peanut butter lids and tangerine netting are more important than such immediate issues? Of course not.

But if we *are* in a position to choose what we eat or wear or buy, the ramifications from those decisions are significant, especially over the long term. One day we who have the luxury of choice may wake up and realize that all those short-term decisions have added up to something really bad, and could even become future sources of acute problems, including further instances of food insecurity and ecological disaster. The prevalence of trash in oceans, landscapes, and our bodies today makes the argument that, in fact, this is already happening. So I view focusing on the choices we make, when we have them, as actually a pretty grave responsibility. If I don't care about where this peanut butter wrapper or orange net ends up, or who it hurts along the way, who will?

Speaking of choices, I was a vegetarian of one kind or another for twenty years. So when it came down to it, if necessary, I could do no meat. And I have also been known to make some pretty decent homemade bread. But *cheese?* This one I honestly did not see coming. Just try finding a cheese, a single cheese product, in your local supermarket that doesn't incorporate any plastic wrapping. I'll wait.

See what I mean? It's crazy. It's as if cling wrap had to be developed first, just to pave the way for the invention of cheese.

I adore cheese. At this point in my life, I'm pretty sure my body is made up of about 95 percent cheese. I may or may not be getting emotional right now at the very thought of a cheese-less year.

But before abandoning all hope and barricading myself in the basement with a tear-stained copy of *Cheeses of the World,* it occurred to me to check in with our friends Robin and Patty, who own an Italian specialty food shop in the next town over. Patty assured me they'd be happy to cut from any wheel of cheese in the big glass case and . . . *wrap it in paper for me*. (Cue the Hallelujah Chorus.)

And, as it turns out, they also sold several types of homemade bread on-site that came in plain brown paper bags *with no plastic windows*. (Cue even louder Hallelujah Chorus.)

Sure, the ladies working the counter looked a little confused when I asked for Parmesan cut from the wheel when they already had about twenty different wedges presliced and wrapped in Saran Wrap, so rather than argue the point I settled for Romano instead. Heck—Parmesan, Romano, Velveeta—*who cared*? I was getting *cheese*, people. (Cue the Hallelujah Chorus, hip-hop/extreme dance club version.)

I know, I know. You've probably already guessed that this was expensive cheese. *Bougie* cheese. Which brings us to the inevitable conversation of whether living more lightly on the earth is a luxury only available to people who can afford it. This was a recurring theme with No Sugar as well. Hearing about my project, and how hard it was to avoid sugar in our daily lives, some would gripe, *Oh, sure, you can spend hours reading ingredient lists, cook homemade food, and buy more expensive products that have better ingredients, but* most *people can't. Most people don't have that luxury.*

And they were right. But part of my objective in doing a year-long project is not just to demonstrate how hard it may be to live in a way that's different from our cultural norm, but also to ask the questions: *Why is this so hard? Should it be? Are there good reasons to rethink things we have till now accepted?*

Change has to start with people showing up and asking for it. Organic produce, bulk shopping, co-ops, health food stores, farmers' markets, and even electric cars are now more popular and more accessible than ever before, and as the audience supporting those institutions increases, prices will decrease.

Acknowledging that everyone may not be able to spend the time or money necessary to go zero waste, doesn't let us all off the hook. We're still on the hook. And it's a *big* hook. Planet-sized, to be precise. But we can all start somewhere.

Even if it's just by changing how we think.

CHAPTER TWO

TRASH IS IN THE EYE
OF THE BEHOLDER

One day in February, as I was walking through our house I stepped on a piece of gravel, tracked in from our driveway, and picked it up with annoyance. Without thinking, I headed for the trash, when I realized (as I had done nearly every day since January first) that there *was no trash to put it in*. I stopped, stymied.

I looked at the piece of gravel. What the heck was I *doing*?

What, I wondered, had I *ever* been doing?

I mean, seriously. *It's a freaking rock, Eve*, I admonished myself. *Rocks aren't garbage . . . they're nature*. Why would I throw a *rock* in the trash? To be trapped in a nonbiodegradable plastic bag, hauled to the landfill, and sit there, smothered for eternity? Sure, it was tiny, the size of an M&M, but how many times had I thrown away a piece of gravel, and how many other people have done just the same thing? That, like anything, adds up.

How much more effort would it really have been for me to open the front door and toss that pebble out into the yard? At some point I must have made the mental calculation, *Oh, I'll just put gravel in the trash because that's easier*, but the difference was truly miniscule: between opening a door and not opening a door. And I knew I was guilty of myriad other, similar infractions. How many times had I tossed out a paper clip or a safety pin just because the trash was closer than the drawer or box? How many pencils have I thrown away because they were missing erasers, or simply weren't sharpened, or because we just had too many?

We live in a time of material abundance unprecedented in human history, and clutter is the thoroughly modern phenomenon that comes along with it. Surely, I can't be the only person who has ever thrown "perfectly good" things into the trash out of a strange sense of pure, unadulterated self-defense.

But what gives me the *right*, I wondered for the first time, to send something to the landfill? When did we become such masters of the universe? When did we become so careless with our resources?

As if to emphasize the point, the piece-of-gravel revelation was playing out in our house over and over like a broken record: what once we would have thrown out, now we were, for the first time, being compelled to really look at . . . and find another way. I'm sheepish to admit that in the past whenever a clothespin came apart I had considered it "broken" and would pitch it: *too hard to fix! Probably impossible.* I'd think. But when that happened to me now, I sat down and in about a minute and a half put it back together. I felt quite unreasonably proud about it, when I wasn't feeling a twinge of shame for not bothering till now.

And when Greta was visiting home and came across a huge entanglement of random yarns and craft scraps that had somehow all been shoved together in the bottom of a tote bag, she looked at me questioningly . . . what on earth were we going to do with *this*? Any other year, we would certainly have thrown it away. Instead, we sat down and started untangling. It sat on the coffee table for a few days getting progressively better in installments. Every time I was sitting and had a few moments I'd absentmindedly run my fingers through it some more, until one day it was no longer a horrible mess at all, but a neat pile of several different balls of yarns and fabric strips. Again, I felt both proud and a little ridiculous for feeling proud. I kept thinking: those bits and pieces can now be used. *Used!*

I felt like an alchemist who had discovered how to turn garbage to gold.

But the real discovery, I think, was that it *was never trash in the first place*. For the first time I could see it: trash is a made-up idea, invented in the name of convenience, which I was beginning to consider a dirty word. Because that lovely idea, as it turns out, comes at a terrible, terrible cost.

So sure, I had saved a teeny tiny rock from the landfill and who cares. But it was a teeny tiny rock that represented something much bigger, so instead of throwing it outside I brought the bit of gravel up to my office and placed it on a little wooden box as a pedestal on my desk, to remind myself that just because our culture accepts something, doesn't mean it makes any sense. Sometimes it's just a matter of stopping to really look at something for the first time that can change your point of view entirely.

Sometimes it can even be something right underfoot.

I had figured out that garbage was an arbitrary definition: trash is in the eye of the beholder. This felt like a key revelation, but it still didn't help me with the one activity that brought more far more new stuff into our house every week than any other: grocery shopping.

Although I had begun the year thinking our family could pretty much follow the same strategy as we had in other projects—simply don't buy *anything* that contains the thing you're avoiding!—that plan was not working. After that first day of New Year's shopping in Brooklyn I had realized we were going to have to break down and purchase some intended-for-disposal packaging if we were going to remain fed, at least for a little while.

So even though I was avoiding the big stuff (package overwrap, hard plastics with no numbers, packages within packages) the small stuff that I didn't know what to do with seemed never-ending. Oatmeal? Came in a cardboard cylinder with a thin plastic pull tab around the top. Anything in glass? (Salsa! Olives! Mustard!) Had a clear, plastic ring around the lid. Virtually all produce came with either little plastic stickers or plastic tags attached to their twist ties. For lack of a better word I'd call it "Ungarbage". . . incidental material that I did not want to keep and probably most other folks wouldn't want to either.

My solution? We just wouldn't dispose of those items. Instead we'd wash everything and keep it in neat little sorted piles till we figured out where it could go that was not a landfill or an incinerator. I firmly believed that all these different wrappers and containers had a purpose, a perfect home, if only I could figure it what that was.

The first order of business was to get a very serious grip on what, in this day and age, was able to be recycled, whether through the single-stream container (were there more things that could go in there than I knew about?) or other, more unusual methods I had yet to discover. (We had an outdoor fireplace, so why not try burning paper products that were not traditionally recyclable such as pizza boxes, tissue paper, and paper labels? I was vaguely aware of the existence of material drop-off bins and mail-in recycling. What was the deal? And what *else* was out there?)

Surely, if I did my research right, this would become a piece of cake. After all, recycling had come such an awfully long way in a relatively few short decades. The seventies, when I sang along with Oscar the Grouch, felt like the Stone Age by comparison with the resources we had at our disposal today, and even in the two decades since we moved to Vermont much had changed in the garbage/recycling scene. When we moved here in the late nineties, we had been instructed to leave our garbage at the end of the driveway in plastic bags, and it was collected by two guys in a pickup truck. Recycling was catch-as-catch-can: a very few recyclable items could be left, separated by material, in whatever container you had lying around—I learned pretty quickly not to use a laundry basket because they'd inevitably just take the whole darn thing. I was pretty sure I didn't want to know what really happened to any of it. Eventually this small-scale operation was bought out, and they got a bigger truck, but then they didn't take recycling at all, so we started taking our recycling directly to the dump, which accepted it for free.

The Dump. It just sounded . . . well, scatological, for one thing. For another, there's something kind of sad and forlorn about it. *This is The Dump. This is where we dump stuff.*

I'd never encountered an actual *transfer station* before. (This is the real name for the dump, which no one actually uses.) I was a little shocked: residents drove right up alongside a series of enormous concrete bays into which we poured our presorted recycling. If you peered over the edge you could see the cascading piles of stuff two floors down, a cavernous open space where the trucks of contractors drove in and out, dropping off construction debris. On most days the place was filled with the sounds of crashing metal and breaking glass.

Using this new system, we got the hang of an elaborate and somewhat grimy arrangement of different bins in our garage for all the different recycling categories: aluminum cans, tin cans, paper, paperboard, corrugated cardboard, certain plastics, green glass, brown glass, clear glass. White paper had its own box, but no staples, no binding, no colored or shiny paper please. Whenever our bins got to overflowing, we'd load up the car and dutifully cart it all over to the dump.

At that time only a very few, specific kinds of plastics were accepted. This was the first time I learned to check for what seemed to be the universal plastic recycling symbol, the number in a triangle, after which we had to separate within those categories: opaque plastics (such as laundry detergent bottles) went in one bin while translucent plastics (like milk containers) went in another.

Mind you, *no envelopes with plastic windows.* No glossy paper. No newspaper circulars. There were hand-lettered signs and admonishments posted all over the facility. Yeesh.

You can imagine our relief when our most recent garbage removal service was purchased by yet another, even larger one, and at last we graduated to a real, big-city-style garbage truck with mechanized arms that not only included recycling, but featured a new magical system called *single stream*. Ooooo! Paper, plastic, tin cans, everything now went into the same blue bin that sat at the foot of our driveway and we felt very up and coming and modern about it. No more trips to the dump! Forget trying to decipher if the can was aluminum or tin! Forget diligently sorting by color and opacity . . . you didn't have to puzzle over such minutiae. *Just throw it in the bin! No problem!*

We went on in this manner for years. Like most people, I had a vague understanding of what was deemed acceptable to recycle in this way, but didn't really focus on the matter. A lot of my "recycling" was based on assumptions rather than facts. Over time, more plastic "numbers" were added to the acceptable list. Eventually, as long as it had a chasing arrow triangle, regardless of which number, you could place it in the single-stream recycling bin. This was where we found ourselves today.

And this seemed like great news for our No Garbage project, because wasn't it true that the majority of plastics coming into our home had these numbers imprinted on them? The fact that the arrows looked like a sign for recycling made it seem quite intuitive: the presence of a recycling symbol meant the item was recyclable.

Only, as it turns out, that's *not* what the symbol means, and ostensibly it was never meant to. As I began to look into it I learned that the chasing arrow triangle system, also known as the Resin Identification Code (RIC), was introduced in the 1980s as a means of helping identify the plastics which were recyclable, but just because a plastic has a number on it isn't any guarantee of recyclability. Additionally, these seven numbers only represent a tiny fraction of plastic types. Many people see RIC numbers 1–7 and correspondingly think there are just seven kinds of plastic, when in fact there are tens of thousands.

Just what did these numbers actually represent, anyway?

"Chasing Arrow" Resin Identification Codes (RIC) Numbers: Identify Plastic Type, Not Recyclability

#1 PETE polyethylene terephthalate—water, soda, and cooking oil bottles

#2 HDPE high-density polyethylene—milk jugs, detergent and shampoo bottles

#3 PVC polyvinyl chloride—pipes, tubing, insulation

#4 LDPE low density polyethylene—flexible plastic film such as supermarket shopping bags, Bubble Wrap, bread and newspaper bags, Tyvek envelopes

#5 PP polypropylene—many "tub" style food containers such as yogurt, sour cream, takeout containers

#6 PS polystyrene—plastic utensils, Styrofoam, coffee cup lids

#7 *Other*—anything not #1–6—such as nylon, fiberglass, acrylic, and many many many more

---

But I'm getting ahead of myself a bit here. At this point in the project, I knew all I wanted to know which was this: if a plastic item had a RIC number, our single-stream recycling provider would accept it.

What about *non* plastic usual recycling suspects? In that area I felt like I was in pretty good shape. Here was a breakdown:

GLASS

According to Friends of Glass and the associated nonprofit European Container Glass Federation,[1] most types of glass are eligible to be crushed, remelted, and formed into new products. They only need to be clean and dry. The exceptions are: glass cookware (such as Pyrex), light bulbs, window glass, mirrors, drinking glasses and vases, eyeglasses, nail polish bottles, and actual crystal. In all these cases, coatings of different chemicals have been applied which can cause the glass not to melt or reform properly. For any of these objects which are still usable, they may be donated to a charity shop. Eyeglasses can be donated to the Lions Club, who will get them to a new user; look for eyeglass donation boxes in your local post office or Walmart, or go online and google "Lions Club Eyeglass Recycling Centers." Burned-out light bulbs depending on what kind they are, can contain mercury, lead, or arsenic, so look up take-back programs for CFLs (compact fluorescent lights), LEDs, and fluorescent tubes. LampRecycle.org and the industry-funded National Electrical Manufacturers Association is a good resource.

Red-alert items
Broken mirrors, broken drinking glasses, and broken window glass have nowhere good to go that I knew of, so I crossed my fingers those objects wouldn't come up this year.

PAPER, CARDBOARD, AND PAPERBOARD
Office paper, newspaper, colored paper, magazines, catalogs (even glossy ones), and phone books can all be fairly easily recycled. What paper can't be recycled? Waxed paper, shredded paper, and paper that's been decorated with crayon or water-based paint. However, all of these can be composted or burned. Even if they are clean and unused, paper napkins, paper tissues, and toilet paper can't be recycled, because the paper fibers are too short, but they can be composted or burned. Paper products that have been contaminated with food such as pizza boxes or paper plates cannot be recycled, but they too can be composted or burned.

Most paper coffee cups have a plastic polyethylene interior coating, rendering them unrecyclable, not compostable, and a source of microplastics that slough off and mix with your drink when the hot liquid is added. They are evil and should be sent directly to hell where they belong.

No paper that is mixed with plastic can be recycled, burned, or composted. Not sure if a paper contains plastic? The website Almost Zero Waste recommends crumpling it up: if it is just paper it will stay crumpled. Another test: try ripping the paper: if it contains plastic it will be hard to tear.[2]

What about cardboard boxes with shipping tape on them? Although many recycling experts say that removing that tape constitutes "best practices," there seems to be a wide consensus that the most important bit is simply breaking the box down flat. And indeed, if you watch videos showing how cardboard is recycled, there is a process to remove "foreign materials" including plastic.

Red-alert items

Because they contain plastic, most kinds of wrapping paper, receipts, photographic prints, stickers, sticky notes, and paper painted with acrylic paint have nowhere good to go and are best avoided entirely. Ask for no receipt or email receipts when possible. Look for wrapping paper marked 100 percent paper, or use old maps, aluminum foil, posters, or newsprint. (Steve has very fond memories of receiving presents as a kid wrapped in the Sunday funnies.) In my family I am famous for being the "ribbon saver." I have a box in the closet where I keep all the old ribbons and bows from presents past for reuse. Now I was saving pieces of wrapping paper smoothed out for reuse as well. I was amazed to realize that it really did still look nice the second or third time around.

If you have extra fabric lying around, try googling "furoshiki" cloth wrapping techniques. I feared this would be in a league with making an elaborate origami swan but in fact can be as simple as folding an envelope.

Of course gift bags made of paper or fabric are a great reusable option, but beware the Amazon gift bag: you know the one. It feels kind of crunchy and paper-like? Don't be fooled. It's made with plastic.[3]

What about tape?

To avoid plastic cellophane tape and shipping tape too, I pledged to try a recipe I found online from the renowned zero waste Chef Anne-Marie Bonneau: wheat paste glue. (Could this cure me of my extreme label-maker addiction?)

Wheat Paste Glue

- 1 cup water

- 3 tablespoons all-purpose flour
- Heat water in a pot over medium high heat and whisk continuously while slowly adding flour. Let paste bubble while whisking a few minutes as it thickens. Turn off heat.
- Store leftover wheat paste in a glass jar in the refrigerator.[4]

METALS: TIN, ALUMINUM, STEEL

According to zero waste expert Kathryn Kellogg, metal is the most valuable of recyclable materials. This category includes aluminum cans, aluminum foil, steel cans and lids, lids from glass jars, and even beer bottle caps. And did you know that metal aerosol cans can be recycled? Just remove the plastic nozzle. All metals need in order to be recyclable is to be clean and dry. Labels can stay on because they will get burned off in the recycling process, and yes, many cans have a thin, inner can coating of plastic but that gets burned off as well. Because most recycling has a hand-sorting component, Kellogg recommends minimizing sharp edges by shoving steel can tops back in the clean, dry can before recycling. Used safety razor blades sometimes come with a metal box for safe collection, but if not, Kellogg gives instructions for making your own on her website.[5]

Red-alert items

Well, anything made with heavy metals, such as mercury or lead, is problematic, so appliances fall into the difficult category, and batteries also incorporate metals that can be toxic. The good news is that although not recyclable in your single stream, all of the above items can be valuable for their components and therefore need to get to the right people for harvesting, scrapyards and e-waste collection programs being the best bets.

In our area, for example, electronics recycling is available at the transfer station at the next town over every Sunday. I have a bin in our basement for anything that runs on batteries or has an electrical cord attached to it that has given up the ghost, and when it is full I bring the whole bin to them. It may take some asking around or noodling on your computer, and once you've found a collection point be sure you're following their guidelines—some places have amount limits or fees for certain items. I think the effort is well worth the knowledge that you've done your best to keep all those heavy metals from contaminating the environment.

As for batteries, Call2Recycle is an industry-funded organization with third-party verification that specializes in battery recycling, you can visit their website to find drop-off locations in your area.[6]

Contaminated cans from oil-based paint or motor oil are the one red alert Item that there is no good solution for at all. These items may have toxic chemistry that is persistent and they need to go to household hazardous waste collection, do not pass go, do not collect $200. They will ultimately be landfilled or incinerated.

BUT WHAT IF I HAVE A CHOICE?

When presented with multiple options, is there a material that is a clear best environmental choice? In fact there is, and I bet you already guessed it isn't plastic. According to Earth 911, which has been around for thirty years and lays claim to being the largest online recycling database in the world, given the choice between plastic, aluminum, and glass, the most environmental choice is aluminum that has been 100 percent recycled, closely followed by the more ubiquitous glass. (This is because new aluminum is made with pit-mined bauxite, which causes erosion, habitat loss, and water contamination.)[7] What about steel cans? A similar problem to aluminum: the process to mine iron ore and produce steel is highly energy intensive and highly polluting.

More often than not? *Glass*, ladies and gentlemen, is where it's at.

Of course, even better than the very best recycling, as any Zero Waster worth their salt will tell you, is not to consume in the first place, if you can help it. "Reduce, Reuse, Recycle" is in that order not only because it sounds catchy but because that's the suggested order of desirability. One of the very best ways I can think of to start reducing is to eliminate the things that come into my house that I didn't even want in the first place. Pretty much everyone gets it too: I'm talking about junk mail. And since every year we cut down about a hundred million trees just to mail everyone this stuff,[8] it's worth spending a few minutes on.

JUNK MAIL

Here are some simple steps you can take to cut down on unwanted junk mail, with the caveat that no one solution will take care of all of it, and they all take several weeks to take effect:

Credit card applications

Don't you just love having to endlessly shred unsolicited credit card applications to prevent identity theft? Visit optoutprescreen. com to opt out of unsolicited credit card and insurance offers. You can choose between opting out for five years and opting out permanently. Don't worry! If you ever feel like you miss all that extra mail, you can revisit the site and opt back in again. They will ask for your Social Security number and birthday, which is encrypted, and if you want the permanent opt-out you must take the additional step of printing out a page and mailing it in. Opting out of unsolicited offers does not affect your credit score. This is the only legit way to decline preapproved offers from the four major credit bureaus, and it is recommended by the Federal Trade Commission.[9]

Catalogs

The Christmas Catalog Onslaught is real and it's a problem. To opt out of unsolicited direct mail marketing such as catalogs, magazine offers and donation requests, you have three choices. The first two are website services that are free and the last is an app that has a monthly fee.

DMAchoice.org

At this website you will be directed to a form asking for your name, address and email. A nonprofit organization, DMAchoice will remove you from lists as a "prospect," but be aware that if you have purchased from a company in the past, you are instead considered a "customer." In this case you will have to contact the sender directly to ask to be removed from their list. Yes, probably even if the only thing you ever purchased was a pair of whimsical socks for your nephew fourteen years ago.

There is a charge of four dollars, and the opt-out is good for ten years. If this, or the rudimentary look of the website, makes your wonder "Hold on, is this for real?" it is. This service is recommended by the Federal Trade Commission.

Catalogchoice.org

For a more hands-on approach visit Catalogchoice, a nonprofit that is part of the Story of Stuff Project, and if you know anything about them, then you know that they are doing wonderful things to save the world. On their platform you can search for each catalog you'd like to stop receiving by name. They have more than nine thousand catalog titles listed, as well as some political and charitable organizations.

You will have to type your name and address in for each and every catalog, which is annoying, but also allows you to target mail that misspells your name or lists your address in different ways. But the very cool part is that they will then contact that company and ask specifically for your name and address to be removed from their list. A personal dashboard keeps a tally of each title and when you requested the removal, which I must say feels extremely satisfying, and also a little addictive. Like a video game for the absolute nerdiest of eco-nerds. If you love this service as much as I do, make a donation—this funds their good work.

PaperKarma.com

This is a phone app that made its debut in 2012, and the concept is super simple: take a picture of your junk mail, and PaperKarma will contact the sender and ask them to unsubscribe you. You can try it for free for the first four items, after which you can enroll in a membership of three months, six months, or a year. Again, it's weirdly fun and like a mobile game for the very nicest

Earth weirdos. What I found most exciting about this option was that I could also submit other kinds of junk mail like big box chain flyers and mailers from meal subscription services. Which is great, because I thought I was going to have to put a restraining order on HelloFresh.

Okay, I admit it. After those three you actually have a fourth choice, because you really could call the 800 number on each and every piece of junk mail and sit on hold waiting to ask them to remove your name from their list, which they may or may not do. Which I've also done. The three methods listed above are way easier and more effective, and if you are serious I recommend trying all of them. The one thing you should *not* do is mark it "Return to Sender," because chances are very good they will just throw it away at the post office.

BUT BACK TO PLASTICS

Why was trying to buy only plastics that had recycling numbers turning out to be so much more of a challenge than I had anticipated? One reason, I was beginning to understand, is that many plastics aren't just one category of material, but a smooshed-together combination. Think: snack bags, like for potato chips. Is the material basically plastic or is that shiny interior aluminum foil? In many cases it's an amalgam of both (unless the shiny interior is Mylar, in which case it's *another* kind of plastic.) Other packages, such as for cuts of meat, might use a plastic tray that had a RIC number, but topped by a cellophane film that did not.

Yet another flaw with my flawless plan, it turned out, was that even when I was exceedingly careful to buy a recyclable outside package, I'd frequently find that—whoops—there was something unrecyclable on the inside of the package. At one point, Greta called to ask me what to do with the horrible little absorbent pads hiding underneath your chicken or steak, inside the outer packaging. I had never really noticed them before this year, but I sure did now: in a house where you can't throw anything away, this item was a clear early front-runner for The Most Revolting Thing You Could Ever

Get Stuck With. That's because even if, by some miracle, you found creative homes for the cleaned and dried outer tray, do you think there is a single, solitary place on earth that *wants* these soppy plastic pillows soaked in chicken blood and finely aged salmonella? Greta called these abominations *meat maxi-pads*.

Of course one obvious solution was to ask around and find out which places would let me bring my own containers, thus eliminating packaging altogether.

In the first few weeks, I learned that none of our local supermarkets would allow me to bring my own containers to the store to buy things like meat and cold cuts. That was a hard *no*. However, there was a butcher and a sandwich shop/deli that were fine with it, as well as a fish store—*yes*! I could hit my friends' Italian specialty shop on the way back for the cheese and bread in either paper-only wrappers or my own containers if I brought them. Plus, there was a health food store that sold some items in bulk: beans, spices, rice. One day I mustered up the courage to use their complicated-looking peanut butter grinder, so now I knew I could bring my own container for that as well.

After all that, for anything else left on my grocery list I would go to the supermarket.

You can see how buying a week's worth of groceries in this driving-all-over-the-place way could take up a whole honking lot of time and fuel. By the time I was done, I had visited six different stores, most of which were in a town thirty minutes from my house. I was making some progress on eliminating packaging, but there was a definitive cost: grocery shopping for the week that once took me not more than an hour was turning into practically an all-day endeavor, *and* I was spending more money on both gas and food *and* increasing my carbon emissions. It occurred to me that, oddly enough, living in the country was proving to be a major obstacle to living more lightly on the earth. If we lived in a more urban area I might not save any money, but I'd probably have a lower carbon footprint.

It reminded me of when I was a college student, studying for a semester in Rome. At that time, I was quite amazed at how many different specialty stores the Italians regularly visited just to gather their basic pantry staples: butcher, baker, pasta shop, outdoor markets. Part of this I think comes down to a European emphasis on very high-quality, very fresh ingredients, made by hand . . . something we Americans say we want, but often aren't willing to pay for.

Another factor is that so many European cities and villages are by American standards mind-bogglingly ancient and consequently have long been set up to accommodate a pedestrian lifestyle. Although there was decent public transportation in my Italian neighborhood, to buy food I never needed to use it; everything I needed was a short walk away. It was assumed you'd have your own basket or bag, and most things were wrapped in a bit of butcher paper and twine, juuuust enough to get your purchase home in one piece, instead of the bombproof packaging we Americans seem to prefer.

But dreaming about strolling around Rome shopping for fresh pasta wasn't going to help me now. I had to get creative, and fast. Because even with the running-all-over-town approach, the piles of clean, dry, what-do-I-do-with-this-no-RIC-number plastic were building up at an alarming rate. It didn't take long for things in the kitchen to reach a level of desperation.

For weeks, our house had been slowly devolving into a state of . . . *disarray*. What with all the careful washing and drying and not-throwing-out of various mysterious food packaging I had been doing, there now were piles: by the dish drainer, on the kitchen counter, in a corner on a chair. It occurred to me that an experiment in being zero waste was essentially a *machine* for clutter. All the I-don't-knows and the what-about-thises were quickly stacking up.

I'll look it up! Had become my new favorite phrase, but what I meant was: *I'll look it up later.*

I stopped to take inventory of the turmoil: on the kitchen counter I had a bowl of wine corks, right next to a pile of wax pieces from some blocks of cheddar cheese, each waiting for me to find a use for them. On the floor, a clothespin held a festoon of Mylar-lined items such as snack bar wrappers awaiting further investigation. Next to that was a supermarket shopping bag filled with other plastic bags that I was pretty sure could also be dropped off at a poorly marked bin I had seen at the supermarket near the aluminum can recycling. I thought this because I had read it somewhere. Always a foolproof strategy.

Next to all this I had a clear plastic bin holding all manner of other serious question marks. What about the penny-sized plastic spout that pops out of the top of the olive oil container? What about the plastic tag welded to the rubber band that comes on a bunch of scallions? What about a broken hair elastic? What about this postage stamp-sized silica gel pack? And foil lids from the tops of bottles! Were they shiny plastic or actually metal? I bent them and they didn't feel like foil, they felt like paper . . . What dark magic was this?

On top of all this, I had recently read that recycling companies apparently frown on our attempts to recycle the Small Stuff—anything smaller than two inches or so can supposedly jam up the sorting machines, or just get lost on the facility floor entirely. What did that mean for us—no small recycling?

Oh dear.

To deal with the situation I set up what I called the Super Awesome Recycling Center but was actually a three-foot wooden bench in the corner of my kitchen. On the floor underneath I repurposed some clear plastic shoe drawers and clear glass jars to sort the difficult, the tiny, and the weird. On top of the bench, I placed a bunch of open baskets for larger items, and bigger questions. Yes, everything was meticulously washed and dried, but I still didn't know where a lot of this stuff was ultimately going to, you know, *go*.

Details, details.

Life went on, and we pretended the Super Awesome Recycling Center wasn't starting to look alarmingly like a growing pile of very clean trash.

Then one morning, in the back of a kitchen cabinet, I had come across some ancient, expired boxes of yogurt starter. What normally would have been a two-second flip over my shoulder into the garbage can turned into twenty minutes of me opening each individual foil packet and dumping the powder into our compost, all the while fuming that the mysterious foil packaging was going to be the Next Problem.

As I sat there getting yogurt starter powder on my feet and all over the floor, I imagined a conversation with the yogurt company that began with me yelling at the folks in the packaging science department.

EXACTLY WHAT are we supposed to do with these after they are used? What do you mean you don't have a plan? These are just supposed to go sit in an airless, non-decomposing mountain for the rest of ETERNITY—is that it?

Ah, the poor yogurt starter people. After yelling at them in my head I felt kind of bad about it. After all, making yogurt starter is a noble profession, and one which enables people to use less packaging in other ways, since they're making homemade yogurt and not buying yogurt cup packaging.

Sitting there, looking a lot like a resident of Grey Gardens surrounded by my sorted but unruly piles, I wondered for the first time: Why on earth was the worldwide packaging industry *allowed* to make things that we had no plan for after their initial use is done? Not being able to throw anything away was making me aware of this giant invisible loophole in our produce-and-consume economy that no one wants to talk about.

In fact, even *I* didn't want to talk about it. Every time Steve brought up the looming pile of crap in the kitchen, I would feign ignorance ("What pile of crap? Could you be more specific?") and hide in the pantry.

"I know this is the Family Project, but we've got to start finding solutions for some of this stuff," he'd say. "I didn't sign on for keeping all our garbage in the kitchen corner for a year."

He wasn't wrong. At the rate I was going, we'd be on an episode of *Hoarders* before the first day of summer.

I was going to have to Sherlock Holmes the shit out of this.

CHAPTER THREE

I BECOME THE SHERLOCK HOLMES OF RECYCLING . . . OR AT LEAST WATSON

Remember when recycling was really *hard*? Like stupid hard. I had almost forgotten it, somehow. Back before we even moved to Vermont, in the 1980s, back when recycling required a near-fanatical level of commitment by people who were willing to do things like remove the staples from catalogs, steam the labels off of tin cans, and cut the little plastic windows out of envelopes.

It was the Era of Ridiculous Commitment Recycling. It was the province of only the most hard-core earth-lovers who drove cars with "Love Your Mother" bumper stickers. The kind of people who could cite the benefits of wheatgrass juice and knew to write the tare weight on the jars they brought to the co-op from home. These were the select few who brought their own reusable grocery bags to the store back when it was kind of a weird thing to do.

Up until my senior year in college in the early 1990s, *my* efforts to save the earth had consisted mostly of me wearing long flowery dresses and Birkenstocks. It was going pretty well. I stopped buying green grapes because . . . something about Cesar Chavez? I dutifully cut up six-pack rings so they wouldn't strangle turtles.

It was at this point that the city I lived in debuted its progressive new curbside recycling program.

Curbside recycling? Who had ever heard of such a thing? I was excited to be in the absolute forefront of green technology.

Immediately, though, I was frustrated by the fact that after rinsing and separating all my items and placing them carefully by the curb in a laundry basket, about half the items would get left behind by the city trash collectors.

In retrospect I find it kind of amazing that the trash people had the time to sort through my proposed recycling as if it were my senior thesis. What was I doing wrong? "Oh, that's because you can't put in any container that could stack with another container," one of my more eco-savvy friends said. "Like yogurt containers or sour cream. It has to have a smaller top opening so things don't get stuck inside one another."

I don't even know if she was right. It just felt like I was failing some kind of earth-loving class, to which no one had given me the textbook. I clearly recall thinking, *Seriously? If they want people to recycle they can't make it this hard to figure out.*

And here I was thirty years later, having that very same thought again.

Going into this year, I *knew*. I knew I'd want to be No Garbage Zero Waste Superstar right away, which was, of course, preposterous. I kept trying to remind myself that the very fact that trying to live without garbage is super difficult—and at times virtually impossible—was the whole darned point: if it were easy there wouldn't be much to write about, and everyone would probably already be doing it, and the earth would be a happier, less trashy, more equitable, less cancer-filled, less disaster-prone place. The End.

Nevertheless, I still felt like I was failing, right out of the gate. I was doing it completely wrong, all the time, and I knew it, and it was kind of killing me.

What I was starting to realize was that virtually every single object I brought into our house on a regular basis—every grocery, every toiletry, every cleaning supply, every piece of clothing, periodical, or mail—now needed to be rethought. That's hundreds of things. Thousands of things.

I realized I needed to seriously interrogate all the piles about my house before they ate me and my family.

I would ferret out the truth. It certainly didn't help that the rules of the recycling world have been in constant flux ever since I encountered them for the first time three decades ago. One by one I would have to zero in on each material and find its own, particular solution.

I decided that every time I looked at one of the piles of clean, dry detritus threatening to overtake my kitchen, household and life, I would start with a supposition:

Someone, somewhere wants this.

PLASTIC BAGS

For a while now I had wondered what the deal is with those mysterious boxes at the front of the supermarket offering to recycle your plastic shopping bags. You know the ones: near the cash registers or the aluminum can recycling, a big carton or barrel with a slot in the top and a green recycling arrow on the side. I mean:

Who collects the bags?

Where do they go?

What can you make plastic bags into anyway? More plastic bags?

Can you recycle other *plastics in these boxes?*

I set about to find out. After a little online research, I ended up on the phone with Alexandra.* Alexandra works for Trex, and Trex is one answer to the question *Who wants a bunch of empty plastic shopping bags?* This is because Trex, among other companies, turns them into composite decking for outdoor porches and railings.

Yes! There is a company that actually wants these plastic shopping bags.

But it got even better. Because Trex didn't *just* want my plastic shopping bags; they wanted all my *low-density polyethylene*, which

---

* Names of customer service reps have been changed.

includes plastic film and a whole lot of things that I imagine most people throw away without a thought—I certainly had. With Alexandra's help I found an informational poster on the Trex website that I printed out and hung in our kitchen to remind me of all the many things that—as long as they are clean and dry—can go into this magical box at our supermarket. I was amazed at how many things this included in addition to plastic supermarket bags, many of which are not labeled with any RIC number, probably because, although they are technically #2 (HDPE) or #4 (LDPE), most single-stream recycling providers *do not* want flexible plastic film because it gets stuck and gums up their machines. The list included:

What Can Go in the Supermarket Bag Recycling Bins
- bread bags
- ice bags
- produce bags (both the kind that come on rolls in the store and the kind apples and oranges are already bagged in)
- plastic overwrap (from things like paper towels, toilet paper and water bottle cases)
- Bubble Wrap
- bubble mailers
- Tyvek mailers
- air pillows (deflated)
- dry cleaning bags
- Ziploc® bags
- newspaper bags
- cereal box liners (unless they tear like paper)

Now, if you don't find that list super exciting, then clearly you are not me. For one thing, this now opened up a whole host of products whose packaging I had thought was going to be extremely problematic, from sandwich bread to cereal. Yes, I'd still make my own bread or buy it from my friends' bakery. Yes, I'd still be bringing my reusable mesh produce bags with me on my shopping expeditions. Yes, I would still always choose the lowest-plastic option of any product, because at 300 million tons of new plastic made per year the world certainly didn't need *my* encouragement to make any more, whether it gets recycled or not. But still. One day when Ilsa felt crappy and asked for toast, it was a relief not to have to drive for an hour or wait for bread dough to rise all afternoon. I could just buy her a loaf at the store ten minutes away.

Now, as you are no doubt aware, wherever there are recycling guidelines, inevitably there are recycling *warnings* too. This is the part that says, in effect: IF YOU PUT ONE WRONG ITEM IN HERE YOU WILL DESTROY AN ENTIRE BATCH OF RECYCLING AND PROBABLY MURDER A POLAR BEAR IN THE PROCESS. These dire warnings all end with the same message: "When in doubt, throw it out."

I take issue with this. *We don't need more encouragement to throw things into the landfill.* What we need is better information.

Which is why I like people like Alexandra at Trex so much. Her job has everything to do with giving people more information so they can recycle correctly. It occurred to me that more companies should have an Alexandra, to answer questions from the public: not just about their products, but about their product packaging, and what exactly they expect us to do with it so as to not strangle the planet.

Alexandra answered some other questions I had too. She told me that when the plastic film recycling boxes at the supermarket are full, they get returned to the supermarket's distribution centers where they are converted into one thousand-pound bales. She explained that most distribution centers ship one tractor-trailer load of these plastic bales to Trex every two weeks.

Wow. Added up, that's a *lot* of not-landfill.

Most importantly, she told me a few simple steps to help people avoid putting the wrong kind of plastic film into the Trex boxes. Here they are:

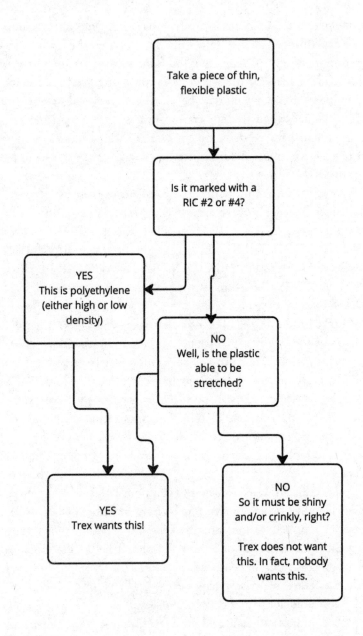

Things that fall into the shiny/crinkly NO! category include: prewashed salad mix bags, frozen food bags, candy wrappers, chip bags, and six-pack rings. In any case, anything going to recycling must be clean and dry: no food, no dirt, etc.

I'd heard much skepticism on the part of shoppers who theorize that these bins of plastic bags just get tossed in with the rest of the trash in the alley behind the store where naive shoppers can't see. And like any system, I'm sure there are abuses and some people not doing what they are supposed to do for whatever reason. But Trex seemed to be sincere in their desire to take and use this plastic again, which is certainly worlds better than having it all go sit in a landfill or get incinerated and disperse more chemistry into our environment.

On the other hand, as I began using the plastic film recycling bin, I saw firsthand that far too often it *was* being treated like a trash bin by careless passersby, which could surely render the entire container unusable.

Just like any kind of recycling, people need to do it properly for it to work, but most of us probably don't have a spare afternoon to track down the Alexandras of the world, so it occurred to me that companies like Trex and supermarkets ought to work together to make sure the public is better informed. Like, how about posting those informational posters nearby the bins? Or, I don't know, making sure supermarket employees can knowledgably answer questions about plastic film recycling? (Which, in my experience, they can't.)

Since it was now clear that, even while doing my earnest best to not buy disposable plastics at all there were going to be some I just couldn't avoid, I was happy to have a place for plastic film to go, while crossing my fingers that everyone else in the transaction did what they were supposed to do.

And then, I was off on the trail of another unsolved mystery. *What was the deal with cartons, anyway?*

CARTONS

When I was a kid, a mysterious aluminum cube sat outside our front door. Once a week it would fill with fresh, new glass bottles of milk.

I never saw the milkman, so it seemed a bit supernatural: put empty bottles in and—*poof*—new milk appears!

It kind of boggles my mind to think about it now. At the time no one seemed particularly worried about the milk spoiling out there in the non-insulated box . . . or freezing . . . or getting stolen . . . or that someone would try to put poison in our milk. The bottles each had a little round foil cap that peeled off the top, and once opened it never sealed quite perfectly again, but no one seemed too concerned about that either.

I know this makes me sound like perhaps I grew up sometime just before the invention of the icebox, but this was just the seventies, people. Plaid pants and avocado kitchens.

Fast-forward to my No Garbage project of today, and here I was obsessing about *milk*. Before this project began, I must admit, I used to rinse milk cartons and place them in the single-stream recycling thinking: *paper*. But soon after beginning the project I looked closer and thought: *Wait—no. Paper coated with* **plastic**. I was just beginning to understand that Frankenstein combinations of materials—such as paper and plastic squashed together by heat, say—are not only ubiquitous, but also, quite possibly, inherently evil, unrecyclable landfill fodder. Researching it, I learned that they are collectively referred to as "multilayer," and include everything from frozen food packaging to the thermal paper used for receipts.

While searching for answers online I came upon something called the Carton Council, an industry organization that promotes carton recycling. *Oh, hooray!* I thought. *Answers.* On their site you can input your zip code and it will instantly tell you whether single-stream recycling *that includes cartons* is available in your area. Now, when you live in Vermont nothing is ever available in your area, so I was sad, but not terribly surprised, to see that recycling in our area apparently did not include cartons.

Fear not! the Carton Council website assured me, because you can *mail your cartons in* for recycling. To places like Virginia and Nebraska.

Okay, at least there's something *I can do,* I thought. I didn't love it, first because any additional level of complexity or cost is going to make it that much less likely for the average person to actually do it, and second because the environmental footprint of mailing boxes of cartons across the country to recycle them seemed to me to raise serious questions about the net environmental impact of the whole endeavor.

Then I took a closer look at my garbage service "recyclable" list. Waitaminit! Contrary to what the all-knowing Carton Council website had indicated, milk cartons *were* on the list!

Then I noticed something else intriguing on the list for my curbside recycling: they also accepted something called *aseptic cartons.* What was that? The lady who answers the phone at my garbage service provider had no idea.

Back to the internet.

Aha! It turned out that in the world of cartons there are two kinds: refrigerated "gable top" (like the kind milk comes in) and shelf-stable "aseptic " (the rectangular boxes that hold shelf-stable things like juice, soup, and chicken broth.) Both are combinations of polyethylene and paper, but aseptic cartons include a layer of aluminum as well. (Just to make things more confusing, the Carton Council calls aseptic cartons "Tetra Paks," which is a brand name. They're the same thing.)

The good news seemed to be that unlike many other paper/plastic amalgams, both gable top and aseptic cartons *can* be separated back into their components for recycling.

The bad news was that this process requires a fair amount of energy and effort, such as trucking giant bales of the cartons hundreds of miles for elaborate processing. Although it keeps these materials out of the landfill, this still seems counterproductive to the purpose of being sustainable and earth friendly.

Hmm. So it turned out I could put my cartons, both gable top and aseptic/Tetra Pak, into our existing curbside, single-stream recycling, and putting them in recycling was surely better than not putting them in recycling, right? But better still would be to find alternatives, avoiding such packaging altogether.

Raw milk was one possibility. Several dairy farms in our area offer raw milk in glass returnable bottles for pickup at the farmers' market or farm. However, after a farm had a listeria scare in our area a few years ago, raw milk had lost some of its charm for me.

I knew the days of the magical Dellwood milk box were long gone, but I lived in hope of finding a local dairy that had regular, pasteurized milk in returnable glass bottles just like those of my youth. This is Vermont, after all, famous for having more cows than people. Which we don't. But we do have the highest *ratio* of dairy cows to people, which ought to count for something.

But alas, it was not to be. Although I hunted high and low, at least in our area, milk in glass bottles seemed to be a thing of the past.

PAPER TOWELS

So, there'd be no return to the hallowed era of the ruffled tuxedo for me. Still, the past was a place I'd started to find a lot of inspiration. Whenever I was confronted with the idea that plastic, and disposable plastic especially, was impossible to live without, I'd ask myself what people had done before there was plastic, and our current acceptance of disposability. After all, plastic was only invented in in the early 1900s, and only truly came into widespread use in the 1950s with the invention of Tupperware parties and Saran Wrap. So it's not that big a stretch to ask: How would our grandparents have done it?

It's curiosity about questions like these that make me a big fan of historical reality television. One of my favorites shows of all time is *Frontier House*, which premiered on PBS in 2002. This show took three modern American families and had them live as nineteenth-century pioneers somewhere in the Montana wilderness.*

Before being transported "back in time" some of the participants were asked what things they thought they'd miss most. They said things like makeup, showers, video games . . .

No one said paper towels.

---

* I would LOVE to do this, by the way. Steve wants to go to outer space; I want to go live in a log cabin. It figures.

The whole time I was thinking: *I know what* I'd *say: paper towels!* I mean, NO PAPER TOWELS! How did people *live?*

Ever since watching that episode I've wondered somewhere in the back of my mind if I could ever, truly wean myself from my fully absorbing paper towel addiction.

(See what I did there? I even like bad paper towel puns. Clearly, I need help.)

As if in reply to my question, on social media I had come across a tutorial on how to make your *own* paper towels out of cloth and then sew little snaps into the sides and snap them together one by one to form a reusable roll. As in so many of these DIY videos, the slick editing makes this idea seem completely brilliant. Wow! Look how easy it could be. *And no waste!*

However, after the idea sank in a bit, I was made of questions: hold on a sec here Pinterest people. How long would it take to make this gigantic reusable paper towel roll, *without* time-lapse photography? And once you had used the towels up and washed them all, how many *hours* would it take to snap all those tiny little itty-bitty snaps back together? And what if you sewed one snap just a liiiiiittle to the left or right and suddenly your lovely DIY project is NOT COOPERATING? And you *accidentally* throw the whole thing out the window after lighting it on fire? *That's* not very zero waste, now is it? If you ever did manage to roll the whole thing back up again— you know, say, three weeks later—is there any possibility it *wouldn't* look like a giant wad of used Kleenex?

So I had kept right on using regular paper towels at a rather alarming rate, despite the fact that I have an extensive collection of dish towels and cloth napkins. I mean, you know, sometimes the napkins were all dirty and I hadn't had a chance to wash them yet. Paper towel. Or, what if it was just a little bit inconvenient to go grab a dish towel? Paper towel. What if it was a messy, stain-y job involving spilled wine or something that I didn't want my pretty dish towels being exposed to? You get the idea.

So, in the beginning stages of our Year of No Garbage, I wasn't quite sure how I would tackle the Paper Towel Conundrum. I had discovered that paper towels are compostable, so that was good news, but it was also kind of bad news, because my kitchen compost container—which I use to collect food scraps to take to the compost pile at the edge of our yard—was getting filled up approximately every ten minutes. People were using one-use, disposable paper towels for jobs that could easily have been going to the dish towels, silly things like drying their hands off or wiping the countertop off. It was simply out of habit and because we knew we could.

It was hard to retrain myself and virtually impossible to keep everyone else away from the siren song of old, bad habits rooted in one thing: convenience.

Should I just do away with paper towels completely? I thought. That was one solution. I kind of felt like that was zero waste Ninja level. I hoped to get there someday, but at this point I still wanted to use them a little, if only for the very slimiest jobs such as wiping grease out of cast-iron pans and drying off raw meat and poultry.

Instead, I decided to switch the narrative: if the problem was convenience, how could I make paper towels the most *inconvenient* solution? I took the tempting roll of convenience and put it in the laundry room waaaaaay on the other side of our house from the kitchen. In a way I felt like I was just trying to hide them from myself, which seemed silly. I mean, *I knew where they were.* And anyway, surely something that simple would never work.

It totally worked. It worked so well I was kind of shocked. One day I was sighing and emptying yet another compost bucket containing 75 percent paper towels into my poor nutrient-starved compost pile in the backyard, the next it was like "Paper towels? Hmmmm. I'm not sure I'm familiar with those. Could you describe them?"

In the old days, it was not unusual for us to use up an entire eight-roll package in one week. Now that the paper towels lived in the laundry room, we'd use *one roll in six weeks.* Another strategy that's ridiculously simple but worked: don't buy more than one or two rolls at a time. Buying paper towel bundles the size of hay bales not only involved plastic wrap, it encouraged us to use more;

conversely having only one roll in the house at a time forced us to be judicious.

Maybe someday I will get to a point where we're *so* organized we have a separate batch of ratty dishrags for those greasy, ooky jobs, along with their own separate container to hold them between washings. But for now I felt really good that this worked. It all came down to an appallingly simple idea that I wanted to be sure to remember: *make the things you want to do easy, and the things you don't want to do, difficult.*

Now, if PBS came knocking, I'd be ready.

Ever since January first, our trash bin had been languishing in the garage, while the recycling bin was putting in overtime, recycling all the usual suspects: cardboard, paper, tin, aluminum, glass, and plastics #1 through 7. Now, in the basement were two additional bins: one for plastic film for deposit in the supermarket bin, and one for cartons intended to mail to the Carton Council (since I had gotten mixed messages about placing cartons in single-stream this seemed like a way to play it safe.) I felt like I was at last finding solutions and making progress.

But even though I was finding new information about packaging and ways to handle it all the time, it just never seemed fast enough. My kitchen piles were still gaining on me, spilling out over onto the floor like the Blob.

Even after incorporating the butcher, the fish shop, the health food store, the local deli, and the Italian store on my weekly rounds, I was still disappointed at the amount of nonrecyclable plastic I was getting in the bargain. Anything with a top came with a shrink-wrap plastic cuff around the lid. Anything in a box invariably involved crinkly plastic bags or sleeves. The closer I looked the worse it got. Not only did all the boxes of tea come wrapped in cellophane, but I then found out that often tea bags *themselves* were made of plastic. Even when a plastic container itself was recyclable, for products such as sour cream, guacamole, raisins, or nuts, there was inevitably a whisper-thin plastic sheet to be removed between the lid and the contents that was not.

Our supermarket snack choices became limited to fruit and . . . more fruit. I stopped packing Ilsa's school lunches because I just couldn't figure out what to put in them. At least at school they had a really good recycling and composting station, and the cafeteria had already dealt with the food packaging. It was loophole, but I was desperate.

You'd think plastic food packaging wouldn't be such a big deal. After all, our family doesn't buy lots of prepared or convenience foods: like many folks trying to avoid unnecessary additives and preservatives, I shop the perimeter of the supermarket, focusing on whole foods, and making as much as I can myself from scratch, from tortillas and chicken broth to yogurt. Given all that, how bad could the packaging really be?

The answer is really, *really* bad. All one had to do was look around my kitchen to see the evidence: plastic wrappers, containers, seals, caps, bags and boxes of every shape and variety in various states of being washed, dried and sorted—mind you, this was all *while I'm actively thinking about avoiding plastic all the time.*

I shuddered to think, *How much plastic had we been going through when I paid no attention?*

I resolved to double down. We were lucky enough to have a year-round farmers' market, so I would attend that more often, so to avoid things like vegetable tags and frozen food wrappers. I vowed to redouble my efforts on the *No receipt please!* front, although it is difficult when so many places don't ask you first if you *want* a receipt. They just hand it to you. Some cashiers seemed so intent on completing the standard customer-cashier script that sometimes I just didn't have the heart to tell them I didn't want it. Other times saying you don't want it doesn't mean they don't print it, it just means they throw it immediately in the trash after they do.

I still hadn't figured out how to buy chicken without plastic at all. Although the butcher who graciously allowed me to bring my own container did sell chickens, everything came to *him* shrink-wrapped in plastic from the farms. He explained that wrapping slaughtered chickens in plastic was "as per regulation." He kindly offered to remove the plastic and dispose of it for me, but that felt like a loophole too far.

Curious, I did a little digging to find out *why* I couldn't buy a whole chicken without plastic and ended up talking to the Meat Safety Compliance and Enforcement Specialist Briton Laslow at the State of Vermont. He explained that the law for packaging meats after processing was actually not as specific as all that. Citing the Code of Federal Regulations, he said meats simply had to be packaged in material that was food-safe, sanitary, and moisture resistant. For example, butcher paper with a wax coating would, in his estimation, also fit those guidelines.

So buying a plastic-less whole chicken was not technically illegal, however it might as well have been, since there were none to be found. Do you recall the *I Love Lucy* episode in which Lucy and Ethel accidentally buy seven hundred pounds of beef and end up putting it in all in a walk-in freezer in the basement? Filmed in 1952, what do you think all those piles of different meat cuts were wrapped in? White butcher paper, string, and tape. What that tells me is that we've done it before, and we could do it again.

For the moment, though, when it came to chicken I was stuck with what existed in my community today, which was inevitably plastic and more plastic. As a result, I couldn't shake the feeling that I was failing spectacularly at my self-assigned endeavor. The funny thing about feeling like you're doing something "wrong" though, is that you're presuming that there is a "right."

Truly, I was starting to wonder. Zero Wasters of the internet fitting their annual waste into a thimble notwithstanding, was living in today's world without throwing anything away even . . . possible? Before we began I had been so sure it was just a matter of pure tenacity, but even as I chipped away at finding certain solutions, gradually whittling down my kitchen pile, new plastics arrived to take their place just as fast. It felt like I was trying to shovel the walk while it was still snowing: could I ever make any real progress?

Steve wasn't happy with this; I wasn't happy with this. At a certain point, a pile of clean *UNGarbage!* in your kitchen is still a pile of garbage in your kitchen. Was it possible to do this project without having to either: a.) subsist solely on bananas and homemade bread, or b.) fill our entire house up with used plastic packaging?

We were not quite three months in, and for the first time I was faltering in my confidence. It occurred to me to wonder: *Is this something we can even really do?*

And then, while I was in the midst of this existential conundrum, something else happened.

It was called COVID-19.

CHAPTER FOUR

....

DID WE PICK AN AWESOME TIME TO DO THIS OR WHAT?

Remember that scene from the 1980s satire *Airplane!*? As things are looking ever more grim for the beleaguered folks on board Flight 209, a tough-talking air traffic controller played by Lloyd Bridges realizes he picked the wrong week to quit smoking. And drinking. And amphetamines. And sniffing glue.

After weeks of trying to decide whether the coronavirus was a head cold or the next bubonic plague, on March 11, 2020, the World Health Organization declared the disease an official pandemic. Major sporting events were canceled, schools started closing. For the first time in my life I saw my supermarket's shelves stripped eerily bare, whole aisles empty, while Ilsa and I, like everyone else, piled our cart with long-term staples: canned tuna, boxes of pasta, dried beans, bags and bags of flour. For the first time since January first, I didn't give a single thought to recyclability. I had been shocked out of my fixation on packaging, neatly eclipsed by fear of starvation, disease, and death.

Dr. Anthony Fauci appeared before the House Oversight and Reform Committee and said, "Bottom line, it's going to get worse."

It was starting to look like we had picked the wrong year to quit garbage.

Suddenly, a surprising amount of my energy every day was being devoted to the task of not being terrified. Even before the pandemic I was the kind of person who struggles not to hide under the bed every flu season. I already sang the alphabet song when washing my hands. Now I sang Wagner's Ring cycle.

Lucky for me I had a bunch of other things to keep my circular thought patterns at bay: I suddenly had a large house full of people to keep fed.

This is because Greta's acting classes had been canceled until further notice, and things were getting even weirder in New York City than they were here in Vermont. At the rate things were going, we didn't even know what would be possible from one day to the next: would the trains stop running? Would there be a citywide lockdown? Nobody seemed to know anything and that was the scariest part of all.

We thought Greta should come home. Yes, her boyfriend, Steven, could come too. Yes, her good friend Cristy could come too. Panic was in the air. It felt like the great flood was coming and our house was Noah's Ark. Luckily, we have a small guesthouse across the driveway that we often use as an Airbnb, so they could all stay there while we waited to see what would happen.

Overnight we went from being a household of three to being a household of *six*. Not long after Greta and her friends arrived home, Ilsa's school closed and began fully remote learning, so that meant everyone was home, all the time, and for every single meal.

I was delighted to have them all here, because at least then we knew our family was together and as safe as we could manage. I was delighted too, to cook for everyone, because that always makes me feel that I am caring for people. It gives me purpose, makes me feel that I'm literally making the people around me more happy and healthy.

The problem was that I'd never cooked for the Brady Bunch before, and I kept wondering where the heck Alice was. Between the fact that I make pretty much everything from scratch, and was doing all the dishes? Three meals a day? And with all the restaurants closed, no "Hey! Let's go out tonight and give Mom a break!" in sight?

It knocked me for a serious loop. I was going to bed exhausted, planning meals in my head, and waking up exhausted, planning meals in my head. At first, I was too stubborn to ask for help, although another part of it was probably my unconscious, deciding that it was better to be on the brink of exhaustion than to think about the things that were going on in the world just then. Social media was filled with images of body bags, pleas for ventilators, and rumors of mass gravesites on the small islands around New York City. People started rehanging their Christmas lights in a desperate attempt at cheer. As all six of us gathered around the dining room table, Steve and I tried to be reassuring to the young adults when in fact we knew nothing, *nothing* about what came next. We told them they were welcome and encouraged to stay as long as possible. We assessed our resources and liabilities like it was the end of the world, which felt both like an overreaction and exactly appropriate at the same time. We made plans to plant extra food in the garden this summer. We were down to three chickens in our backyard hen house, so we went out to the local Tractor Supply and bought a dozen baby chicks, who began their tiny new lives living dustily in the corner of our dining room in an aluminum tub.

I began to feel like the stress of uncertainty, and the round-the-clock eatery I was running was burning me out. With Steve's encouragement, I finally set up a calendar of chores so everyone in the house began contributing every day. After two weeks, Cristy made the decision to fly home to her parents in Chicago, which made us sad to lose her company, but in sheer practical terms it also meant one less mouth to feed.

I was struck by that old-fashioned phrase: *one less mouth to feed.*

In addition to keeping everyone fed, the other thing that was keeping my worry factory of a brain occupied was, of course, No Garbage.

The world is ending? Don't mind me, I'm just gonna wash some tinfoil and tie some broken rubber bands back together! Everyone around me is acting out the screenplay from *Contagion*? Pardon me, I have to figure out if staples are recyclable. Everyone I knew was running around with their hair on fire, trying to buy toilet paper and here I was having regular, fairly elaborate dreams about sorting recyclables and googling whether or not shredded paper is compostable.

My mind became a crazy seesaw between pandemic problems and No Garbage conundrums. I had so many questions about both—and so few answers. One day I sat down and wrote a list of things I was wondering at that moment:

When will Ilsa's school reopen?

It *will* reopen, right?

What does "anthropogenic"* mean?

Do I have time to write today *and* drive forty minutes to try to find milk in glass bottles?

I now have a houseful of kids—I mean, *young adults*. Can I keep them all fed *and* stay No Garbage?

On a related note, are Greta's friends gonna think I'm as crazy as a soup sandwich?

Would they think that anyway?

Saran Wrap *seems* to be made of polyethylene.

Is it?

And if so, does that mean it's recyclable in the plastic film bin at the supermarket?

Is there anything harder than trying to wash Saran Wrap?

Giving a chicken a bath, maybe?

On a related note, what the heck is TerraCycle?

Is it really all that?

We are now out of toothpaste.

How, exactly, will my husband react if I present him with toothpaste homemade from baking soda?

Toothpaste can't be grounds for divorce, can it?

I probably have to stop despising hand sanitizer now, don't I?

Damn.

Are the kids—I mean young adults—bored yet?

How about now?

Don't we have a soccer ball around here somewhere?

---

*   See Chapter 11, "All the Ridiculous Terms Translated."

Should I make another trip to the forty-five-minutes-away
butcher to stock the freezer?
Or, perhaps build a tree fort where no one can find me?
(Note to self: bring stuffed animals.)
Is it wrong to try to be No Garbage when the world seems to
be going to hell in a handbasket?
Or, is it an excellent strategy to stay sane?

It was a strange time: pandemic limbo. Everything was closed, and
Ilsa's high school remained shut, scrambling to figure out how to
switch to online classes. Besides lots of cooking, there was nothing to
do. I got out puzzles. Steve got out the archery set we had purchased
at L.L.Bean but never had any time for and taught everyone how to
aim for the paper target on a hay bale, peppering the shed behind it
with pockmarks. I took the young people for long, muddy walks in
the countryside around our house, up the hill behind our house, and
all around the dirt roads of our neighborhood. For the first time ever,
we walked not only to the top of our hill, but down the other side,
coming out in a strange meadow behind houses that in the last twenty-some years we had only ever seen from the road. We wandered the
nearby cemetery, reading ancient, lichen-encrusted inscriptions. We
ran into some nearby homeowners we had never met before as we
emerged from the woods behind their house and waved and yelled
greetings some fifty feet away from behind a line of barbed wire.
We were all marooned on our own little islands. There was a strange
sense of wonderment to it, as if we had lived on our land, in our
neighborhood, for decades without ever really knowing it at all.

Steven, Greta's boyfriend, was funny. A young actor who Greta
had met at drama conservatory, Steven had been born in Shenzhen,
China, and raised between there and Limerick, Ireland, where his
mother had later moved and remarried. Of course, he has the same
first name as my husband, so *that* had to be sorted out. It was decided
that whenever we were talking about Dad/my husband, it was Steve,
whereas when we were talking about Greta's boyfriend, it was Steve*n*.
(Which is not terribly creative, but every time one of us tried to

use his given Chinese name, which is Jia He, he would make a face as if I had just called him something surprisingly nonsensical, like "Wandering Taco.")

Steven had never lived anywhere but in a major city, so the idea of not being able to even, say, have a pizza delivered to the house, was a bit unfathomable to him. Looking for something to do, as well as to supplement the hastily packed wardrobe he'd brought with him, he kept asking if he and Greta might venture out to "the shops," even though I assured him most of them were a thirty-minute drive away *and* closed, besides which we really didn't want anyone getting exposed to any other people right now. In desperation he asked if he could borrow a bicycle to ride the three miles into town, but I explained "town" consisted of two restaurants (both closed for the pandemic), one general store that had been closed for several years, and a gas station that accepted cash. There simply was, perhaps for the first time in his entire life, *nowhere to go*.

As the days went by, not being able to be productive in any way seemed to be torturing Steven. Walks were okay, but pointless. Archery was fun, but then what? And he hated puzzles. Ilsa suggested, since he was an actor and all, that he check out this social media app that she and all her friends enjoyed. It was called TikTok. Maybe he could do something on that?

He scoffed a little. Social media videos . . . wasn't that just a bunch of kids doing silly dances for each other?

Nevertheless, after a few weeks of isolation, what did he have to lose? He decided to try it.

It was right around this time that I pretty much abandoned the whole idea of the Whoops/WTF box. I now knew that even before the pandemic had begun, I had been thinking way too literally about things. I began to realize that the idea of a concrete "mistake" that took the form of singular objects or pieces of packaging was quite beside the point—it was way murkier and more confusing than that. Now that we were strictly limiting our contact with the outside world this fact seemed plainer than ever. I finally and reluctantly accepted that feeding a household while limiting ourselves to only plastics with RIC numbers 1–7 on them was unrealistic. And during a pandemic? Impossible. All the zero waste experts I followed online seemed to agree with this unfortunate fact, posting messages about not judging yourself harshly if you couldn't be quite as zero waste as you had in the past.

Meat was reportedly starting to be in short supply, so I started making a monthly pilgrimage to the butcher to stock up my freezer. My butcher now operated on a "call us and we set your meat aside for you in lovely vacuum-sealed plastic packages" system. Besides that, in the interest of limiting our exposure I was pretty much only going to one store once a week for one hour, and logically, that was the place where I could get the most foods we needed all at once: the supermarket.

Previously, during our Year of No Sugar, I had learned that sugar was present in three-quarters of the items for sale in the supermarket. I had learned how to shop super carefully, avoiding all the dozens of different words that *meant* sugar, and learned how to make from scratch the things I couldn't find without it. My black-and-white, literal-minded way of thinking worked in this scenario. It was hard, but we found ways.

This, though, was different. Although I couldn't find a statistic for how many items have plastic packaging in the average supermarket, I was guessing it was even more than the three-quarters that have sugar in them. Once you get past the produce section, with few exceptions (flour, tinfoil, canned goods) the product packaging is almost entirely plastic. Previously, with careful planning, I had gotten to the point where I could buy everything our family needed at the store without added sugar in any of it. But after visiting the grocery store with this project I began doing a tally: no matter how careful I was, 60 percent of the items I purchased *still* involved plastic in one way or another. When limited to shopping at my supermarket, more than half of the products I needed to buy gave me no other option but to buy disposable plastic: mayo, crackers, cat food, lemons, chicken breasts, milk. It felt like we were at the mercy of the Single-Use-Plastic Mafia.

It was an offer I couldn't refuse.

Sixty percent.

Black and white didn't work here, it was all gray. As hard as no-sugar had been, this was *much* harder.

Ilsa had been right.

When my first book had been published, one reviewer accused me of writing a "how-to manual for an eating disorder." She had been wrong, because avoiding sugar never, ever meant that we deprived ourselves in any real way or went hungry, any of us. But I thought of that now as I saw that avoiding plastic really *could* turn into an eating disorder. That's how much worse the situation is: there simply would not be enough readily available food that didn't either come wrapped in plastic or have those little plastic bags, nets, tags, or stickers on them. Later, I found an article in which another woman wrote about trying to go plastic-free for a month and she arrived at much the same conclusion, saying "Before long, I found that the easiest way to consume less plastic was to eat less."[1] I had no intention of going down that path.

So we had started out planning not to buy plastic, or at least not buy anything without a RIC number 1–7. Now we were *avoiding* plastics, and washing and holding onto all the pieces of non-RIC number plastics we ended up with in hopes of finding a recycling solution for them.

Just because we weren't doing the project in the manner we had originally imagined didn't mean we were throwing in the towel, and didn't mean we were throwing anything else away either. Just like the pandemic was causing everyone to do, we just had to see things differently. Reassess.

I started to realize there was more connection between our Year of No Garbage and the global pandemic than my long list of unanswered questions. It occurred to me that the coronavirus came to us with a message that we ignored at our own peril, and it was this: we are all much closer than we think. Watching the news reports day by day, as reports of confirmed cases were leapfrogging from one country to the next, I had been struck by the fact that all of these infected people were linked, one to the other: the trail of the virus was like a spider web that spiraled ever outward.

The virus knew something fundamental we often seemed to forget: *we are all connected*. And much more closely than we might like to admit.

Which reminded me why garbage is such a colossally bad idea. And "throwing things away" is a human strategy that involves a willing suspension of disbelief that such a thing is possible on a planet that is round and finite. Because of course garbage doesn't "go away," it just goes somewhere else. This may be okay with you, unless you happen to live in the neighborhood of the landfill. Then again, at the rate we're going the landfill will soon be in everybody's neighborhood. The Great Pacific Garbage Patch is now twice the size of Texas. Ocean garbage patches now take up more surface area on the earth than land.

And what about if that landfill ends up in the neighborhood of your body? Microplastics, for example, have started showing up in everything from fish and shellfish to beer, bottled water, tap water, and sea salt. Our garbage is everywhere, all around us, in our very bodies, and we don't even realize it. Microplastics have been found in humans' blood,[2] lungs,[3] the placenta of unborn children,[4] and, most recently, breast milk.[5]

It reminds me of that old quote from the comic strip *Pogo*: "We have met the enemy, and he is us." Cartoonist Walt Kelly knew that fifty years ago, but the rest of us still can't quite seem to come to grips with it. Acknowledging it would mean changing the way we do business, the way we live our lives, and, well, everything. And the suggestion of fundamental change freaks people out, a *lot*. Even more than the coronavirus, maybe.

Mutating pandemics and polymer particles in our rainwater have this in common: they don't pay any attention to the walls that humans have built to make ourselves feel safe, whether figurative or literal. So when we talk about the merits of universal health care, as I had no doubt we would in the wake of this global panic, in the next breath it now occurred to me that we might consider another radical proposition: *socialized garbage*. This would mean that every company who makes anything, ever, has to be able to answer is this: *What happens to this, and its packaging, when the consumer is done with it?*

We could take our linear consumption of all products and make it circular.

There was a moment, an ever so brief, flickering moment, when it did occur to me: maybe the Year of No Garbage stops here. All those great plans I had started out our year with, bringing food containers to the stores and buying in bulk were suddenly utterly off the table. Not only did no one want to so much as *look* at my nice glass containers, most of the smaller specialty stores where I had been able to purchase items in bulk or paper were shuttered until further notice. The health food store managed to stay open by improvising a new online ordering system and drive-through pickup, but that necessarily involved lots more packaging, not less. Everywhere people were enclosing foods and other products with extra packaging as a way to make people feel safer, which of course was an important thing, but definitely the opposite of where we and our project had been trying to go.

Was this a sign? Was the pandemic trying to tell me something? Maybe this was just too hard on everyone.

Steve and I talked about it. We didn't get too far into the pros and cons list before it became apparent that, deep down, we both felt we needed to keep going. It was only March, but we already felt like we'd come so far. Plus, it was a welcome distraction. Most of all we felt that: this is life. The planet isn't going to wait around for humans to have "the right year" to tackle all the harm that's been inflicted on the environment. There was never going to be an ideal time to rethink the way we live—significant change is always inherently uncomfortable and messy.

Deal with it, I thought.

Staying away from the world as a family meant we were turning inward, slowing down. I found myself moving slower, having more patience, even driving slower. I was lucky: I didn't have anywhere to get to in a hurry. Spending so much time in our home was giving me a whole new perspective, making me look at home all the more, think about it even more, use it differently. Not going out meant we needed to use everything we had more efficiently and wisely: food, space, things.

Even in a house in rural Vermont, being so steadily homebound could make a person feel a little anxious or claustrophobic. My husband was one such person. Some days it was as if the pandemic made him want to crawl out of his skin. On the other hand, I was surprised to find that I rather liked our new hermity existence and the intense ability to focus that came with it.

And in part because I had lots of time to think, to continue to scour the internet, and make persistent phone calls, I was about to find out a lot of unsettling things.

I was about to discover Dark Recycling.

CHAPTER FIVE

....

SECRETS AND FRAUD:
WHEN "GREEN" PLASTIC
GOES HORRIBLY WRONG

One night, I dreamed I had invented a way to turn clear plastic wrapping into food.

I had made a lovely plastic salad that looked a bit like transparent coleslaw. Fortunately, I woke up before eating it.

Probably this was evidence that plastic had clearly emerged as enemy number one, as well as the fact that the concessions COVID-19 had wrangled from me were weighing heavily on my mind.

In the grand scheme of so much illness, hospitalization, and death, was it important that I couldn't stick to my guns? No. Nevertheless, it was hard not to feel like I was somehow giving up as I sliced open yet another plastic package (sigh), admitting that at least for the moment I was in some ways choosing the higher priority of keeping the family fed and safe, over a project about the health of the planet.

Nevertheless, I dutifully washed and air-dried each and every plastic package, unsure of what would come next. I was determined to adhere to my No Garbage pledge: maybe it was disposable plastic, but *this* plastic, at least, was not headed for the landfill. Not on my watch. Where it *was* bound was becoming a more desperate question by the day as the recycling corner of my kitchen had become Krakatoa, ready to blow.

What *was* all this stuff anyway?

THE INSIDIOUS SMALL STUFF

Ever stopped to wonder what the T-shaped thread that connects the price tag to your clothing is called? Or what the "safety band" is made of, the one that once primarily appeared on bottles of over-the-counter medicine but has now proliferated in a Tribble-esque fashion to include virtually every item with a lid or cap in the entire store? What about the plastic pull tabs that come off cartons of milk? Are *they* good for anything?

I repurposed a peanut butter jar as a container for the smallest of the plastic stuff and labeled it "Doohickeys," and that's where all these itty-bitty things ended up, along with lots, lots more. Research revealed information, if not solutions. I learned that the fiber-thin plastic thread that attaches price tags to clothing, as well as the information labels on everything from pineapples to mattresses, is called a "swift tack," and that it was invented in the early 1960s.[1] I learned that the ubiquitous safety bands are made of PVC (which means endocrine disruptors such as phthalates and BPA) and shrink to encase the product lid by use of a "heat gun." I learned that there are many questionable DIY projects you can make with the little circular milk pull-tabs. (Although I admire the ingenuity of the plastic milk tab crafters, I fear that the world probably can't use enough miniature pin cushions or Barbie earmuffs to truly make a difference.)

Where on earth could any of these little bits and pieces ever actually go besides being made into ugly jewelry? I planned to find out.

MULTILAYERS

I had first encountered the concept of "multilayer" packaging— *extruded combinations of paper, foil, and/or plastic*—while researching cartons, but little did I realize that it represented much more than just containers for milk or soup. Frozen food packaging, plasticized produce tags, pull-off seals, stickers, thermal paper tickets, coupons and receipts were among the items that showed up repeatedly in our kitchen's I Don't Know pile. I was coming to understand that *all* of them were multilayers.

Of particular urgency in terms of shrinking the pile was finding out more about the vacuum pouches meat often comes in. A few months back we had purchased half a pig for our freezer from a local farmer, and it was all packaged in vacuum-seal pouches, dozens of them. I needed to know: *What kind of plastic is this, and is it recyclable?* I asked the farmer who we had bought it from, my friend Rico, who didn't know, but directed me to the local facility that had processed the meat: Locust Grove Farm. Locust Grove Farm didn't know, but directed me to their wrapping supplier: the Teri Equipment Company. I called the Teri Equipment Company, and they didn't know, but they directed me to *their* supplier: UltraSource. Is this starting to sound like one of those circular nursery rhymes where at the end you go right back to the beginning?

But no, at last I got Andrea from UltraSource on the phone. During the pandemic, she was working from home, as evidenced by gurgling baby sounds in the background. And wonderful Andrea solved my problem because she was happy to send me the actual spec sheet on the plastics used in their vacuum-seal plastic.

That was the good news. The bad news was that clear, vacuum seal plastic looks like it is made of one kind of material, but it is in fact made of a whole buffet of different kinds of plastics, including: polyethylene (either plastic #2 or 4), polypropylene (#5), ethylene vinyl alcohol, and ethylene vinyl acetate (as far as I can tell both fell into the "other" category.)

These materials are sandwiched together—what they call "coextruded"—resulting in something called "multi-film" or "multilayer," although I think a much better name would have been Intergalactic Space Plastic. And the problem with coextrusion, as I've touched on previously, is that different materials that have been scientifically smooshed together are Very Bad News for recycling, because most of the time it is too costly or difficult to un-smoosh them, and so pretty much no one does it. Poof! Intergalactic Space Plastic becomes land-fill contents for all time.

Doing a cursory online search of the properties of each of the different materials that made up our meat-wrapping pouches, I could see that each plastic lent a different property to the overall material. I'm sure if I were a packaging science major, I could tell you much more about how amazing and revolutionary the invention of coextruded, multi-film packaging is, and all of that would be true. Before the Year of No Garbage, did I love that I could buy a package of lovely, sealed, organic ground beef at the super-market that would keep good for much, much longer than other, mere mortal organic ground beef? Of course—it's convenient and efficient. It reduces food waste and saves money. Longer shelf life probably even made my supermarket more likely to carry organic meat in the first place.

But where Intergalactic Space Plastic reduces waste of food, it creates waste of something arguably even worse: permanent, forever garbage. At least wasted food, if composted, can degrade back into the environment.

On top of that we have our health to think of: how much of these different plastics leach into our meat and end up in our bodies? BPA, PVC, PFA, and PFOAs have all gotten a lot of attention in recent years for being cancer-causing and endocrine-disrupting, not to men-tion present in the bloodstream of pretty much everybody (accord-ing to the Centers for Disease Control and Prevention, 95 percent of Americans have PFAs in their bloodstream). Consequently, those chemicals have been removed from some—but not all—of food packaging. Does that mean we can assume what's left is definitively safe? Not at all. History tells us that replacement chemicals are often just as toxic, or more so, than the ones being replaced. Joseph Allen from the Harvard University's T.H. Chan School of Public Health explained in a *Washington Post* opinion piece that this is precisely the case when the similar chemical BPS is used to replace BPA, or when flame-retardant PDBEs and TPPs are used to replace PBBs: the health risks are just as bad, if not worse. He calls this phenomenon hazardous chemical "whack-a-mole."[2]

So both for health reasons *and* for No Garbage reasons, it made the most sense to avoid plastic wrapping for food as much as possible, especially multilayer. But this did me no good when it came to the pig already in my freezer.

Nope. I'd have to find a home for this forlorn, unwanted, Intergalactic Space Plastic.

So far, I'd identified two promising options. One was TerraCycle, the private US company that offers to recycle your hard-to-recycle stuff, for a fee, if you send it to them in the mail in a prepurchased box (read: pricey). The other was Precious Plastic, which is an open-source alternative plastic recycling movement supported by grants and volunteers (read: will I have to join a cult?). In either case, I suspected that multi-film plastics that couldn't be recycled normally would be chipped, melted, and molded into new recycled plastic products, but I didn't really know for sure.

More research was required: more on that in chapter 7 and in the epilogue.

PLASTIC WRAP

Next on my list of Big Mysteries was *plastic wrap*. Also known as "cling wrap" or "plastic film," it presents perhaps one of the toughest of all zero waste conundrums.

Only those who are trying to avoid it can fully appreciate how everywhere plastic wrap really is. Whole aisles of meats, entire walls of cheeses, all sealed off from the world in tidy little flexible packets! Even organic produce is safely—if ironically—secured with it to little bio-degradable trays. It's hard to imagine how utterly magical plastic wrap must have seemed to consumers in the 1940s when it was first marketed, back when glass, metal, and paper were the primary materials for storing food. One ad I found from that time cheerfully extols plastic wrap's ability to keep flies from landing on the foods of the buffet table.

Fresh! Easy! Lightweight! Cheap! I suppose it makes sense that the supermarket has a long-standing love affair with clean, clear, oh-so-sanitary plastic wrap. Even before the pandemic severely limited my shopping/food packaging choices, the stuff just kept popping up in my house like an uninvited guest who can't take a hint.

> **Friend:** *I brought you some lovely cheese, Eve!*
> **Me:** *CRAP.*
> **Also Me:** *I mean, thank you, it's lovely!*
> **Me (quietly):** *CRAP. Guess I'll put this next to the plastic wrap I found in the freezer and the plastic wrap a friend brought me leftovers in, and the plastic wrap that fell out of the freaking sky on my head.*

Ever since this year began, whenever plastic food wrap had reared its ugly head in my kitchen, I had carefully washed it in the sink, in much the same way I do tinfoil: flattening it against the sink bottom and wiping with my dish sponge in one-directional strokes, draping it delicately over the dishes in the drainer to dry, and later be stored for future repurposing yet to be determined. At some point, though, it occurred to me: how is *this* thin, flexible plastic any different than, say, the thin flexible plastic of supermarket shopping bags? It felt the same. It used the same industry terminology: "plastic film." If food wrap *is* the same plastic as supermarket bags, wouldn't it stand to reason that you could—after cleaning and drying it—recycle it in the plastic bag recycling bin at the supermarket?

So I googled it. When one googles "is plastic wrap recyclable?" the resounding answer one invariably gets is: *NO. NO. NO. DON'T EVEN THINK ABOUT IT NO.*

But I wanted to know *why*. Most online sources give no reason at all, but a few say it's because plastic food wraps are made of #3 plastic: PVC or PVdC (polyvinyl chloride or polyvinylidene chloride).

The thing is, this is not entirely true. When you dig a little deeper you find that, due to a growing awareness of the toxicity of chlorine in PVC and PVdC most plastic wrap films are no longer made with these materials, notably including Saran Premium Wrap, which changed its formula in 2004.

So what are they made of? Well, when you get an actual person on the phone at these companies, you find out that two of the leading food wraps, Glad Clingwrap and Saran Premium Wrap, are currently both made with . . . *polyethylene*. (Stretch-Tite, sadly, is still made with PVC.)

And because I was well on my way to becoming a Certified Recycling Nerd, this was when I started to get excited. Because polyethylene, you may recall, is exactly what makes up all those plastic film products that are suitable for recycling into outdoor decking by the good people at Trex. Dry cleaning bags, bread bags, plastic overwrap from toilet paper and paper towels, produce bags, etc. You'll recall I had found out that all of these things are made with polyethylene (plastics #2 and #4) and can all go into the plastic film recycling bin at the supermarket.

Wouldn't it stand to reason then, that Saran Wrap and Glad Wrap could go in that recycling bin too?

I sent an email to my friend Alexandra at Trex to confirm my hypothesis. I was disappointed to get her response: "*Hi Eve . . . Glad Wrap and Saran Wrap are not plastic films that Trex accepts. It's my understanding that the chemical does not behave the same as typical PE film. Please do not include.*" This struck me as odd, because both of the company representatives I spoke with confirmed that their plastic wraps were *100 percent* polyethylene—there are no other chemicals hiding in there. So what made this polyethylene film different than any than other polyethylene films?

When I pressed for more info from Alexandra at Trex, this is the response I got: "*Saran Wrap is PE (polyethylene) but it's a modified form of PE and . . . it does not melt like traditional PE.*"

Wait, was that true? More phone calls.

This time I spoke to a public affairs representative at SC Johnson, the makers of Saran Wrap. That's when I got a response that blew my recycling mind. Here's a quote from the official statement they sent me:

We can confirm that clean and dry Saran Wrap® is recyclable at most major US retailers similar to Ziploc® bags by dropping off in the bins located in stores that collect plastic bags and films.

On the phone, Margaret, a customer service representative at Glad Products told me the same thing about their Glad Wrap: "100 percent recyclable."

Wow! Great news! But hold on. One thing I'd been learning this year is to be more skeptical about things companies say. What does "recyclable" *really* mean, anyway? The term *recyclable* is meaningless if no facilities actually exist to accept it, right?

"Dear Loyal Consumer: We are delighted to inform you that our product is 100 percent, guaranteed, fully recyclable. On Pluto. Thanks for your inquiry!"

Was I just back to square one? After all, even though the manufacturers *say* their product fits the parameters like those used at Trex, remember Trex said: *Glad Wrap and Saran Wrap are not plastic films that Trex accepts.*

But . . . *why?* I was starting to sound like a persistent four-year-old, but there had to be an actual reason, right? Is it just because recyclers are afraid customers won't wash and dry the stuff properly? Or are they afraid customers will put in *non*-polyethylene films that look identical, but are chemically very different? And if so, would this contaminate the recycling process? And how?

At this point I'd just like to pause and state the completely obvious: *it should not be this hard.* I should not have to make forty-seven phone calls in order to know what chemicals are being used in the packaging of our foods. It should not be this hard to recycle our food packaging. I do think Trex and other polyethylene recyclers are doing a wonderful thing by turning plastics that were heretofore unrecyclable into new products. They are to be deeply commended, and I mean that.

But. Why did I feel like I was getting the runaround?

Were they just hoping I'd give up and go away? Because if so, they were truly not understanding the level of Lady Macbeth obsessiveness I was operating on.

So I gave Trex one last try, emailing Alexandra yet again, asking: *What is the modification that makes 100% polyethylene plastic food wraps unrecyclable with other 100% polyethylene plastic films?* And at last I *was* able to get a more specific answer:

It is true that saran wrap plastic films are 100% PE, but are XPE— cross linked polyethylene. Trex process does not handle well XPE as it doesn't move through the process of melting and material flow the way that non XPE does. Our whole business, machinery, and technology are designed to use a consistent or homogenized material source and XPE causes major chemical shifts.

Apparently, XPE can gunk up the whole recycling process, creating clogs in the line and irregularities in the new product.

After all this rigmarole with dueling representatives I kind of felt like it was time to get an outside viewpoint on the recyclability of plastic wrap. So I had a phone call with a woman named Debbi, at MORE Recycling, a consulting company that specializes in facilitating recycling and sustainability.

According to Debbi, the other concerns I had suspected are, all by themselves, enough to put the kibosh on the whole endeavor, even before you get to the issue of the polyethylene being cross-linked. "[Many recyclers are] probably worried about contamination," she explained. "Most people probably won't take the time to wash and dry the film properly." Which can not only contaminate the recycling, but also invite pests.

Add to that the fact that, while Saran Wrap and Glad Wrap *are* polyethylene, others are not.

"It's confusing enough for people trying to recycle right," she said, without people trying to keep track of whether their plastic wrap came from Saran, Glad, or Stretch-Tite. And once the plastic is out of the box, they're indistinguishable: there's no way to determine whether a food wrap is PVC or HDPE just by look or feel.

And, most importantly, she confirmed once and for all: *"XPE is not currently compatible with the PE recycling stream."*

So just as in the Mysterious Case of the Meat Plastic Vacuum Pouches, I had at last gotten to the bottom of a difficult recycling question, only to find a not-very-satisfying answer. In this case the answer was: *yes!* But really, no. Yes, some manufacturers are *saying* plastic food wraps are "recyclable," but are they really? In reality, no one wants to recycle them, because it just too hard: too complicated, too arduous for consumers, too messy, too confusing. The recycling industry is simply not set up to do this.

But that's okay, because I think the easiest, most sensible thing we can do as consumers is to avoid food-wrapping plastic films altogether. Don't buy them for your kitchen—instead use beeswax wrap or glass storage containers such as Pyrex—and try not to buy products that come wrapped in them. One of the favorite tricks I'd developed to avoid plastic wrap was to use a rubber band or two to resecure food packaging once the product had been opened. This worked well for so many things: blocks of cheese, bags of sauerkraut, a package of smoked salmon. It was bad enough they all came in plastic, at least I didn't have to compound the problem by then using more plastic once it was open.

What about in cooking? A surprising number of recipes actually call for the use of plastic wrap—from wrapping dough to various stages of food prep—but I'm pretty sure Laura Ingalls Wilder didn't cover her bread dough with Saran Wrap. What I've discovered is that a plate on top of the bowl as a covering works every time.

"COMPOSTABLES"

Next up for further investigation was a product that promised to assuage the guilt of our modern throwaway lifestyle: *compostable packaging*! Now here at last is something garbage-conscious people can feel good about, right?

I got to thinking about compostables one day while on a supplies run with Ilsa: fully masked and plastic-gloved, and wishing for a hazmat suit. Hastily posted signs indicated new instructions for patronizing our favorite bagel shop. We went to a different door around the back, waited obediently six feet from all the other patrons, did the hokeypokey, and ordered a dozen bagels and a smoothie (with a paper straw) to go. When we checked to be sure the cup was recyclable it appeared to be even *better* than recyclable. It was something called "Greenware," and a cheerful message across the bottom of the cup read: "yay! i'm compostable so don't trash me already"!

Nice! *Compostable plastic!* It was a cup that *looked* like plastic, *felt* like plastic, but, as I discovered after we got home and I looked it up, was actually made from "Ingeo," the trademark name for a "PLA resin derived from plants." "PLA" stands for polylactic acid, which comes from corn, sugarcane, or beets.

Ilsa was impressed. But then she said: *Waitaminit. If it is possible to make compostable disposables, why don't all takeout places use them?* I explained what I knew: that eco-friendly products made with natural, renewable materials like bamboo or corn are usually more expensive, so using them is something the company has to believe provides "added value" to their brand for customers.

And for sure, we were those customers if anyone was, willing and able to go out of our way, and pay a few cents more, to "do the right thing." I feel very fortunate to have that option of choice.

But is the option of choice real or an illusion? Let's find out.

After the smoothie had been drunk and I had washed the transparent cup, I wondered: Does this very, *VERY* sturdy-looking thing *really* go in our compost bin? It just didn't feel right throwing something so . . . so *plastic-resembling* in with all our squishy banana peels and grainy coffee grounds.

So, I researched it further, and that's when I fell out of my chair. Greenware "compostable cups" are . . . (wait for it) **not compostable** . . . in a backyard compost. Their website explains: *These products are compostable in actively managed municipal or industrial facilities, which may not be available in your area. Not suitable for backyard composting.*

There are other brands out there of similar products: Ecotainer is another one I've encountered; in the United Kingdom there's Vegware. All the websites contain the same message: *Compostable? Yes! But hold on! Don't try this at home.*

So let me make sure I understand this. I'm supposed to get my one-use, takeaway cup, and as the name indicates, *I take it away.* And then when I'm done I . . . bring it to the nearest industrial composting facility? Oh sure, I think there's one of those at the mall in between the Hallmark Store and the movie theater.

To be fair, yes, in-store our bagel shop does have a designated bin for these "compostables," which presumably goes to the mythical industrial composting facility in the sky. If you consumed the drink in-store (presumably during a non-pandemic time when people did such wild and crazy things) then this all *might* make sense. But in this scenario surely it's far better, and more to the point, to have the vendor provide a real glass cup that gets washed and reused.

Alas, the point of the takeaway cup is to Take. It. Away. Am I really supposed to drive the thirty minutes back to town to return my "compostable" cup? And if I did wouldn't I get pulled over by the Irony Police?

But wait! It gets worse. Although the cup is labeled with a recycling code number (#7), the Greenware website also explains it is not really a normal #7 plastic made of things such as acrylic, polycarbonate, or nylon, so it should not be put with single-stream recycling, lest it contaminate actual plastic recyclables. What do they recommend instead?

If a commercial composting facility is not available, please dispose responsibly in a trash receptacle.

So it goes to . . . the landfill. Where, despite the fact that it is made from plants, means it never degrades. And Greenware *knows* this. Again from Greenware's website:

The sealed anaerobic environment of a common landfill severely limits the ability for compostable materials to break down. Oxygen and microbial activity are necessary for the breakdown of all compostable items and unfortunately is not present in most landfills.

To recap: You've come home with this awesome good feeling about being kind to the planet with your better choices. Yet, when you discard your feel-good cup, you end up either: a.) messing up your home compost, b.) contaminating your recycling, or c.) adding to the landfill.

It's enough to make a regular recyclable plastic cup look downright sustainable by comparison.

If you think all this is confusing or misleading to customers, it turns out we aren't the only ones. I called up the shop where the cup had come from and asked the employee who answered if I could put the Greenware smoothie cup into my home compost pile. She said, "I don't know. . . . I *think* you can."

Now, I love my bagel shop. And right at that moment, in particular, I applauded them for being open, heroically feeding hungry, COVID-19-panicked patrons, not to mention taking the time to answer weird, random questions from some crazy lady on the phone. But if the very people who work at the shop can't tell you about the cup, I ask you: *what good is it?* (More on PLA and so-called "bioplastics" in chapter 10.)

Not long after this episode, a package arrived at our house in a flexible mailer that had a familiarly cheerful message emblazoned upon it: *Hey! I'm a 100% Compostable Mailer.*

As you can imagine, I was deeply suspicious. First of all: why are all these inanimate objects talking to me? Second: why are they all so friendly? Third: Compostable? Yeah, *right.*

But as it turns out *these* mailers—made by a company called Noissue—really, truly are what they say they are. Again—they look like plastic, feel like plastic, but when you are done with them you *can* throw them right into the backyard compost bin. In six months there will be no trace of them. I learned from the Noissue website that there is a technical term for this capability: *home compostable.*

So, the upshot is: beware of greenwashing. Just because something presents itself as an earth-friendly alternative, doesn't mean it actually *is* one. Sometimes I wonder if we aren't all just so busy feeling good about *trying* to be better to the planet, we don't stop to realize we might actually be being *worse* to the planet instead.

At the risk of sounding like a broken record, it shouldn't require a host of Google searches to get to the heart of whether a product is what it claims to be, but until we get better regulation and public awareness around such issues, the onus will still be on the consumer to ferret this stuff out on their own. We could all benefit from clearer, legally defined terminology that recognizes the difference between "industrial compostable" and "home compostable."

Noissue is clearly the real deal, and kudos to them for walking the walk. As for products like Greenware, Ecotainer, and Vegware, I'd like to think that they are well intentioned. But the problem is that using these products alone isn't enough, because *using them improperly can be worse than not using them at all.* Informing the consumer and the vendor about what a product can and can't do is key, and obviously that isn't happening enough. In cities that offer curbside compost pickup, these products probably make more sense than they do elsewhere. But there are an awful lot of places, like my town, that don't fit that description.

Until the pandemic receded, and we were allowed once again to bring our own reusable containers for takeout, I realized it would be better to choose a recyclable plastic container over products that are only compostable in an industrial setting. At least then I know it's part of an attempt at a circular economy, and not necessarily destined for a landfill.

Then I'd know I'm doing something real, with intention, and not just accepting the veneer of sustainability as fact. Sometimes, when you peek behind the curtain, that shiny "Green" veneer? Turns out to have been just a mirage after all.

"FLUSHABLE" WIPES

Amazingly, there seemed to be no end to the disposable items that had lived in my house and been used on a regular basis, that I had never really thought about. To wonder what they were made of had simply never occurred to me before. Between buying them and tossing them there was simply no moment encouraging me to stop and ask. Once I had gotten through the more obvious suspects, I began to see still more suspicious characters lurking.

Like *wipes.*

Disposable wipes are sneaky. They have the look and feel somewhere between a cloth and a tissue. Intuitively, they seem to hold no more potential harm than a paper Kleenex. Antibacterial wipes, makeup removal wipes, baby wipes, "personal" wipes: When you start to look around, you find them everywhere.

But what *were* wipes?

Were they paper? Were they plastic? Some combination of the two?

Were they bad for the environment? (I was starting to notice the pattern that if you have to ask, the answer is: yes.)

And if they *were* bad, *how* bad, exactly?

Let's start with the kind of wipes labeled "flushable." Flushed right into nothingness! Like magic!

That should've been the first clue. If I was learning anything at all during this year, it's that upon closer examination "magic" is just like it sounds: wishful thinking.

The packages proclaim: "Designed for Toilets!" and "Tested with Plumbers" so one might think these wipes decompose along with human waste in sewers and septic tanks. But then again "tested *with* plumbers"? What did that actually mean? Were they having coffee in the same room or something?

It turned out I was right to be suspicious. Virtually all wipes—from Stridex pads and Wet Ones to baby wipes to one-use facial "spa" masks—are made of something called "*spunlace*." And this material, it turns out, is a bit of a hot-button issue in the plumbing community.

This is because spunlace is, in fact, made with plastic. It is a fabric made of a combination of materials including polyester, polypropylene, rayon, cotton, and Tencel. The fibers are bound together by something called "hydroentanglement" which is to say a treatment of high-pressure water. Reading more, I found out that because of the plastics involved, not only is spunlace *not* biodegradable, it is also notorious for clogging up sewer systems and wastewater treatment plants all over the world.

When this happens "fatbergs" occur. These are rocklike masses composed of things like disposable wipes and congealed grease. Fatbergs can cause city sewage systems to overflow with untreated sewage. And if that isn't enough of a party for you, then you will love what happens next: the fatberg must be excavated, and then . . . you guessed it! Landfilled or burned.

(You can peruse a nice list of "Notable Fatbergs" on Wikipedia. In 2017, excavated pieces of a 140-ton fatberg on display at the Museum of London apparently became one of the museum's most popular exhibits.)

The Wet Nap hand wipe originally trademarked in 1958 has grown and morphed into literally thousands of different wipe products on the market today. The term *fatberg* was coined around 2010, and in 2015 a British sewer company reported that *two-thirds* of their blockages were caused by disposable wipes.

So we've established that under no circumstances must a disposable wipe no matter how tissue-like be flushed. But what about so-called "flushable" wipes? It turns out that any wipe marked "flushable" *cannot* contain plastic, and are made entirely of paper. However, there is clear disagreement in the plumbing and wastewater community about whether even 100 percent paper wet wipes break down fast enough to avoid causing problems.

On their website, the popular brand Cottonelle's defense against such accusations is to tout the fact that their product is "approved by JEA"! Great! But who the heck is the JEA, and why are we supposed to be impressed by that? If you noodle around for a little while you can eventually discover that JEA stands for Florida's "Jacksonville Electric Authority."

So waitaminit. One wastewater treatment facility *in the entire country* approves this product? One out of the approximately fourteen thousand wastewater treatment facilities in the United States? Maybe we shouldn't be too impressed by this high-power endorsement. I'm more inclined to listen to *Consumer Reports*, whose test in 2013 determined that all four of the leading "flushable" wipes failed to break down in an agitation test.[3] Then in 2019 *Forbes* reported on an independent study that tested 101 different wipes, 23 of which were labeled as "flushable," for disintegration and flushability and— wait for it—*not one of them passed.*[4]

What experts will tell you is that it has yet to be proven that paper-only wipes are any less harmful than spunlace wipes. For folks who are on a public sewer system, the wipe just doesn't have enough time or agitation to disintegrate before it reaches the sewage pump in a matter of minutes. If we are lucky the wipe gets filtered out, and set aside to be either landfilled or burned. If not? Fatberg.

But are they safe for use for those not on a sewer system? We live in the country, and whenever someone in my house uses a "flushable" wipe, it gets deposited in the septic tank buried in our yard. While liquids run off and eventually deposit into a nearby leach field, the wipe will fall to the bottom with the sludge.

Maybe it degrades in there. Since we only need to pump our tank out every seven to ten years, it's likely that the paper does get broken down by bacteria and enzymes in the septic system, but that's a guess.

And opening up my septic system to investigate further is on my list of things to never, ever do. But all this new information has brought me to two conclusions:

First: Unless verified by an objective third party, don't trust companies' claims. Ever. (You'd think I'd have learned this by now, yes?) "Flushable!" in most cases, probably isn't.

Second: As an admitted fan of the previously thought to be flushable "personal" wipe, " I realized it was time to at least entertain at least the possibility of a bidet attachment. When the pandemic began, and a bizarre toilet paper shortage ensued, bidet attachments had suddenly become wildly popular and much discussed in the popular media. Although I knew it was also a great way to cut down fewer trees for toilet paper, I wasn't ready to devote that much of my conscious thought and financial resources to the process of keeping my tush clean. Yet.

Speaking of unmentionables, a man in our neighborhood named Terry Tyler is well known for being a classic Vermont storyteller of the more . . . *profane* variety. Years ago he wrote a hilarious, bawdy, and offensive-to-pretty-much-everyone book of stories and anecdotes entitled *Don't Scratch Too Deep!* I hadn't been sure what the title meant until I got halfway through the book at which point the phrase is used to describe an obnoxious local.

As in: *You don't have to scratch very deep on him to find an asshole!*

Although blunt, this warning kept coming to my mind. It felt relevant to my current investigations. As in: *Don't scratch too deep! You probably won't like what you find out!*

All these answers to my package labeling questions, when I finally got them, were unsatisfying at best. At worst, they felt like real deception. But I was at least glad now to be getting to the bottom of some of the *real* stories . . . cross-linking, non-flushable warts, and all. Because as long as we are willing to take the word of industry who tries to brush us off with: *You wouldn't understand it, lady. Because, you know, Science,* we can't effectively argue for change.

And as the year progressed, it was becoming increasingly clear to me that change is what needed to come next.

Too bad then, that the pandemic was causing everyone to run in exactly the opposite direction. As Earth Day 2020 rolled around in April, the fiftieth anniversary of the first Earth Day in fact, my supermarket had shut down all recycling—redeemable bottles and cans, the plastic film bin—*and* was actively discouraging reusable bags. There was talk of banning them altogether amongst the cashiers.

Meanwhile, the Environmental Protection Agency had suspended enforcement of environmental laws.[5] Yes, all of them. After mounting pressure from a variety of industries including Big Oil, the EPA had decided the pandemic made complying with basic protections for human and environmental health just too darn difficult.

That's right! No more pesky monitoring, lab analysis, or reporting! In the United States there were now effectively no penalties for breaking pollution rules. And COVID-19 necessitated this because . . . if we can't pollute our own country the germs win?

In a press release, the EPA explained that they *expect(ed) all regulated entities to continue to manage and operate their facilities in a manner that is safe and that protects the public and the environment.* Translation: big corporations were now operating under the honor system.

What could possibly go wrong?

Even curbside recycling services were in jeopardy. Sure, everyone agreed waste removal was an "essential service," but whether or not recycling was included in that had been left up to the local governments to decide. Here in Vermont—*Vermont* mind you—there was a movement brewing to landfill all recycling and postpone the soon-to-be-enacted ban on sending food scraps to the landfill.

It was the fiftieth anniversary of Earth Day, and saving the earth seemed to be discontinued until further notice.

Things felt upside down. There was so much depression, boredom, isolation, and fear, but at the same time there were moments of unexpected beauty. Social media showed us that polluted skylines the world over were clearing because the world was standing still. The polluted canals of Venice became crystal clear. Wild boar were reported to be wandering the streets of Barcelona, and viral video showed a herd of deer cavorting on Indian streets. We were all watching from our windows, taking videos with our phones. We were a captive audience, literally and figuratively. In our absence, what would nature do to surprise us next?

What could we find to celebrate in such a Through-the-Looking-Glass Earth Day? I wondered. I read an article on the World Economic Forum that had a good answer. It argued that what the pandemic offered us was the chance to see the huge difference humans can make when they make individual change.

"Our collective ability to address the damage we've done to nature has seemed impossible. Until now. . . . The virus is raging, but we all can help stop it. When's the last time you felt you could freeze a glacier, or actually help extinguish a forest fire? What we do here—and what we learn—could save lives and help us all endure and thrive as individuals, as communities, as a species."[6]

Meanwhile, our family was limping our way along in our Year of No Garbage turned The Year of Keeping All Our Nice, Clean, Washed Garbage In A Pile In The Kitchen. One day, while cooking, I held up yet another piece of plastic food packaging and shook my head and sighed. Was I disappointed in it, or in myself?

At that moment Ilsa walked in and caught me wistfully contemplating a plastic food wrapper as if I were Hamlet regarding a skull. "Alas, poor Yorick . . ."

She laughed.

A PLASTIC PRIMER

Because it has emerged as the Darth Vader of our No Garbage Year, it seems like a good time to let you in on the birds and the bees of plastic. Where does plastic really come from? Why is it so evil?

Plastic begins its life in the ground as fossil fuel. "Fracking" is the means of extracting natural gas by injecting a combination of pressurized water, sand, and chemicals into the ground. Raw natural gas, which is primarily methane, is released but so are gases like ethane, butane, and propane.

Ethane is the building block or "feedstock" of plastic.

It used to be ethane would be burned off as a valueless by-product of oil extraction. Today, ethane is collected and transported to "cracking facilities." Maybe you've heard controversy about building new cracking facilities; these are the places where ethane is turned into ethylene (aka ethene) when the molecular bonds are broken through the application of extreme heat.

This is what that looks like, before and after cracking:

My profound apologies for resorting to actual chemical diagrams but the important takeaway for our purposes is that the bonds between carbon atoms have changed from single to double. Meaning? In a process known as polymerization, it "reacts easily with other chemicals and can be strung together into long molecular chains—sort of like Legos," as one chemist described it.[7] Or beads on a chain. This is what that looks like:

This is how ethylene can become: *poly*ethylene.

Mind blown. But let's keep going.

So, through cracking we have created ethylene. Is it evil yet? No. Ethylene is a product that does occur naturally as a gas given off my maturing plants.[8] (You know how you can ripen fruit faster by putting it into a brown paper bag? That's because of the ethylene the fruit is putting off.)

So we have a whole bunch of ethylene we've created, but at this point it is still a gas and a flammable, explosive one at that. Now it gets converted into something more transportable: solids that can take the form of powders, pellets, and granules that are shipped to production facilities around the world. Often that takes the form of *poly*ethylene, as described above, but alternatively ethylene could also be turned into propylene, which through polymerization becomes? *Poly*propylene! Or it could become polystyrene, polyvinyl chloride, or other plastics depending on the exact process.

No matter what type of plastic is involved, the most common form this new solid takes is known as "nurdles." Nurdles, or "preproduction pellets," are lentil-sized plastic building blocks that are trucked or shipped to production facilities to be melted and re-formed into plastic products. Along the way, *lots* of them get spilled into the environment, including a shocking 230,000 metric tonnes into the ocean every year.[9]

Now because we are terribly sharp cookies—you and I—we both know that fossil fuel comes from fossils. An excellent question would therefore be: if plastic is made from organic material, why can't it break back down into its organic roots?

The answer is that the carbon-carbon bonds in plastic formed through heat and pressure, create a *synthetic polymer* (synthetic meaning artificial or manmade and polymer meaning molecular chain, or literally "many parts"). These bonds are so strong as to be irreversible, as well as unrecognizable to the bacteria and enzymes that eat/break down organic material. "There aren't the metabolic pathways to do it," as one organic geochemist put it.[10]

We still aren't done, though, because according to Dr. Jenny Davies, who is the public and environmental health director for Cafeteria Culture, a nonprofit that works with schools to achieve zero waste cafeterias and which founded Plastic Free Lunch Day, plastic needs one more thing in order to be born: toxic chemicals. There are at least ten thousand different man-made chemicals that exist solely to create different properties in plastic; according to the E.U., a new synthetic chemical is created every 1.4 seconds, most of which is driven by the plastic industry.[11]

In a talk she gave to the Manhattan & Brooklyn Solid Waste Advisory Boards, Davies explains that all these thousands of synthetic chemicals fall into one of two groups: persistent organic pollutants (POPs), and heavy metals. We all know heavy metals—lead, mercury, chromium, antimony—are highly toxic, but what about POPs?

Persistent organic pollutants are, as you might guess from the name, bad news. "Persistent" applies to the fact that they are not water based and therefore instead of being eliminated by our body's waste removal system, they build up in the body (what's known as "bioaccumulation") and get stored in our fatty tissues, where they wreak all kinds of havoc. They can interfere with normal cell functioning, they can disrupt our endocrine system with implications for everything from our growth and development and reproductive systems, to the growth of cancers. Have you heard of "obesogens"? These are endocrine disrupting chemicals that mess with your metabolism and appetite.

"Okay, sure," I can hear you saying, "maybe they *use* all those different chemicals in the production of plastics, but that doesn't necessarily mean plastics shed those chemicals, does it?"

Turns out they do shed those chemicals, but at what rate and in what amounts can depend a lot on the circumstances. Many folks today know that plastics should never be microwaved, because the application of heat can cause plastic chemicals to leach into their food. Fewer people are aware of the fact that the older a plastic is, the more chemicals it will give off or "leak."

But what about new plastics? Because they are brand new, mightn't we presume they'd be fairly stable and *non*-leaky? A recent study showed that even in new plastics, toxic chemicals are being given off at an alarming rate. Danish scientists put room temperature water into a new, reusable plastic water bottle, the kind you might give your kid to take to a sports game, say. After twenty-four hours they found *400 different plastic chemicals* present in the water. Then, after washing the bottle in a home dishwasher and refilling it? They found *3500 plastic chemicals*—plasticizers, heat stabilizers, processing aids, not to mention the toxic pesticide DEET, which may have been formed inadvertently by the combination of other chemicals.[12]

So while we are helpfully hydrating our kids at soccer practice, at the same time we are unwittingly nourishing them with an array of hundreds, if not thousands, of man-made, toxic chemicals, the kind that our body can't get rid of: bisphenols (BPA, BPSS, BPSF), flame retardants and water repellants (PFOS, PFOA, PFAS, PFBS) and heavy metals. When I studied sugar, I learned about the difference between an "acute" poison (the kind that makes you keel over and die) and a "chronic" poison which builds up and creates ill effects over time. With the chemicals of plastic, we are all effectively poisoning ourselves slowly, over time. We use these plastic products every day, all the time, taking in thousands of chemicals in innumerable combinations from something as simple as taking a drink of water. Is it any wonder that today we suffer from so many diseases for which no one knows the exact cause? (We'll talk more about the health effects of plastic in a bit.)

But back to why plastic doesn't biodegrade. When that very specific natural gas meets the application of extremely high heat and pressure in the presence of one of the tens of thousands of synthetic, toxic chemical catalyst(s), it's something that would never occur in nature, and consequently, results in the transformation of an organic product from the ground into a material that no organism on earth recognizes as food. *That's* why it won't break down, and *that's* where the evil comes in.

Do you recall the late seventies margarine commercial that proclaimed "It's not *nice* to fool Mother Nature!"? Turns out Mother Nature isn't so easily fooled after all.

CHAPTER SIX

....

"HAS MOM LOST IT?" NO ONE EXPECTS THE GARBAGE INQUISITION

I t was May. And not just May, but May after *seven weeks of quarantine.* In January I had posted pictures of little glass jars holding tiny piles of colorful bits and pieces on social media and it all seemed quite adorable. It was not adorable anymore. My Super Awesome Recycling Center continued to overflow rather alarmingly. Perhaps it was best that the isolation required us not to have guests over, since the most popular room in the house was now occupied by a pile of indeterminate proportions, possibly escaped from a low-budget horror film entitled *The Garbage Blob That Ate My Kitchen.*

Here's my strategy when things like this develop: *Ignore. Ignore. Ignore. Ignore. Ignore. Igno-*SUDDENLY FREAK OUT. I am very good at this. So when Steve walked in and saw me sitting knee-deep in a pile of what most people would call "garbage," carefully separating tangled thread from a wad of I VOTED! stickers and the disembodied wire from a long-lost spiral notebook, he knew not to assume I'd lost my marbles any more than usual.

This is what happened the day the wishful recycling blob finally destabilized and started cascading all across my kitchen floor. Once

I had to wade through plastic bags and random pieces of cellophane to get to the stove, it was time to take action.

Fortunately, Ilsa was there to help. The two of us pulled everything apart and began sorting up a storm. Because there were still so many items still awaiting official answers as to where and how they might be recycled, I knew I needed to abandon the dainty little system I had begun with in favor of something a bit more rugged.

Out with the pretty mason jars and baskets. The Super Awesome Recycling Center was now composed of six, round, identical plastic bins, each one large enough to hold a twenty-five pound bag of flour. What warranted its own bin? What could do with something smaller? This is, of course, something I would have ideally set in place at the beginning of our project, but back then I had no idea what the categories would be, or how much of each one we were likely to collect; now as we crept up on the halfway point of the year, this pile was now the big, ugly answer to that question.

In the end, Ilsa and I came up with a system that I was quite unreasonably proud of. Here were the six major categories, one for each large, round bin:

1. **POLYETHYLENE #2 AND #4:** The flexible, stretchy plastic also known as "plastic film," one of the first major breakthroughs we had discovered of non-single-stream recycling.
   To recap, this included:
   - plastic supermarket bags
   - produce bags (both the kind that come in rolls at the store and the kind apples and oranges come in)
   - plastic overwrap from things like paper towels, toilet paper, and water bottle cases
   - dry cleaning bags
   - Ziploc® bags
   - Bubble Wrap and bubble mailers
   - deflated air pillows and plastic mailing envelopes
   - newspaper bags

- cereal box liners (unless they tear like paper)
  SOLUTION: Recyclable at the supermarket bag
  recycling bin, once that opened up again. Free.
  Difficulty level: Easy

2. **MULTILAYER/ MULTI-FILM PLASTIC:** These are the
   plastics that are coextruded (aka scientifically smooshed
   together) and therefore use several different kinds of
   plastic. This makes storing food wonderfully easy and
   recycling impossible very, very hard.
   Included:
   - pouches used for vacuum sealing, such as for meat
   - plastic bags used for frozen vegetables
   SOLUTION: I was still working on it.
   Difficulty level: Tough.

3. **PACKAGES USING FOIL:** These are also multilayer
   packages, but in this case Mylar (a form of plastic itself) or
   foil (which is aluminum) is smooshed together with paper
   and/or plastic.
   Included:
   - snack bags
   - chip bags
   - coffee bags
   - candy, granola, and breakfast bar wrappers
   SOLUTION: I was still working on it.
   Difficulty level: Tough.

4. **CRINKLY PLASTICS AND CELLOPHANE:** This is
   any flexible plastic that is shiny, and makes crinkly noises.
   Unlike polyethylene, it does not stretch when you pull it.
   Included: The heat seal shrink-wrap that comes banded
   on the top of so many products. Also, packaging for
   practically every product you can think of. If it didn't fit in
   any other above categories it was probably this.
   SOLUTION: I was still working on it.
   Difficulty Level: You're killing me here.

5. **WINE CORKS:** Because apparently I'm a wino. I blamed the pandemic. Also, I blame wine. (Note that this bin was reserved for actual *cork* wine corks, which are made from the bark of the cork oak, not plastic ones.)

   Included: Um. Wine corks.

   SOLUTION: Start a business making wine cork keychains? Check Pinterest? Note to self: buy a glue gun. Also, I read you can soak them in alcohol and use them as fire starters, so my inner pyromaniac found that promising. Failing all of these options, you can always home compost wine corks since they are made entirely of tree bark. If you want to speed the composting process up you can try shredding them on a cheese grater. (Make sure they aren't plastic: plastic corks are entirely smooth and denser feeling; real cork is lighter, spongier, and has small imperfections.)

   Difficulty Level: Easy to Moderate

6. **I DON'T KNOW!:** This is where I put the fun stuff.

   Included:
   - deflated birthday balloons
   - broken Pyrex
   - two pieces of Styrofoam
   - a burned-out light bulb
   - plastic produce netting
   - hard plastic with no identifying numbers
   - used-up ballpoint pens
   - old mascara containers
   - empty mailing tape dispenser
   - irredeemably bent coat hanger
   - a forlorn winter glove that had no soulmate
   - a plastic pickle holder that looked like a parasol for a leprechaun

   SOLUTION: I swear to God I was working on it.

   Difficulty Level: Ninja.

Beneath the large bin area, I also had eight smaller containers for things that didn't come up as much/didn't require much room. They were labeled correspondingly: Tinfoil, Wax, Silica Gel Packs, Batteries, Stickers, Plastic Doohickeys, Caps, and Plastic Wrap (as opposed to plastic film).

I know what you're thinking. "Eve? Hadn't you just, you know, washed and dried and kept all your garbage instead of sending it to the landfill? I mean, what was the point of all this sorting if there *was no solution* for these things?"

I know you're probably thinking that, because I was thinking it myself about once or fourteen times a day. I consoled myself with the realization that all of this stuff, *all* of it could have fit into one ninety-six-gallon trash container. That's the same trash container that until January we used to cart to the curbside, full to bursting, every single week. If I my calculations were right, at eighteen weeks in, we'd avoided sending 1,728 gallons of garbage to the landfill.

A whole year of filling up our trash container amounted to 4,992 gallons. I realized that even if, at the end of the year, we ended up with, say, two containers of *I couldn't solve this*—192 gallons—I could probably still feel pretty good about the other 4,800 gallons we had saved from the landfill, primarily because we decided to start paying attention.

Just to be super geeky, I tried to figure out what weight was represented by those 4,800 gallons of trash. Would it equal a small elephant? A grand piano? Unfortunately, because gallon is a measurement of volume, not weight, that's a very tricky thing to figure out. Online I found wildly different estimates as to how much an average gallon of household trash is supposed to weigh. Is it a half a pound? Four pounds? Depends who you ask.

The online consensus seemed to be that the average American throws out four pounds of trash per day,* or 1,460 pounds per person per year, which is to say three-quarters of a ton. In a household of four people that would equate to about three tons per year.

---

* More on this in a bit.

That's like throwing away a full-grown rhinoceros. That, however, is a very conservative estimate. Author Edward Humes cites a study by Columbia University and the journal *BioCycle* as calculating the actual figure to be more like *seven* pounds per day.[1] Now that family of four is throwing out a full-grown elephant every year.

If that's not depressing enough, consider that these estimates don't include the extra burden represented by all the plastic associated with the pandemic: plastic gloves, masks, all that additional takeout plastic, the online shopping package material, cylinders of Clorox wipes and home tests, as well as medical waste generated by the hospitals coping with the requirements of dealing with COVID-19. Worldwide, the pandemic is estimated to have generated somewhere between eight and eleven million tons of additional plastic waste.[2]

At our house, after beginning the pandemic in washable cloth masks, we had gotten the word that disposable N95 masks were considered much more effective, and we dutifully bought a big box of them. However, how to determine when a mask had lived its whole life was less clear: how many hour-long trips to the grocery store was it good for? What if I hung it up to air it out in between? Did I really need to wear plastic gloves too, or was that overkill? There were no definitive answers at this time and of course it always seemed better to err on the side of caution. Even though it was technically allowed by the terms of our project I still hated having to put old PPE in our "health and safety" garbage, because I knew nothing good would be happening to it down the road.

At last, summer was here and for Ilsa school was out. Greta and Steven had settled into routines of their own, Greta working on knitting projects and beginning the process of learning to apply for acting jobs online—of which there were precisely none. Steven had done a complete about-face on TikTok: he had started by making short, jokey videos and over time they became more elaborate and sophisticated. Favorite recurring characters and tropes began to appear that were gaining him a small but steady following, and he was happy to have a self-appointed "job." He talked about being an influencer and chatted with the kids who made up his primary audience during periodic live streams. First three people showed up. Then twenty. He started to have a couple dozen fans, all of whom kept asking him why he wasn't famous yet.

For the most part, things were continuing on a fairly even keel in the No Garbage department. Steven resolved to do the dishes every night after dinner, and he was admirably steadfast in this, which helped me tremendously. Greta and Ilsa would (perhaps a wee bit less reliably) take care of the dishes during the day. Quite understandably, what no one wanted to do, however, was to wash the weird plastic packaging that inevitably went along with those dishes—that job was oh-so exclusively mine. Not just bottles or cans for rinsing, but plastics, foils, and multilayers, wet with food-related goo in various stages of smelliness, sticking to each other and themselves each awaiting their own separate rubdown and spa treatment. Sometimes I just wasn't sure I could face it.

"Wow. We take such good care of our garbage," Ilsa marveled one evening as I draped a freshly massaged and buffed piece of Saran Wrap atop the overflowing dish drainer.

Every once in a while there'd be a bit of excitement. I'd taken to occasionally becoming possessed by the spirit of the Spanish Inquisition.

"SO *WHO* PUT AN *ENTIRE ROLL OF SOGGY TOILET PAPER* IN THE 'HEALTH AND SAFETY GARBAGE'? HMMM? COME ON! OUT WITH IT!"

I don't know why everyone looked at me like I was crazy when this happened.

Once Greta casually mentioned *throwing out* (!) an empty shampoo bottle. The logic was that she had heard someone say at some point that the guesthouse "didn't count." Of course, this notion had been uttered before COVID-19, back when we still rented the guesthouse to actual *guests*.

"Are *YOU* an Airbnb guest?" I asked her with poorly concealed exasperation.

"No . . .?"

"Then *it counts.*"

If I ever questioned Greta's commitment to the project, though, she'd remind me of the trials and tribulations of being No Garbage in Brooklyn before coming home. There was the trekking all over the city in vain, trying to find a butcher who still wrapped in paper, rather than plastic. There was buying a twenty-dollar horsehair dish-scrubbing brush to replace plastic sponges that cost $2.50 for a pack of three. There was the time she unthinkingly threw her banana peel in the trash can at school and then realized what she had done.

"I stood there trying to figure out if I should put my hand in the garbage to take it back out! And my friends were like what's wrong why are you so upset looking and I told them and they're like GRETA. *You do not put your hand in the garbage*—**no**."

"*MOM*," She had phoned me the next day racked with remorse. "I have *banana guilt.*"

My husband, Steve, had been known upon occasion to skirt the spirit of the project too, if not the actual rules. I'm sure he found it just adorable when I harangued him about putting the perfectly recyclable cardboard toothpaste box in the much-discussed Health and Safety Garbage, using the justification that brushing our teeth falls under "health." Or, when his foil photographic film wrappers somehow ended up in the "can be used for kindling" bag that we had started keeping for campfires.

"This *isn't* paper, *darling*!" I call to him across the kitchen, waving the foil wrapper at him as daintily as a linen hankie.

"It *does* burn, though, my love" he smiles back at me.

"But my *dearest,*" I say, batting my eyes sweetly, "IT SHOULDN'T."

Although everyone had signed on for this Year of No Garbage, it suddenly occurred to me that maybe, perhaps, they were less than enthusiastic. I'd been finding that instead of throwing things in the trash, people in my family were instead throwing things at *me*. And then I'd take care of getting it to where it needed to go.

One thing that I found especially absurd was mail packaging. Like many people, in an effort to avoid pandemic exposure, we were now getting far more packages delivered to us at home than ever before. The good news was that I had figured out how virtually all mailing materials may be recycled, with cardboard going to regular recycling, and Bubble Wrap, Bubble Wrap mailers, air pillows, and Tyvek mailers all suitable for the plastic film bin at the supermarket.

The bad news was that it didn't seem like anyone else in the house had absorbed this knowledge. When Steve tried to hand me a Bubble Wrap mailer one day, I told him he could put it in the recycling himself. Steve protested he was afraid he'd do it wrong.

A little while later Greta did a very similar thing. A cellophane bag needed disposing of, so instead of taking care of it for her, I gave her a quiz: where do you think this goes? She guessed Polyethylene recycling, which was close but no cigar. No, I explained, any plastic that is *stretchy* may go to Polyethylene (supermarket plastic bag) recycling, but any plastic that is *crinkly* must go into the crinkly plastics and cellophane bin.

I realize my reactions sound suspiciously like the ravings of a Recycling-Obsessed Lunatic: *No! Not the low-density polyethylene bin, you cretins!* But I genuinely was surprised to realize that just because *I* had been consumed by thinking and writing about zero waste for the last half a year, didn't necessarily mean that my family had absorbed that information. But come to think of it, why would they?

And if my own participating family didn't internalize the hard-won lessons learned from a Year of No Garbage, then who would? If I was the only one actually living No Garbage in our house, then wasn't that a failure of the project on some fundamental level?

The $64,000 question that led me to was: *can* people change?

If you lead a horse to water, can you make him recycle?

So I approached Steve and Greta and asked them. Was I wrong to interpret their behavior as lack of interest?

Turns out that they were not uninterested; they were intimidated. They didn't want to mess up my elaborate system, and the hard-won lessons I'd learned regarding the distinctions between the materials in plastics, hadn't been absorbed by osmosis. Hanging up recycling flyers in the kitchen and placing neat labels on bins wasn't enough. I needed to actually talk to my family when they had something to discard. Every time. For a while. Change takes not only time but investment, and I realized that I had made some assumptions that just didn't follow.

So now that we had cleared the air things were changing. I was trying to be more communicative about my hard-won system, and they, for their part, weren't just handing me stuff anymore. I noticed Greta checking in with me when discarding packaging. "Mom? This goes in polyethylene, right?"

I was so proud.

When it came to making less trash and being more sustainable there was at least one category where Greta was way, way ahead of me: and that was in getting away from "fast fashion." Ever since high school she's been taken with vintage fashion from a variety of time periods, the 1940s being a favorite era. Online, she has discovered an entire community who shares her passion for the styles and culture of this period (but, Greta is quick to point out, not the prejudices or politics). Want to know how serious she is? For her seventeenth birthday we celebrated with a "V-E Day" party that featured big band music, a Victory Garden, and signs pointing to the nearest Anderson air raid shelter. Over the years she has added to her collection of vintage clothing, as well as taught herself to sew her own clothing in period styles.

Ilsa's no fan of poorly made contemporary clothing either. Her favorite shopping opportunities are thrift shops where she's learned to pick up items that are better made than anything she can find new, and, after working on costumes for the school play, she now has the sewing skills to alter and repair just about anything, bringing items back to life.

And this is important because the fashion industry has a very serious environmental impact, in water usage, in climate emissions from transport, and in being an enormous driver in the production of plastics. Sixty percent of material made into clothing today is plastic.[3] Your yoga pants? Your fleece jacket? Check your clothing labels, and I'm sure you'll find that most of them, either in whole or in part, are made with plastics: nylon, polyester, acrylic.

Bear in mind too that anything "faux" is almost always plastic. Faux fur? Pleather? Imitation suede? All plastic. One popular "vegan leather" I found recently is made of 60 percent polyurethane and 40 percent polyester. So are you wearing a chic "vegan leather jump-suit," or are you wearing a glorified plastic bag?

One thing this means is that during their useful life these items are all shedding microplastics all the time: into the air we breathe while wearing them and into the water in our washing machines when we clean them. On top of that we have the problem that when their useful life is done, none of these items will ever degrade or break down. There are "clothing graveyards" springing up around the world, notably in Chile's Atacama Desert, where 35,000 tons of used clothing has been dumped in the desert.[4]

On top of all this there's just the sheer wastefulness of our current relationship with clothing. According to Earth.org, between 2000 and 2015 clothing sales doubled, while in that same time garment usage has declined by thirty-six percent.[5] The world currently discards 92 million tons of clothing-related waste each year, representing a loss of $500 billion.[6] After realizing the ever-accelerating wasteful cycle that the fashion industry is currently in, I resolved not to buy new clothes anymore. I mean, underwear and maybe shoes I buy new, but otherwise? Shopping used is, in my opinion, both more economical *and* more fun. More importantly, my two girls who represent the next generation, agree with me.

And they're not alone. One of Greta's favorite online personalities is Bernadette Banner, whose specialty is knowledge of Victorian era garments and who makes YouTube videos about using traditional techniques to make and repair clothing. I was struck by these words from her in her recent book on the topic:

It is worth keeping in mind the difference between being a caretaker versus being a consumer. Consumerism makes sense within the context of products that are, well, meant to be *consumed*: food, drinks, soap, and so on. Textiles—and clothing as a result—are not easy to consume, and so they must by default fall into the caretaker category: Once a garment enters our lives, we become responsible for it, including taking on the task of helping it on to the next stage of life when we no longer have a want or purpose for it.[7]

She almost makes our clothing sound like our children, doesn't she? I think this is brilliantly expressed, and perhaps may even be expanded beyond the category of clothing: we have *responsibility* to our things, and to make sure good things happen to them. In modern contemporary life, of course, that is swimming against the entire tide of our culture. Having such an attitude will definitely make you the resident weirdo sooner or later, but I'd advise against worrying about that. I find normalcy to be highly overrated.

STRANGE TIPS FOR THE UBER RECYCLER

- When opening packaging never fully remove pull tabs. Leaving them attached to the original packaging means they are more likely to get recycled too. Likewise, any package you cut open with scissors: make a tiny slit and then only cut one side of the package, so that it stays intact and you aren't left with smaller strips that recyclers say fall through the cracks of the machinery.
- Collect even the tiniest bits of foil—like the little circle you remove from the top of the wine bottle. Once you have enough to make a potato-sized ball of foil, put it in the recycling (again, anything smaller may get lost on the floor of the sorting center aka the materials recovery facility or MRF).*
- Cut plastic tags away from the rubber bands and twist ties on produce. The plastic is almost certainly not recyclable but the

---

* Please note not all recycling programs accept aluminum in this form. For example, here in Vermont they do, but my friend Andrea says in Ohio they don't.

ties and bands are infinitely reusable. (Use these for resecuring food packaging instead of plastic wrap!)

- A broken rubber band can be tied and reused.
- Birthday candles can be washed and reused.
- Wash Ziploc® bags, produce bags, deli packaging for meat and any other plastic bags that are destined for the plastic film bin at the supermarket—or to be reused—by turning them inside out. To dry, place bag inverted over a bottle or hang from a clothespin. I have a hanging herb-drying rack in my kitchen that does very nicely.
- When it comes to recycling, the small stuff is the most problematic. I keep a few glass jars near the kitchen sink to collect bottle caps, wine corks, silica gel packages, and random plastic doo-dads. Once I have accumulated a big bunch of something I make a post on a local online bulletin board, Facebook group, or on Freecycle and offer them free as art supplies or whatever. A local acupuncturist picked up my entire year's supply of silica gel packets for the preservation of her herb collection, and a craftsman in the next town took my year's worth of plastic bottle caps.
- If you can, have a small burn pile for small, nonplastic items that can't go to recycling. In my kitchen I keep a container for things like tiny pieces of paper, paper-only takeout containers, toilet paper cores, and used disposable wood chopsticks. I put these in a brown paper bag, and Steve uses it to start our outdoor fireplace. Pizza boxes with food on them meet this fate as well.
- Itty bitty metal things such as bent screws, springs, old hardware, and yes, even staples, I collect in a bin in the basement. Once in a blue moon, I pour this into the metal recycling bin at the transfer station. But will they fall through the cracks like other small items? Items that have steel or tin in them have a better chance at the materials recovery facility as they are collected and sorted magnetically.

When I was a kid my dad used to play for me the Arlo Guthrie song "Alice's Restaurant." If you've never heard it, it's a hilarious, loopy, partly spoken twenty-minute song about how a visit to some friends' house ends up endangering Guthrie's eligibility for the draft due to the fact that he tried to do a good deed and take his friends' trash out but ends up getting arrested for littering.

(When a police officer asks if he has any idea how an envelope with his name on it ended up in the illegally dumped trash he confesses: he *did* put an envelope under that big pile of garbage.)

It was the first time I had ever thought about where trash actually went when it left our house, or the fact that it could represent a real problem. Enough of a problem that people could get in actual trouble for doing it improperly. So, when it came to garbage, what was "proper"?

As I zeroed in hard on each and every item that our household felt ready to part ways with, I was giving a lot of thought to the two primary ways we deal with garbage in our society today. When something leaves our houses in one of those wheeled, black plastic bins, the fate of its contents ultimately comes down to just one question: to bury or to burn?

BURY

The vast majority of trash in this country—about 88 percent—is buried, which is to say landfilled. What began as the largely unregulated practice of putting stuff we'd rather not deal with into a hole in the ground—which, surprisingly, lasted in this country all the way up through the 1970s—has evolved today into a complex system intended to prevent the contents from contaminating the surrounding environment, meant to every leakage manner possible: solid, liquid, or gaseous. Thus, the modern-day landfill incorporates layers of clay and plastic liners, systems of liquid collection for "leachate" (aka "garbage juice"), and gas collection for methane (a potent greenhouse gas linked to climate change.)

Think of the modern landfill as a kind of wall made of garbage "bricks": sequential sections or "cells" are lined with clay, plastic, and dirt before trash is dumped in and compacted with machinery.[8] At the end of each working day, whether the new cell is full or not, several inches of dirt called "daily cover" are laid on top in order to limit odors and discourage pests. Shredded tires, automobile pieces, incinerator ash and/or biologically, chemically or, yes, even radioactively contaminated material may be combined with or used in place of dirt for daily cover.[9]

Although the system for landfilling has become orders of magnitude more elaborate in just the last half century, that's no guarantee that it actually works. In fact the Center for Health Environment and Justice issued a report in 2016 that convincingly asserted that "all landfills leak,"[10] citing concerns such as the inevitability of cracked and leaking liners, and silt-clogged leachate collection pipes.

One of the report's authors comments dryly: "Since humans have no experience maintaining anything in perpetuity, perpetual maintenance is an untested and unproven, and, one can only say, silly non-solution. If we took it seriously, perhaps we would develop a large army of landfill maintainers whose only job in life will be to maintain the toxic garbage left behind by their parents and their parents' parents and their parents' parents' parents and so on for generation after generation."[11]

BURN

Compared to the landfill, garbage incinerators receive a much smaller percentage of the waste disposal market generated in the United States, only about 12 percent. As you can imagine, once upon a time, not all that long ago really, trash incineration was pretty unsophisticated: you got a furnace? Then you can burn garbage. Whatever ash or unburned material that was left got carted off to the landfill. Then in 1970 the Clean Air Act banned uncontrolled burning of garbage, and facilities were forced to install technology to reduce emissions, or close. Currently there are only around seventy incinerators in the United States, and notably, three-quarters of them are more than thirty years old and thereby not subject to the more stringent regulations imposed by the updates to the Clean Air Act made in 1990.[12]

Although each facility is somewhat unique, the most prevalent method for garbage incineration is called "mass burn." In this system, waste is dumped in a storage area, from which larger items may be removed by a crane, and ferrous metals are extracted by magnet. There may be a shredding process to reduce object sizes, after which the waste is moved to a furnace, which is burning at temperatures over 1,500 degrees Fahrenheit. As the furnace burns, water circulating around the furnace is heated and used to drive turbines that produce energy. Because of this, proponents of incineration prefer to call the burning garbage process by the euphemism "waste to energy." It is true: burning garbage does produce energy. It also produces toxic ash and gas.

In fact it's kind of surprising how much material is still left over after burning: in terms of mass, about one-third is left over from the process as ash, and not just any ash, but toxic ash containing furans and heavy metals (we will talk about these terms more in chapter 11). This "incinerator bottom ash" (IBA) or "fly ash" as it is also known (although the latter term also may apply to ash from coal-fired power plants), must then be removed and—you guessed it!—buried in a hazardous waste landfill. Which is bad enough but, for the last few decades it's also been extremely common to "reuse" IBA in the production of cement. How do you like the idea of the cement used to build your kid's new school being composed of, say 30 percent toxic incinerator ash?

It seems there's always someone out there trying to find a new good use for this nasty, potentially hazardous stuff: IBA has been proposed for making clay for "land reclamation" in which land is built out into oceans and other waterways,[13] and even suggested as an agricultural soil amendment.[14] Proponents term such uses "recycling," although I am tempted to rename it "hiding toxic crud in plain sight."

And we are still not done, because remember the gases? As burning is taking place, gases are also being released, known as "flue gas." These are then collected in a mechanism called a "scrubber" which works to remove particulate matter and chemically neutralize acidic gas, before releasing what's left into the air. I have to admit that no matter how much "scrubbing" goes on, I wouldn't be running to be first in line to breathe that air, but *especially* not for the air released by one of the fifty-five incinerators in the United States that predates more stringent regulations.

If you find yourself thinking, "That's it? When it comes to getting rid of garbage that's the best we've got?" then you're not alone. Municipal garbage treatment options leave much to be desired, which is where private enterprise may come in.

And the name of the company that came up more than any other in that category? You may recall I kept hearing about this company called "TerraCycle."

CHAPTER SEVEN

···

IS TERRACYCLE FOR REAL?

TerraCycle is one of those entities that seems to be both every-where and nowhere at the same time. Even if you've never heard of them, I'd be willing to bet TerraCycle's infinity symbol logo is emblazoned on the packaging of a fair number of the products you have in your home right now. A self-described "waste management company with a mission to eliminate the idea of waste," they were making millions of dollars doing what was supposed to be impossi-ble: recycling *everything*.

How did they do it? Could this be for real?

Get any group of eco-obsessed folks together and you can imme-diately start a heated discussion on the merits of this New Jersey–based specialty recycler, and its boy-wonder founder, Tom Szaky. "This Guy Makes Money Off Your Cigarette Butts and Flip-Flops" exclaims one Bloomberg headline. It's a quintessentially American story: Szaky started the company in his college dorm room, feed-ing cafeteria compost scraps to worms to create plant food, which he then packaged in reused plastic bottles. Today the company gets a lot of media attention for things like turning juice pouches into backpacks.

But one place Terracycle reliably shows up is in those articles entitled "Recycling! Ten Ways You're Doing it ALL WRONG!" Incidentally, what I hate about Top Ten "listicles" is they purport to give you good advice about important issues, like recycling, but actually end up just skimming the surface in a way that isn't at all helpful. We feel good about reading the article, but don't end up with enough information to effectively *change* anything.

I give you Exhibit A: in the article "10 Household Products You Never Knew You Could Recycle" posted on Food52, the author breezes past the thorny issue of what to do with used toothbrushes and toothpaste tubes with the advice to "mail toothbrushes to alternate recycling systems like TerraCycle" adding, "TerraCycle's got you covered"!

Wow! Great! I'll use TerraCycle! we think.

But . . . what does that actually mean? Like . . . can I just write TerraCycle's address on an envelope and mail them my old toothpaste tube? And once they get it, what on earth do they do with it?

Unfortunately, TerraCycle's website doesn't do much to clear up the confusion. I had visited TerraCycle's website at least a dozen times since the Year of No Garbage project began. Every single time I, a reasonably intelligent, ordinary person, came away utterly defeated. The TerraCycle universe is rife with made-up copyrighted terms like *Loop* and *ReZound*. There are contests, promotions, points, rewards, and initiatives. They have literally hundreds of different programs individually listed, each one customized for a different specific product line or manufacturer. There was a program for recycling Swedish Fish packaging. There was another for recycling Teva sandals. How on earth was this supposed to work?

After speaking to a few customer service representatives and scouring the website still further, I decided to compile my *own* listicle:

TOP TEN FACTS YOU NEED TO KNOW ABOUT TERRACYCLE *NOW!*

FACT #1: No, you can't just mail them your old toothpaste tube.

To begin with:

FACT #2: You have to pay for TerraCycle's services. Unless you have a school group or business that is locally collecting for TerraCycle as a fundraiser or promotion, it is a fee-based program. (More on this in a minute.)

On top of this:

FACT #3: It's unnecessarily complicated. This much was clear: for the pay programs, you order a Zero Waste Box for a fee, which included the postage for mailing it back when it was full; they recycle the contents. So the next logical question was how much does it cost?

FACT #4: The fee varies a *LOT* depending on what goes in the box, and this is where it starts to get complicated, because:

FACT #5: There are *seventy-nine different types* of Zero Waste Boxes, at least by my last count. This includes boxes devoted entirely to subcategories like 3D printing materials, toy action figures, and (my personal favorite) *used chewing gum.* I was not sure I wanted to know what they do with that.

On top of this:

FACT #6: The Zero Waste Boxes come in three sizes, the middle one of which is about the size of a kitchen garbage can.

Between the categories and the sizes, I counted at least 237 boxes to choose from. Overwhelmed yet? Well, they do have an "Everything" box option, in which you can put, well, almost anything.

FACT #7: The "All in One" box is clearly the easiest solution, but it is also the most expensive: the medium box in this category costs $287.

Hmm. I felt a little led astray by "10 Household Products You Never Knew You Could Recycle" . . . if I was trying to recycle that empty Tom's toothpaste container from the article, $287 felt a little steep. How about the "Personal Care Accessories" box? The smallest box measures 11" x 11" x 20" and costs $115.

But wait! In the list of acceptable items for the Personal Care box, nowhere does it mention toothpaste tubes or toothbrushes! Back to the drawing board.

In the TerraCycle search bar I type "toothbrush" and am pointed to the "Oral Care Waste and Packaging—Zero Waste Pallet" available for the low, low price of $1,147.

I try again and type "toothpaste."

Sorry, we could not find a program matching your request.

ARGH.

I *knew* they accepted toothpaste tubes for recycling but darned if I could figure out a way to submit them that made any kind of sense. I flipped over to "Free Recycling Programs." Maybe I could start one of those in our community, like at the local school or library? Then everyone could recycle their toothpaste tubes! For free!

FACT #8: All the "free" recycling programs sound like advertising: "Febreze Aerosol Recycling," "Gillette Razor Recycling," and so on. So does that mean you can only recycle those brands in these boxes? It was not entirely clear, but it turned out that didn't matter, because:

FACT #9: The free boxes seem impossible to get. At one point I went through the effort to register and make separate requests for three different kinds of the free recycling boxes. I got a message for each one saying I've been placed on a "waitlist for this program." That had been several months ago.

Back to the drawing board. A search for "dental" brought up boxes for disposable gloves, garage waste, and pet products.

I was swimming in a sea of random objects. Vitamin bottles! Cassette tapes! Shoes! It was all so frustrating and tantalizing at the same time. I was so very glad to know that someone was out there trying to do the impossible, offering to recycle things no one else would, but so very frustrated I couldn't figure out how to use their system.

From the sheer number of categories, to the huge boxes, to the bureaucratic layout, the TerraCycle website felt designed for industry, not ordinary people. Which it may be, but I was still glad that it is open to ordinary people. Despite the fact that TerraCycle's system was, shall we say, flawed, I'd nevertheless like to point out that:

FACT #10: What they're trying to do seemed groundbreaking and kind of heroic. Yes, I wished it was much, much more user friendly. But as far as I could tell they seemed to be the only game in town trying to recycle everything, and at the time I thought, *Well, that counts for a whole heck of a lot.*

It was time at last to bite the bullet and just try ordering something from TerraCycle and see how it all turned out. I selected a Zero Waste Box called "Plastic Packaging." I had both phone and email exchanges with TerraCycle customer service, to be reassured that this particular box was appropriate for what was building up in my recycling corner the most: crinkly cellophane plastics and coextruded multilayer plastics. Then I checked on the one last thing that had been bothering me.

I emailed: Did I really have to remove *all* paper labels?

A customer service representative wrote back: *With regards to paper labels, we do ask that they are removed before you place them in your Zero Waste Box. I know these can be a bit tricky at times so please know that we sincerely appreciate your efforts in removing them!*

Well, what choice did I have? Buying the "All in One" box at more than twice the price? No. I'd wrestle with those labels.

I was finally ready.

I ordered a medium size box for $134. At some point during the ordering process I stumbled across an envelope I could buy marked "Oral Care Waste"! At last, a solution for my toothpaste tubes! It was forty-two dollars, for a size slightly smaller than a manila envelope but I was so grateful to at last find it, I added it to my cart without hesitation and clicked "PURCHASE."

I was excited, but at the same time I wasn't quite sure how to feel about this pay-to-play recycling. Of course, there's always the problem of what-is-the-carbon-footprint-of-all-this-package-mailing? There's the wondering what really happens to the stuff once it gets to the good people of TerraCycle? There's the hope that this is really doing good things, but the lurking fear that I may just be paying TerraCycle to assuage my first-world-problem guilt.

But for most people, cost is clearly the most obvious deal breaker. *What! PAY to throw things away?* Although, come to think of it, most of us do that all the time. At our house we were paying fifty-seven dollars per month for combined garbage removal and single-stream recycling. So, if I managed to get six months' worth of otherwise-unrecyclable plastic stuffed into that TerraCycle box and recycled by paying $134, and a year requires, say, two boxes, that would work out to just over twenty-two dollars per month. Compared to curbside removal, I'd be saving money.

In cases like this, Steve likes to quote a scene from the movie *National Treasure*. Harvey Keitel's FBI agent is confronting main character Nicholas Cage, who asks if he really has to go to prison, even though they both know he's actually the good guy. Keitel says, "*Someone's* got to go to prison." What he means is someone, somewhere always has to take responsibility, to *pay the bill*. That's what all this disposable packaging is like—an unpaid bill. If the companies who make these almost-impossible-to-recycle products aren't going to do it, we have to. Or the government does. Or the environment does. *Someone* does.

Today it would be me. And when my TerraCycle box showed up, I *was* pretty blown away by how much fit into it. My entire five-month supply of cellophane/crinkly plastic went in, about half of the multilayer plastic went in (the other half had the dreaded paper labels I had yet to figure out) and literally two-thirds of my large I

Don't Know box also. It felt like the first major breakthrough since the supermarket plastic bag recycling. So far I was pretty impressed, and the box wasn't even full.

Things I discovered could *also* go into the Plastic Packaging box, that before now were giving me agita in the nonrecyclable pile:

- plastic blister pill packaging
- plastic produce netting
- hard plastic with no recycling numbers
- plastic mailing tape dispensers
- plastic ribbons
- those little plastic tags they sneak onto the rubber bands around vegetables
- Styrofoam
- heat-activated shrink-wrap seals (those bands around the cap or lid of products)

I still, however, had a sticker problem.

The funny thing is, I used to adore stickers. When I was in middle school I had a whole three-ring binder full of them: puffy stickers, heart stickers, stickers with pictures of unicorns gazing meaningfully at rainbows . . .

These days, my thoughts about stickers were much less fanciful. And occasionally involved adult language.

That's because stickers are another confounding object when it comes to recycling. So many questions and so few answers. I wondered:

When is a sticker a sticker . . . and when is it a *glued paper label*? (There is a difference.)

Will a sticker really interfere with the recycling process (TerraCycle, supermarket plastic film bin, and otherwise)?

Would I rather hang out with roadkill than spend time removing stickers?

I have a confession to make. I did everything I was supposed to do: I cleaned my plastics; I made sure they were all completely dry.

I sent my TerraCycle Plastic Packaging box as densely packed with plastic as any box could ever be, but *I did not remove any stickers*.

I wondered . . . what would happen? Would they issue me the equivalent of a recycling speeding ticket? Would they send me my box of plastic back? Or worst of all, after all that effort from cleaning and drying to shipping and paying: in the end would they just discard my whole box into the landfill? I realized I had entered:

The Five Stages of Wish-cycling
- *Hope*—I crossed my fingers. I really, *really* hoped my box was recycled.
- *Rationalizing*—After all, you used to have to remove paper labels from *cans* before recycling, and now you don't anymore! Maybe it's like that!
- *Pretending I'm an expert*—Well, they're probably melting all these plastics down, so heat will just melt those labels too. I think.
- *Anger*—You know, how on earth are we supposed to remove all these sticky labels, anyway? It's practically impossible! What is this my new freaking *job*? *Sticker-remover*??
- *Acceptance*—Who the heck knows?

The problem was I just didn't know. There are so many things about recycling that we *just don't know*, that prevent us from doing it correctly and efficiently, and I was pretty much spending every waking moment trying to figure them all out.

Ultimately, I let it go; I forgot about the sticker conundrum. Then one day I watched a video featuring a recycling expert who talked about removing stickers from the plastic films you put in the recycling bin at the supermarket. He said that sticker labels must be removed, or cut out. If not, the sticky part of the stickers will gum up the recycling machinery.

Of course, we are talking about two different things here. *Plastic film recycling* and *TerraCycle plastic packaging recycling* are presumably two different processes, so their answers to the Sticker Question may very well be different. But this was the first time I'd heard anything about sticker labels presenting a problem in *plastic film* recycling. There I'd been going along, blithely putting my bubble mailers and Tyvek envelopes into the supermarket bin all this time, never removing any of the shipping labels. Was that a problem?

Was I a sticker offender on multiple fronts?

So I emailed Alexandra, my e-friend at Trex who has been so helpful in the past on questions about plastic film recycling.

And then I contacted TerraCycle again too. Better to resolve all this sticker business once and for all. And TerraCycle's answer was actually surprising.

Their Customer Care Associate Angelica answered in an email: "oftentimes the reason we aren't able to recycle the items is not so much due to the residue itself but rather the fact that many of these labels are made from *paper-based products.* (Emphasis mine.) If you were to send in a clear tape, for example, this would be more easily processed through the Plastic Packaging box then something made with paper products."

Now *this* was good news. At last, it seemed I could relax about all those label stickers in my TerraCycle box, because I was pretty sure they were all plastic themselves.

And then I got more good news from Alexandra. At least as far as Trex is concerned, "paper labels are not an issue for Trex. They can remain on the plastic packaging when dropped off for recycling."

So either the expert video I watched was incorrect, or there are different kinds of plastic film recycling and it all depends who is collecting it. So now I'm supposed to figure out who exactly my supermarket is sending their plastic film to?

Which brings me back to my previous point: Who has time for this nonsense?

Nobody.

I was coming to realize something. Recycling in this country *isn't supposed to actually work.* Recycling is broken. And maybe, just maybe, companies like it that way.

Until recently, we only recycled 8 percent of our postconsumer plastic in America. Which sounds pretty bad until you learn that number has been revised. The nation's plastic recycling rate is now estimated to be 5 percent.[1]

Despite the efforts of companies like Trex and TerraCycle, these are mere drops in the ocean, an ocean of garbage Americans are tossing out every day. There simply isn't enough of a standardized approach in this country to make recycling work in any real, effective, and comprehensible way. Instead, we're just supposed to think it works, so we keep buying the products made with materials we as a society don't know what to do with.

Shut up and buy stuff!

But at least I could relax a little on the sticker anxiety. It wasn't the recycling machinery that had a problem, it was just the whole damn system.

Time went by. I continued to rely on TerraCycle for a solution to the very hardest recycling items, and it was an incredible relief. Things got better in the kitchen Super Awesome recycling nook. I felt like we had turned a corner. And yet there was a question nagging at the back of my brain.

What REALLY happened to the stuff I sent to TerraCycle?

It couldn't all be made into backpacks, so where did it go? Steve, for his part, was definitely suspicious. In fact, everyone I talked to about TerraCycle who had heard of it, found it to be something of an enigma, wondered if it was an illusion that was just too good to be true. Was it?

I had done my research. I had called to ask if TerraCycle conducted tours of their recycling facility; they didn't. I then turned to TerraCycle's website and watched videos posted there, many of which were old—posted eight, nine, ten years ago—and others which were utterly beside the point (how to make a bracelet out of used coffee pods!).

I watched hours of videos of TerraCycle founder Tom Szaky delivering keynote speeches, telling the story again and again of how he started the company in his college dorm room by putting fertilizer into old soda bottles, or giving tours of their headquarters in Trenton, New Jersey, artfully decorated with graffiti murals and partitions made out of old vinyl records, and showing off a variety of upcycled products such as the backpacks made from juice pouches and tote bags made of potato chip bags. But, even if we all wanted to walk around covered head to toe in our repurposed food wrappers, in some dystopian future in which everyone looked like the offspring of Blade Runner and Lay's Potato Chips, it still didn't fix the problem. There were just far too many of them.

So where were the rest of the juice boxes and chip bags going?

After getting diverted by other things I stopped looking, and time went by. Then one day, I returned to the search. Jeez—it was right there! How could I have missed it? It turned out it had been newly posted since the last time I had looked. But there it was: *what happens when TerraCycle opens your Zero Waste Box.*[2]

According to the one-minute video what TerraCycle does with our plastic packaging is this: they turn it into plastic pellets to turn into things like park benches and picnic tables. (This is very similar to what Trex is doing with all that #2 and 4 plastic film.)

How you feel about this revelation depends a whole lot on who you are. Is this "upcycling": creating a product of higher value than the original? A picnic bench is surely more valuable than any amount of disposable food packaging, after all. Should we be delighted that our otherwise useless plastics are being turned into something useful, a fate so much better than being landfilled, ending up in our oceans, or burned in toxic incinerators?

Or should one see this as "downcycling": creating a product of lesser quality than the original? When melted or chipped into new products, most plastics lose "integrity," and the number of things they can be turned into dwindles. The plastic used in the picnic tables is of a lesser quality because it can be used for fewer things. One day the picnic tables will break down and this plastic is back to being a problem. And don't forget—whether it's in the form of a picnic table in the park or a disposable bottle in the landfill—that plastic is still filled with any number of the more than ten thousand potential toxic chemicals—POPs and heavy metals—leaching chemicals into the environment, still breaking off into microplastics that ultimately infiltrate our environment, the food chain, and our bodies.

Which brings us to an important fact to know about recycled plastic: we know that there are literally tens of thousands of different, often patented and proprietary, formulas for different plastics, each with its own unique, often secret cocktail of chemical additives. What you may not know is that, legally, all of them are considered "innocent until proven guilty" or rather, safe until proven harmful. Harmful, since modern life is something of a chemical soup we all swim in, is extraordinarily difficult to prove.

Even if you could say, without reservation that, yes!, *all* of those tens of thousands of chemicals are perfectly safe for humans, there remains the likelihood that many are dangerously toxic *in combination* with one another. I'm going to take a wild guess and say there are therefore, at the very least millions, if not billions, of possible, completely unintentional chemical combinations involved in the prospect of a single recycled plastic product.

The upshot being that recycled plastics deserve a more descriptive name: Frankenplastics.

TerraCycle seems like an unquestionably good thing. But when we look closer, we must ask: does recycling with a program like TerraCycle do more harm than good? Is it truly better for our planet and environment? Or, does it serve to assuage our environmental conscience, so we don't have to do the harder work of committing to bigger, more meaningful change?

I was starting to think that, no matter how grateful I was for the escape hatch that TerraCycle provided to our project, moving plastic around like this without working for actual change is ultimately like rearranging the deck chairs on the *Titanic*—it's not going to matter unless we find a way to right the ship. Plastic is our looming environmental iceberg, and despite some recent positive changes—plastic bag and Styrofoam bans being the best examples—so far we are still full steam ahead.

We need to stop saying "It's okay: It's recyclable!" When it comes to plastic, I was now realizing, all plastic, it's not okay, and it isn't recyclable, not really.

CHAPTER EIGHT

TOOTH TABLETS AND PERIOD PANTIES: WE TRY ALL THE WEIRD ZERO WASTE PRODUCTS

I f I was beginning to learn any one thing this year, it's that we can't recycle our way out of the plastic problem. If I've learned a second thing, it's that we can't buy our way out of it either.

It's too bad, because if there's one thing Americans are really, *really* good at, it's buying things to make ourselves feel better. I don't just mean chocolate-flavored wine or a fuzzy blanket that makes you look like a human burrito; I mean buying specific products to signal our value system, and make us feel like we are creating something good in the world while, incidentally, also buying ourselves more stuff.

"Eco-friendly" products on the market are no exception. In my search for nonplastic products I was visiting sites selling all kinds of supposedly eco-friendly items, and some of them strained credibility. Do we really need to junk up our kitchens with *food huggers*—little silicone doo-dads whose sole purpose in life is to keep our avocado halves from turning brown in the fridge? Do we really need separate sets of bamboo flatware for our kids' school lunches? I've been putting stainless steel flatware in my kids' lunch boxes since kindergarten and so far no one had sought psychiatric counseling over it.

I mean, if you are a person who needs a straw for medical reasons that's one thing, but does the world really need so many metal straws? Do we really need kits for them with little straw cleaning brushes and a convenient container pouch? I wonder how many of these things will end up being discarded after a year or two spent at the bottom of our purses and fanny packs.

Sometimes we're being sold ordinary products, but produced in a way that is supposed to make you feel good. You can often tell they're using the Virtue Strategy by counting the number of buzzwords: *this supersoft throw blanket is made with vegan-organic, responsibly sourced, ethically produced, biocompatible eucalyptus fiber! Made by pandas!*

When at least one aspect of our planet's problem is our addiction to stuff, why do we think buying more stuff will fix it?

So I was making a concerted effort to be thoughtful about any purchases I made this year in the name of No Garbage, and not be swayed by fancy adjectives. Since I wasn't finding real answers among the stainless steel water bottles and fabric tote bags at my local store's "Eco-Friendly" table, many of the solutions were found online. Although this list is by no means comprehensive in terms of what's available, this chapter details all the products we tried and what we found to be truly worthwhile in the process.

First, let's visit a veritable minefield of disposable products.

THE BATHROOM

Toothpaste

For some reason, when people talk about going zero waste, how we clean our teeth is a particularly hot topic. I don't know why. We go around all day long buying bags of chips in throw-away bags, cheese in unrecyclable plastic that may or may not be leaching chemicals into our food, and hardly blink an eye when even at the Farmer's Market they start putting produce in plastic packaging for greater germ protection (*thanks, pandemic!*), whereas the average American uses 400 million toothpaste tubes per year, which works out to about 1.2 toothpaste tube per person.[1] The difference between all that food packaging and one or two toothpaste tubes? Is like the difference between a raindrop and a swimming pool. For elephants.

Nevertheless, for many people being able to brush their teeth in harmony with the environment seems to be pivotal. This is why zero waste proponents are always giving out recipes for making your own toothpaste out of things like baking soda and bentonite clay.

But I liked Tom's Toothpaste. And what the heck was bentonite clay? When I looked it up I found people using it as a kind of miracle cure, good for everything from weight loss to poison ivy rash. But before I ordered a lifetime supply, I found articles warning that because the FDA does not regulate bentonite clay products, it can be uncertain what you're getting when you buy it; in extreme cases heavy metals have been found in some bentonite clay products.[2]

Okay, so bentonite clay was out.

I was relieved at first to be sticking with Tom's, a product I've been buying for years and not incidentally the very first product on which I encountered the TerraCycle logo. I didn't do anything about it of course, but it made me feel good that if I put the effort in, I *could have* recycled the packaging if I wanted to.

Good for them! I thought. (Hel-*lo* greenwashing!)

At some point later on, I graduated from this position to actually taking five minutes to look up the TerraCycle website and try to discern what having this logo on its product was supposed to mean, but I had been almost immediately stymied by the complexity. And then this year rolled around and, as I mentioned, through a combination of sleuthing and sheer pigheadedness stumbled at last upon TerraCycle's returnable "Oral Care Waste" envelope, specifically for toothbrushes, floss, and toothpaste tubes. I felt pretty good about myself for finding a home for our family's four or five combined annual toothpaste tubes. Case closed! I thought. Now on to the other 3,372 zero waste questions I still have.

Then one day I noticed that Tom's Toothpaste (which is owned by Colgate-Palmolive) had made a small but significant alteration to their packaging: no more TerraCycle logo.

?!?

Instead, the tubes sported a small blue recycling triangle with caption below reading: *Once empty, replace cap and recycle with #2 plastics*.

If I was a cartoon, I would've rubbed both eyes with my knuckles before taking a closer, saucer-eyed look. *Single-stream-recyclable toothpaste tubes?* Was I dreaming?

But no, once I looked it up on Tom's website I found a whole page devoted to explaining that they'd changed their packaging and that they haven't totally broken up with TerraCycle, but you know, they just want to see other people.

To recycling geeks like me, this was huge, right? But the thing that truly stopped me in my tracks, was something even more amazing: the website also explained that not only had Tom's paid to develop this technology, but they were also now openly sharing it with other toothpaste manufacturers. According to their website, this is because most recycling facilities can't tell the difference between a recyclable toothpaste tube and a nonrecyclable one, so the sooner everyone is using this technology the better.

How utterly . . . sensible.

Okay! So my new, *new* plan was to use the TerraCycle Oral Care Waste envelope for old toothbrushes and toothpaste tubes, and moving forward, only buy Tom's with the new #2 symbol for eventual placement in single-stream recycling.

You'd think that this might be more than enough thinking about the waste generated by oral hygiene alone, but wait! There was more. Because the more I thought about it, the more I worried about how Tom's website had said most recycling facilities can't tell the difference between a recyclable tube and a nonrecyclable one. And then it occurred to me to wonder if the Tom's tubes shed microplastics. And then I thought about the fact that plastic is not indefinitely recyclable, so it is always going to be best to get away from the plastic entirely.

Was there a way to get the plastic out of my dental hygiene entirely? Enter the toothpaste tablet.

Toothpaste tablets

I'm going to be honest and tell you that I actually thought you were supposed to chew toothpaste tablets up and swallow them instead of brushing your teeth. Fortunately for me, the tiny glass jar of Georganics tooth tablets I bought from EarthHero.com comes not only in entirely plastic-free packaging, but also with the helpful instructions to chew the tablet up till it is foamy, brush your teeth, and then spit it out.

In fact you'll be glad to spit it out, because unlike Tom's Toothpaste at first blush these tablets do not taste fabulous. In fact, the first time I tried them they tasted a lot like I was trying to take a bite out of a salt lick. Steve tried them and was left trying to remove his tongue from his mouth.

Then a funny thing happened. The more I used the tooth tablets, the less the taste bothered me. Coupled with my bamboo toothbrush that can biodegrade in my compost (more on that in a minute), I now felt really good about my new plastic-free tooth brushing routine. Story over? Not yet.

Because then my dentist told me I had a cavity. And not just a cavity, but my first cavity ever. It had been a long time coming and was not the result of my new routine, but it did cause me to look more closely at my Georganics tablets and realize that they do not incorporate fluoride. This resulted in my switching to Unpaste toothpaste tablets, which not only have fluoride but also come in a small bag that feels like paper, and is *home* compostable. And I like them just as much. Now, when for some reason I end up using regular toothpaste again, *that* is what tastes weird to me, and oddly sweet.

I haven't yet convinced anyone else in the house to try the tooth tablets more than once, but hopefully the toothpaste industry is simply delighted to benefit from the investment in tube recycling technology made by Tom's and makes the switch to a #2 container immediately. After which they will all join hands and sing "We Are the World."

I can hope can't I?

Bamboo toothbrushes

Every toothbrush you've ever used in your entire life still exists. Every single one of them, including the ones with cartoon characters on them, sitting in a landfill somewhere, and will still be sitting there in that same landfill when your great-great-grandchildren walk the earth. And although an individual toothbrush is a relatively small item, by some estimates the United States alone disposes of one billion of them every year.

My dentist never mentioned any of this.

I have a friend who is an avid environmentalist and forager, and they tell me toothbrushes can, in fact, be made of willow or birch, frayed at the end by chewing. When the bristles become too soft the end can be cut again, and the entire thing is 100 percent compostable. Although I love that they know this, I'm afraid I have to admit that I am daunted by the idea of brushing my teeth with an actual tree twig, but it's nice to know that if the world ends I'll have a last-resort method for keeping my teeth clean.

This problem seems easily fixed, however, by purchasing a bamboo toothbrush. Because bamboo is a sustainable grass that grows quickly, it is kind of like the Neil Patrick Harris of eco-friendly materials: once you start to look, it's *everywhere*. Bamboo towels, bamboo coffee filters, bamboo iPhone cases, you name it. Bamboo makes a fine toothbrush handle, so it's not surprising to learn that this is what many toothbrush handles were made of before the invention of plastic. However, I'm not sure people are going to be excited about going back to what predated the nylon toothbrush bristle: which, according to the Library of Congress, until 1938 were made from "coarse hairs taken from the back of a hog's neck."[3]

Bristles are where things get tricky. You'll notice that a search for "eco-friendly toothbrushes" brings up many results that talk a whole lot about the Wonders of Bamboo, but carefully avoid telling you exactly what the bristles are made of. That's because the bristles are still made of plastic. You might encounter the term *bamboo charcoal* bristles, which, clever marketing aside, still *use* plastic. Isn't there any bristle material out there that doesn't use plastic and does not involve denuding pigs?

As it turns out there is: Brush with Bamboo makes a toothbrush with bristles made of castor bean oil.

Using castor bean oil means companies can say their toothbrush is 100 percent plant-based, or "biobased." The catch is, they are *not* home compostable. Heck, they're not even commercially compostable. What??

I was getting really confused. The EPA website helped me out by explaining that the Federal Trade Commission defines "degradable" as "completely decompos(ing) within one year."[4]

But they *are* made of organic material. Which means that these bristles *may* eventually break down without any toxic by-products. It might take decades, though, and no one really, truly seems to know. To be clear, this was the best option I was able to identify that didn't involve a pig's barber.

When my new eco-friendly toothbrush arrived the first thing I noticed was that, compared to my old plastic brushes, it felt exceedingly substantial—like something Fred Flintstone might use. Nevertheless, it seemed to work every bit as well as my old plastic one.

So what do you do once you have worn out your bamboo toothbrush? Well, first of all, I demote it to cleaning grout in the shower. After that, when it has been thoroughly smooshed into oblivion and we are ready to part ways, EarthHero's website says the handle is "commercially compostable" and as for the bristles? "using pliers, remove the bristles from the head." After that? "please feel free to dispose based on your personal preference."

Translation: "We've told you it won't break down quickly in your home compost, buuuuuuuut, if you want to put it there anyway, who's gonna stop you?" This seems a little disingenuous to me, because, who wants to find plastic-like bristles in their garden compost ten years from now? What they aren't saying, of course, is that the only other alternative is the trash.

Having no trash myself, what did I do? Well I spent far too long reading a Reddit thread in which a bunch of self-defined nonexperts went back and forth on whether burning plant-based plastic was worse than sending it to a landfill, to no satisfying conclusion. And then, along with a bunch of used paper towels and pizza boxes, I burned my old toothbrush in the outdoor fireplace.

Compostable dental floss

True confessions time. Some people hate the dentist. Not me. I have always hated flossing.

I mean: the imprecision of deciding how long to cut your floss (too long? *don't be wasteful!* too short? *try again!*), the string that cuts at your skin, the sticking your fingers way back in your mouth, the drool that inevitably tries to escape the whole situation and goober up your shirt . . . UGH.

So for the longest time I didn't floss at all. As it turns out I was lucky, because as I mentioned, I've been cavity-free most of my life, but also because according to a study done by Harvard in 2019, at least some brands of floss contain PFAs. The same chemicals that make pans nonstick and clothing waterproof are making the nylon floss glide more efficiently through the interstices of your teeth, and in the process leaving behind chemicals linked to liver damage, immune system damage, developmental issues, and cancer.[5]

At some point my dental hygienist turned me on to flossing sticks—neat little pokers that slide in between the teeth—overnight I was a flossing convert. Hooray!*

Except for now. Because flossing sticks are 100 percent disposable plastic. Sure, I could always put them in the "Health and Safety" garbage with the Band-Aids, and yes they are terribly small, but . . . nevertheless it felt right to try to find a biodegradable alternative.

---

* No word on whether PFAs are used in flossing sticks as well as dental floss.

Enter compostable floss. Made by Georganics, this product comes in its own refillable glass container with metal screw-on cap. It was so cute and pretty that I resolved: I would try to be okay with regular flossing, like a normal person. I could do this.

A few nights went by and I managed to use this product made with "corn-based PLA with vegetable waxes and essential oils." It was vegan! It was compostable! It was phthalate and sulfate and cruelty free! It probably played piano and rode a bicycle to work and had a variety of tasteful tattoos it displayed at parties!

And then it all fell apart, quite literally. The floss began to pull apart in my mouth every time I used it. Repeatedly, threads of floss separated and got caught between my teeth, which is the only sensation known to man to be more skin-crawlingly annoying than flossing itself. And then it finally dawned on me: *this* PLA was in fact the same PLA that makes up all those non-compostable compostables that I have been so irritated by. I realized that even were I entirely prepared to save up all my used dental floss and bring it to the bagel shop in search of industrial compost disposal, it was highly likely that I would be arrested for being too gross to be believed.

Fortunately, another alternative is floss made from finely spun silk thread, which apparently was one of the predecessors to nylon floss. It sounds expensive but, in fact, a container of thirty-three yards is only about four dollars.

After I recovered from my traumatic PLA experience, I ordered silk floss made by a company called RADIUS, in a cute paper package adorned with every buzzword you can think of. Women Owned! Fair Trade! No Impact! Clean and Green! Handspun! Wait—really? There are people in a room in Colombia somewhere hand-spinning my dental floss? I tried not to think: *This is the kind of thing that started the French Revolution. What's next? Ermine-trimmed Q-Tips?*

As bougie as it sounds, silk turned out to be the solution to my flossing conundrum, and it could go right into my compost after use. I certainly don't follow the package recommendation to "Floss after every meal or at least 2x per day" because I actually have a life, but I do floss. Sometimes. And I don't have to use disposable plastic to do it.

Deodorant

It's been a minute, so perhaps it's time for another Eve Confession: I don't wear deodorant.

I know. My daughters are like "*How . . . ?*" but honestly I either don't sweat that much, or my nose is defective because I just don't think I need it most of the time. One less thing to worry about, right? Including the worry of whether or not the aluminum in deodorant or antiperspirant causes breast cancer.

My husband, on the other hand, does wear deodorant. I was delighted one day when instead of coming home from the drugstore with his usual plastic container-ed stick, he had in his hand a deodorant from Hey Humans, a push-up style stick with entirely cardboard packaging. He is the type of person to be immediately skeptical about the efficacy of a product that is made with "gentler" ingredients (read: no crazy chemical crap) but he was game to try it and he was pleasantly surprised to discover: it works. And, as a bonus, it makes a pleasant "boop!" noise when you open it, from the suction. What more could you want?

Bamboo toilet paper

In the category of Most Polarizing Zero Waste Product, "the family cloth" might have to be the winner. Extreme or not, it definitely has its proponents: a search on Etsy for "*reusable toilet paper*" reveals 1,645 results.

Why, you may ask, are there people out there consciously choosing to wash, line-dry, and reuse their toilet paper?

It turns out that regular toilet paper—at 1.5 pounds of wood and thirty-seven gallons of water per roll—*is* surprisingly wasteful. Most of us would hear this and say: *Sure, but what is the alternative?* Well, one fine No Garbage day I stumbled upon the concept of using these small designated cloths instead. I mean, reusable toilet paper sounds like a horrible idea, but . . . was it that far a step from, say, reusable menstrual pads? (which we will get to in a minute).

I was trying to keep an open mind. I did some research, read a slew of articles both for and against. You'll find them easily if you look: the strategies, the arguments pro and con, the dedicated proponents versus the utterly disgusted opposition. An article on Lifehacker entitled "Please Don't Use Cloth Toilet Paper"[6] summed up the opposition this way:

"[Cloth toilet paper] is annoying, time-wasting, and pretentious, but is it harmful? It's certainly not great PR for environmentalism; part of America's problem is we view frugality and eco-consciousness as weirdo hippie bullshit. And in the case of cloth butt wipes, America is right."

The "weirdo hippie bullshit" argument, plus legitimate hygiene concerns lead me to an unambiguous conclusion: Nope. No family cloth experiments.

Still: trees! Water! My environmentalist friend also pointed out that not so terribly long ago the category of toilet paper used to include things like corncobs and most soft plant stems or leaves, all wholly compostable and sustainable, but in a house of between three and five people I can imagine gathering such materials taking a not-inconsiderable amount of time, even in good weather. And don't even *think* about trying to flush a corncob, people. You've been warned.

In the interest of environmentalism, recycled paper toilet paper would seem to be the next best option, right? Unfortunately, I had some prior experience with recycled paper TP and at that time had discovered that it was not only harder to find and cost more but that it also—just as a bonus—sucked. It was either too thin, too rough or both. And either way, toilet paper goes down the toilet and disappears, so even if it wasn't environmentally awesome, it technically didn't present much of an immediate problem for our Year of No Garbage. *It* disappeared.

What *was* a problem? The plastic overwrap.

Inexplicably, even the *recycled* toilet paper at my store comes with plastic overwrap. Why do companies think we'll buy recycled paper to save trees but ignore the This-Will-Outlive-Your-Great-Grandchildren-Overwrap? I'm looking at you, Seventh Generation.

Yes, you can theoretically recycle plastic overwraps of all kinds in the plastic bag recycling at the supermarket, but most people won't, and—repeat after me—*more plastic is always bad.* Not creating it in the first place is far preferable.

Enter the Australian-based company Who Gives a Crap. Besides the wonderfully memorable name, here are some things I found out that I immediately liked about them:

- They donate 50 percent of their profits to help build toilets for people who need them. Eight hundred children around the world die every day from lack of clean water and sanitation.
- Their products are 100 percent plastic free.
- They offer toilet paper made from either recycled paper or bamboo. Because bamboo is a sustainable grass that grows quickly, using it in place of virgin paper reduces deforestation.
- They have a sense of humor. To draw attention to their 2012 crowdfunding campaign, cofounder Simon Griffiths sat on a toilet for fifty hours; he wrote contributors thank-you notes on pieces of toilet paper.

As you might expect—when you're mail-ordering your sustainably sourced toilet tissue—it is expensive. Just how expensive? I ordered forty-eight bamboo TP rolls for fifty-two dollars, which meant I was paying just over a dollar a roll. According to the toilet paper math mavens of the internet, of which there are far greater numbers than I could ever have imagined, this is nearly twice what I should be paying for an ordinary roll of TP.

A slightly cheaper option is Who Gives a Crap's recycled paper line, for which you are paying about a third more.

The expense is one obvious downside. Then there's the global footprint involved in shipping, but where is it really coming from? And how does that compare to the carbon emissions of shipping of products like Cottonelle or Charmin to my supermarket?

Who Gives a Crap addresses this issue on their website. Although based in Australia their blog post tells me, their products are, in fact, made in China.[7] The internet informs me Charmin, on the other hand, is made in Pennsylvania. One could be forgiven for thinking that shipping toilet paper from Pennsylvania to Vermont would seem to be a lot more sustainable than shipping it from China to Vermont, right?

But here's the $64,000 question: is much shorter shipping distance enough more sustainable to counteract the benefits of using recycled or renewable materials? I was quite unhappy to realize that answering this question would probably involve . . . math.

Fortunately, the math cells in my brain were allowed to go on sleeping, undisturbed. This is because in this same blog post Who Gives a Crap* cites a 2020 report by the Natural Resources Defense Council[8] that rates toilet paper companies by sustainability, giving Who Gives a Crap the highest marks.

This same article is at pains to point out that Charmin toilet paper is sourced from 100 percent virgin trees from Canada's boreal forest, and that every second 1,400 square feet of Canadian boreal forest are clear-cut for products such as toilet paper.

Now, we aren't given the basis of the marks on the NRDC scorecard in the article, and so can't see how heavily transport figures in to the overall calculation of environmental impact, but unlike so many of the industry sources who are tap-dancing like mad around such issues, the NRDC is a pretty reputable source in my book. They very clearly choose Who Gives a Crap as the lesser of all toilet paper evils. So I decided to accept that they had, in fact, done the math.

Once my big box of TP arrived in the mail, I was delighted to find that I liked their product a lot: it is surprisingly thick, soft, and comfortable to use. And their subscription service means you never have to worry about forgetting to buy toilet paper at the store ever again. As for the expense? I mean, we are talking about paying up to

---

* In this same blog post they also explain what they're doing to ensure fair pay and ethical treatment of the Chinese workers involved.

twice as much per roll. Well, I see it as analogous to supporting local businesses or buying organic food; if one is both willing and able to pay the higher price for things you believe in, then it is worth it.

My bottom line (so to speak?): The plastic packaging overwrap was gone. So I was pretty happy.

Shampoo and conditioner bars

A few years ago a dear friend of mine got very energized about going "no-poo" which sounds suspiciously like toddler bathroom speak to me but in fact is a philosophy of cleaning your hair without the use of shampoo. While my friend was super excited about it, another friend of ours was downright horrified. It was as if someone had asked her to give up a limb.

Me, I was just mystified. What could be wrong with something as basic as shampoo?

In case you haven't heard it, the no-poo argument goes like this: commercial shampoos didn't come into use until relatively recently in human history—in the 1930s. Whereas in the old days dirt-removing lather was created by combining a natural vegetable oil or animal fat with a base such as lye, most often today's shampoos use synthetic chemical foaming agents known as *sulfates*.

Aha! "Sulfates" sound . . . bad, right? I knew for sure I'd seen "sulfate-free!" promises on products without knowing exactly why that was supposed to be a good thing. It turns out that sulfates have been rumored to be carcinogens for some time, but without any definitive proof.[9] Instead, the biggest reason to avoid sulfates in shampoo seems to be that they can be overly harsh on hair. Sure, you want to remove oil, but you don't want to remove too much oil and damage your hair, or worse still, cause scalp irritation.

So why not just buy a less harsh, sulfate-free shampoo? No-poo proponents say that even then, our society is so addicted to compulsive washing that we shampoo too often, drying our hair out and causing the glands in our scalp to produce ever more oil, known as sebum. This supposedly creates a vicious cycle of oil production and removal, i.e.: the more we clean our hair, the oilier it gets. Some dermatologists agree with this theory, but others flatly dispute it, arguing that no matter how much or little you shampoo, or with what, your scalp will still produce the same amount of oil.

Cleaning my hair was yet one more activity I had done all the time, bought products for all the time, and yet had never given much thought to or really understood. *What is in this goo I put on my head several times a week? What is it actually doing?* I didn't need to cure a scalp condition, thank goodness, or particularly worry about my sebum production, but I did have another goal in mind: I wanted to avoid the plastic packaging of shampoo and conditioner.

So the question arose: what does one really need to get clean hair?

No-poo proponents would approve of my husband Steve's approach: he hadn't used shampoo in years. At all. In the shower he simply rinsed his hair with water. He picked this habit up in the military aboard ship when soldiers went for weeks without showering due to the need to conserve water. Back then his hair was very short, but today his somewhat longer hair doesn't seem to suffer from the lack of foaming agents—natural or otherwise.

If this is a little too bare bones for you (as I suspected it might be for me), no-poo proponents suggest a host of alternatives: baking soda and apple cider vinegar, coconut oil, using conditioner only, rye or chickpea flour, honey and egg. I was intrigued, but kept envisioning my shower smelling like salad, or me on my hands and knees trying to clean chickpea grit out of grout and decided, um, no.

I decided instead to take a more moderate approach and try out another product I'd seen a lot on the zero waste websites: *bar* shampoo and conditioner. If you've never seen these, they look exactly like bars of soap, but are formulated for hair (most hand soaps would be too harsh and stripping on hair.) I imagined myself rubbing the shampoo cake on my scalp—was that how it worked?

That is *not* how it worked. Rather, I found out, one simply lathers the bar in one's hands like hand soap, and then rubs the lather into your hair. *Oh.*

I was pleasantly surprised. Yes, my shampoo bar was somewhat less lathery than liquid shampoos, but it still lathered. After rinsing out, my hair felt clean. On the other hand, the conditioner bar I purchased was a bust. It was difficult to get enough material from the bar onto my head, and after rinsing it off my hair didn't feel like it had been conditioned.

I found out from my blog readers that many people have this problem with bar conditioners and consequently opt to combine shampoo bar use with a more traditional conditioner or substitute an apple cider rinse instead. Online I found Alpine Provisions conditioner available for purchase in a fully recyclable aluminum container, so hooray!

Public Service Announcement: please note that your aluminum conditioner bottle will need a pump. Do not make the mistake of thinking, "Oh, but the pump is plastic. I can get along without that!" This aluminum bottle is *very* serious, and unless you are the Hulk, you *cannot* squeeze the sides to make the gooey, viscous material come out. Instead, you will be left standing in the shower, trying to claw conditioner out with your pinkie finger. I speak from experience. Instead, buy the dreaded plastic pump one time and then reuse it on every subsequent bottle.

My upshot? Shampoo bars yes, conditioner bars no. Chickpea flour? Stays put in the kitchen.

Razors

I've always been bugged by what I see as the tremendous expense and wastefulness of women's razors. Either you use a plastic disposable razor that you throw away lock, stock, and barrel, or you opt for a particular brand's handle and purchase cartridge heads for that handle until the day you die. God forbid you buy the wrong model number of the same brand because now you have to chuck those and head back to the store to fork over another bucket of razor head money.

But at least when it comes to razors, unlike shampoo, what you are buying is pretty self-evident: small handheld blades for cutting off small body hairs. After doing some research Steve found me a rechargeable Panasonic wet/dry razor for $19.99. Yes, it was made of plastic, but at least this was durable plastic intended to stick around longer than those disposable whole razors and heads. It worked equally well wet or dry, with a head that popped off to rinse out the hair. I did have to press down firmly to make sure it actually did the job, and even so, I did not get as close a shave as with a blade. But, it produced nothing disposable, which was the point.

Then, while noodling around the internet, I came across the Mercedes-Benz of eco-conscious shaving: the Leaf razor. Oooooo. Retailing at eighty four dollars for an all-metal, pivoting head razor, and an additional thirty dollars for a custom stand, fifty single-edge blades, and blade recycling tin, the Leaf comes in plastic-free packaging, with a lifetime warranty, and will give you periodic back massages. Except maybe not that last part.

After looking into it further I realized plastic-free safety razors like this didn't all cost this much. A cursory check on Amazon turned up dozens of double edged, all-metal safety razors in a variety of finishes and possible accessories ranging anywhere from $5 to $350. Because I had never used anything but a plastic razor from the drugstore the whole aspect of the safety razor looked a little intimidating. They weren't as alarming as straight razors, of course, but they looked *serious*. Could I accidentally, hurt myself with this thing?

I'm happy to report that regardless of which model you choose, the all-metal safety razor is not nearly as scary as it might appear. I have to admit that after some hemming and hawing I went with the pricier Leaf razor, because I'm a sucker for a beautiful, well-designed object. It gives a perfect, close shave, and in months of use I never cut myself once. At the same time, I ordered a bar of shaving soap to use with it and I liked it okay. I mean, it does lather, but not a whole heck of a lot. In fact, when I compared it to just using regular soap lather I saw virtually no difference. So I figured why not just use soap?

So now in my shower I have two small ceramic soap dishes: one for my shampoo bar and one for my regular soap bar, which is also my "shaving cream," plus my aluminum can of conditioner. With pump.

Eco-friendly tampons

Whenever I was feeling discouraged with how the year was going, I really should've just gone and looked at the bathroom wastebasket.

Pretty much the only thing we had actually thrown away this year—in our "Health and Safety" wastebasket in the bathroom—had been Band-Aids, pandemic face masks, and feminine products. The basket never got full before I emptied it, and it seemed like it was going to take years to come up with enough material to fill an actual garbage bag.

That was something to feel proud of.

And yet. Recently, I had started thinking about modern-day pads and panty liners and the fact that they are composed primarily of plastic (up to 90 percent). Researching it further, I was surprised to learn that tampons use plastic in the absorbent part, so even if you buy the cardboard applicator variety, you're still using disposable, single-use plastic. And pads used today will be littering the landfill, landscape, and ocean for generations to come. Considering that a woman uses between five and fifteen thousand menstrual products in her lifetime, this is bad news, and surely every bit as bad as all the other plastics we've been trying to avoid.

Case in point: menstrual products are number five on the list of top ten plastic items found on European shores and beaches. Ew.

It hasn't always been this way. It's only within the last century that women switched from reusable cloth to sticky plastic pads and tampons with plastic applicators.

When I mentioned to Greta and Ilsa that I was looking around at alternative menstrual products, they both pretty much resorted to the "la-la-la-I-can't-hear-you" response. I could hardly blame them. I mean, periods can be unpleasant enough, without trying to conduct experiments on how you deal with them.

But I made a point of buying something that had just arrived at our supermarket: Seventh Generation Organic Cotton Tampons. That certainly sounded like an improvement, right? No chlorine bleach, fragrances or other harsh chemicals, and no plastic . . . waitaminit.

These tampons from Seventh Generation *did* use plastic: *"plant-based plastic"* or PLA, which in this case, according to the box, was made from sugarcane. Here we go again. Sure, "Plant-based plastic!" sounds better than "petroleum-based plastic!" but I now knew that there was no guarantee that plant-based plastics are significantly better or more degradable than other plastics . . . and don't even get me started on bringing my tampon applicators to the bagel shop.

I wondered, why wouldn't Seventh Generation use a cardboard applicator, like so many other tampons do? For that matter, why do so many other Seventh Generation products use actual plastic: unbleached paper towels wrapped in plastic overwrap, "green" cleaning products in plastic bottles, dishwasher pods made with controversial polyvinyl acetate?*, 10

SIDE RANT THAT WILL MAKE ME SOUND OLD: I recall years ago when the only way I could purchase Seventh Generation products was in bulk, by mail. Back then, the toilet paper and paper towels weren't just made of recycled paper, they came wrapped in it as well. Sadly, what started out as a company that was leading the way towards sustainable, eco-friendly products appears to me to have lost its way in a sea of uncomfortable, self-defeating compromises.

Okay, rant over. Yes, we could purchase no-applicator tampons from Seventh Generation or other organic cotton tampon brands, but honestly I find them to be . . . messy.

I decided I was ready to look elsewhere for viable alternatives.

Period panties

In the zero waste universe sometimes one happens upon a product that champions old-fashioned idea, but with the added benefit of modernized design. Machine washable menstrual pads and panties are among these in the old-idea-but-new-and-improved category.

---

* According to a 2009 study, PVA takes over thirty years to degrade. Which is better than most plastics, which never *truly* degrade, but hardly what most people think of when we say "biodegradable."

After looking around I decided period underwear looked intriguing and was the least intimidating of all the available options. (*Underwear! I know how to wear that!*)

Before long I had ordered three pairs of "Hiphugger" Thinx period panties, using their website's "Know Your Flow" calculator to identify which absorbency model to buy, given my regular period characteristics. According to their calculations, I use nineteen period products every month, and by using period panties could throw out 228 fewer disposables per year. And that's just me: when you consider that we have three women in our household regularly using feminine products, that added up to a lot of single-use plastic.

Of course, guess what period panties are also partially made of? That's right: plastic. All Thinx panties contain some proportion of either Elastane, polyester jersey, or nylon. Their website says Thinx panties should "stay at maximum performance" for forty washes, or two years. I have to admit I was disappointed: only two years? Then again, compared to several hundred plastic pads or tampons it *is* better. (I imagine what would be better still is if Thinx had a take-back program to recycle old panties. Then again, I just had a vision of sitting at a plastic picnic table and learning it was made entirely of old period underwear.)

All in all, I still felt pretty good about trying period panties out. Ilsa had no comment, since she was still pretending this was not happening. Her sister, on the other hand was somewhere between horrified and mystified.

"Seriously, I don't understand how this works," Greta commented when I told her I was trying out period underwear. "Does it *teleport* it somewhere or something?"

After trying them, I could confirm that there was no teleportation involved, and I came away with several further conclusions as well:

I found the design not exactly comfortable, but not exactly *un*comfortable either: thicker than a regular panty, but decidedly not diaper-like, it felt very much like wearing a bathing suit bottom.

I didn't like that the inside material was black, because unlike when you wear a white pad, I couldn't tell how much I was bleeding. How would I know that it was "full" before it was, you know, too late? I know that having the inside a light color would mean constant staining and not look very attractive long-term, but with black material I found I just had to trust the panties were doing their job, because I really couldn't tell. Trying them out when I just happened to be (for some weird reason) isolating at home, turned out to be a very good thing.

Yes, the material is pretty good at wicking and odor control. After a while I got the hang of knowing when it was at capacity. Despite the fact that I couldn't see it, there were other clues, for example it would feel begin to feel a bit clammy.

Washing them is very easy and, as promised, the blood did not stain my other laundry. Importantly, to maintain absorbency you must line dry them. I liked one commenter's suggestion to put them in a lingerie bag throughout the week and then throw them all at once in the washing machine at the end. (Contrary to my expectation, collecting them in this manner did not prove to be an untenable mess.)

My three pairs were not enough for the whole week, of course. But Thinx are expensive: thirty-four dollars each for the ones I purchased, with a small discount for buying three or more. I washed them after three days and kept using them, but a minimum of six pairs would be better suited to get through the week.

Although I had hoped Thinx could eliminate all my other feminine products, I realized that on heavier days I would either need to also wear a tampon (organic cotton ones would avoid chemicals and plastic) or change underwear before the day was out. Other women whose reviews I read came to much the same conclusion: period panties do not absolutely remove the need for any other feminine products.

All in all, I liked the period panties from Thinx, but I wondered if I couldn't find a solution that was less expensive *and* used less plastic. So, next up?

Reusable menstrual pads

After noodling around on a variety of sites I zeroed in on a product called New Moon Pads made in Canada by a woman named Renee whose title was listed as "Owner/Designer/Cloth Pad Artisan."

New Moon makes an array of pads in different sizes and colorful patterns, in regular and organic cotton or flannel. I settled on a trial pack featuring three pads, each a different size. According to Renee, one pad should last ten years, and is equivalent to more than two hundred disposable pads.

While the exterior of the pads is made from natural fibers, the interior does use a Polartec fleece which is made from recycled soda bottles. Cotton-only pads are also offered, with the caution that they are not as absorbent and will need to be changed much more often. Two wing tabs snap underneath to hold the pad in place, and the snaps are also made of a poly resin plastic; it is explained on the website that this decision was motivated by a concern that metal snaps could set off metal detectors, and *wow*—can you imagine how much fun airport security would be if you were holding up the line with your menstrual pads?

Renee seemed to have thought of everything, so again, I took the plunge and ordered my comparatively pricey pads: three for thirty-two dollars.

You know what? I was converted. I loved my soft new pads, and greatly preferred them to the swimsuit-wearing feeling of period panties.

The menstrual cup

After I wrote a blog post on this, several people commented I should look into the "Diva Cup," which is a brand name for a type of flexible plastic funnel that one inserts, wears, and empties. After first encountering this concept when reading Cheryl Strayed's *Wild*, I had been pretty sure this product was only for people who were trying to find themselves in the wilderness, and I had left it at that. I had no idea they were so popular.

But honestly, I didn't feel the need to go there. I was happy with the reusable pads and panties, and liked the idea of keeping any unavoidable plastic outside my body as much as possible.

After trying the reusable pads, I ordered another two sets, and voilà! I was proud to be getting through my entire period every month without using a single disposable product. I spent $105, less than I would spend in a year on disposables, and they were good for ten years.

Not that I'll likely still be menstruating ten years from now, but you know what? Let's move on.

THE KITCHEN

Once upon a time, I imagine there wasn't really any such thing as a *leftover*. Rather, there was prepared food, which you ate, and anything that didn't get eaten went to an animal, which you used for protection, food, or food products.

Today, by comparison, our relationship to our food is very, very different: we have on hand a whole menu of preservation techniques to keep it fresh and young long after the fact of its preparation. Whether you're packing a lunchbox sandwich, refrigerating the rest of a noodle casserole for tomorrow, or freezing a batch of soup for next month . . . how do we do it? *Plastic*: plastic wrap, vacuum seal plastic bags, plastic Tupperware, and the ubiquitous Ziploc® bag.

But there had to be a time, pre-plastic, when we knew how to preserve food in other ways, right?

Beeswax wrap

When you google "who invented beeswax food wrap" you will come up with at least three different articles, each featuring a different, smiling, entrepreneurial woman who wanted to find a better way to pack her children's lunches sometime in the early 2000s. What they all admit to a greater or lesser degree, however, is that beeswax food wrap wasn't so much invented in the last decade as it was *re*invented. My favorite version is found on the Apiwraps website, which tells the story of founder Freyja Tasci studying colonial poetry for a degree in literature when she came across the concept of wax-infused cloth that had been used as far back as the Middle Ages for purposes of waterproofing. They just knew it by a different name: *oilskin*.

Today beeswax wrap has become so wildly popular that odds are good you have some of it somewhere in your kitchen. Made from cotton fabric which has been coated with a combination of beeswax, resin, and oil, beeswax wraps can do practically anything that tinfoil or plastic wrap can do: wrap sandwiches, cover bowls, preserve cheese. Wash them in the sink—flattening against the sink bottom and sponging in strokes and laying over the dish drainer to dry—and they're ready to go again.

Here's what I don't like: they're expensive and they don't last, you know, *forever*, which, strangely, I expect every product I purchase to do. In my experience, beeswax wraps work well for a good long time, perhaps a year, and then they start to become gritty feeling and lose their grippiness. At this point, because the ingredients are all biodegradable, they can be home-composted, which is great, but at nineteen dollars for three little squares of the stuff, you could be forgiven for wanting it to last longer. Many DIY people have recipes online for making your own from scratch for a fraction of the cost, but like knitting your own socks or making your own soap, this enterprise might not be for everyone.

Beeswax wrap is a great product, but my conclusion was that it didn't do anything that tinfoil couldn't do, and, at least where I live, tinfoil is both fully recyclable and cheaper. I wash and reuse tinfoil in just the same way, and when it is no longer usable I can ball it up and place it in recycling. Pro tip: as long as you make sure it is the size of say, a baked potato, it won't get lost on the floor of the materials recovery facility.

In addition to tinfoil, I also use food storage containers. Which brings me to:

Glass jars versus Tupperware

I have a very respectable collection of food storage containers I've accumulated over the years. Some are made of plastic, some are glass with plastic lids, and some are Pyrex, which is to say glass with glass lid, or enamelware, which is metal coated with a thin layer of porcelain. (Those last two I often find in local thrift shops or antique stores.) I discovered that the Vermont Country Store, which specializes in old-fashioned and hard to find products, sells the only fully clear, top and bottom, glass food storage I've yet found for purchase new. The ones with clear glass bottoms are my personal favorite, because not only do I not have to worry about weird chemicals leaching into my food from a plastic container, but I can immediately see what is in the container, which greatly reduces the risk I'll forget all about the lentil stew I left in there until it's developed sentience and applied to college.

But my favorite Tupperware isn't Tupperware at all, and it is free. Sort of. That's because every time I buy straight-sided jars—of peanut butter or olives or tomato sauce—I save them. Most often I use these for my homemade chicken broth, which I make in large batches and then freeze in portions of varying sizes.

But doesn't freezing glass make it break? It definitely can. After breaking my fair share of peanut butter jars, I learned:

The Three Secrets of Freezing Liquids in Glass:
1. Let hot foods cool before placing in containers.
2. Leave a large amount of headspace—an inch to an inch and a half to leave room for the expansion as the liquid becomes solid. (If you're nervous you can freeze without the lid and add the lid soon after.)
3. Defrost *slowly*. I like to thaw the jars in my fridge overnight, but in a pinch I place jars in a saucepan of *room temperature* water and let sit while I prepare other parts of the recipe. After twenty or thirty minutes I will place the pan on the *lowest* burner setting on my stove, so it can warm super gradually. Going any faster results in broken glass and shattered dreams.

Silicone Stasher bags
Thankfully, there are a lot of great resources out there these days for folks who want to go zero waste or just want to cut their waste down. In Brooklyn my daughter Greta took me to a "sustainability shop"

called Salter House. It is a gorgeous shop: white porcelain dishes artfully arranged, tiny enamelware chocolate pots in pastel shades, chopstick rests that look like tiny dolls and gigantic scented candles that I'd have to mortgage my house to afford.

I've been there several times, but I can never find anything to buy. That's because what they *have* is a $310 sustainably made hand-stitched winter plaid corset, or an eighty-eight-dollar "arenga fibre porch broom," but what I *need* is . . . toothpaste tablets.

I've heard it called "consumerist environmentalism," and it hearkens back to my frustration with all the glass and aluminum straws that come with their own carrying cases. To be clear: I don't think there's anything wrong with buying a beautiful object if you love it and it will bring you a little bit of aesthetic joy every time you use it, especially if it avoids the use of the ever-problematic plastic. But there's a lot of stuff out there masquerading as useful and sustainable, when it's really just more stuff.

This is how I feel about the big push on environmentally themed websites to sell *silicone-based* products. When I see the websites that market Stasher silicone bags as "the last food storage bags you'll ever need to buy," alarm bells go off in my head. I worry it is yet another deceptive switcheroo, an attempt to trade one bad, landfill-ready product for another: *Throw away all your plastic Tupperware and replace it with earth-friendly silicone! And next week we'll come up with something else to replace that!*

Silicone products are marketed as flexible, safe food storage that doesn't contain the things we worry about leaching into our food from plastic (BPA, BPS, lead, latex, phthalates, formaldehyde, etc.) and they can be washed in the dishwasher. Which sounds great, right? It's all the benefits of plastic without the actual plastic!

Or *is* it? Stashers—and food containers like U-Konserve that pair stainless steel bottoms with silicone lids—are marketed as "non-plastic," but I had to admit that silicone certainly looks and feels like plastic, so I was suspicious.

It turns out I was right to be suspicious. Because when you look beyond the surface, whether or not silicone is a kind of plastic depends—like so many of the definitions I've been seeking out this year—a whole lot on who you're talking to.

The argument goes like this: silicone is made from sand, and therefore is a natural product more akin to rubber than plastic. But hold on! The website of Life Without Plastic, which is another eco-friendly online vendor, argues pretty convincingly that silicone should *not* be considered harmless or eco-friendly:

"Like any plastic polymer, silicones are synthetic and include a mix of chemical additives derived from fossil fuels. . . . Silicone does not biodegrade or decompose (certainly not in our lifetimes)," they explain on their website. "Silicones are very persistent in the environment."[11]

Uh-huh. So silicone presents all the benefits of plastic, with many of the same problems of . . . actual plastic. *Right.*

I'd be sticking to my Pyrex and glass jars. If weight is a concern, on a hike or a picnic say, I can use aluminum foil, some of my collection of metal tea tins. As for my Tupperware, the more I was learning about fully plastic containers, the more I was wanting to deaccession these from my storage collection. (More on that in a bit.)

Coffee, tea, and me

Heaven forfend we should have to imagine a life without our hot beverages. Unfortunately, the practice of making and drinking coffee or tea in this day and age represents a veritable plastics minefield: why don't disposable hot beverage cups leak? They're lined with polyethylene. Tea bags are often made of polypropylene terephthalate (PET) and nylon, or, at the very least, are sealed with plastic. K-cups for the ubiquitous Keurig machine are made with nonrecyclable multilayer plastic lined with polyethylene.

What's worst of all is that new research has shown that trillions of nanoparticles are released when liquids interact with polyethylene lining, even at room temperature.[12] But the hotter the liquid the more nanoparticles get released. Did I say trillions? Yes.

Truth be told, as of this writing no one has proven that ingesting microplastics causes any particular health problems. Yet. But, scientists note that these particles *are* small enough to slip into the bloodstream and become lodged in different tissues and organs of the body.

First of all: ew.

Second of all, I'm pretty sure it's just a matter of time before we find out the hard way. In an article about this new research regarding hot liquids and plastic nanoparticles, one expert pointed out that even a material like asbestos is "relatively benign," but what makes it so dangerous to humans is when "tiny particles are inhaled and accumulate in lung tissue, causing inflammation that can lead to scarring and cancer."

Bringing your own mug everywhere you possibly can is one obvious way to avoid drinking nanoplastics by the trillions. Another is skipping the Keurig machine at home and investing instead in a Nespresso. Their capsules are made of aluminum, *and*, if you check a little box on your capsule order form, they arrive complete with a prepaid mailer in which to collect your used capsules, coffee grounds and all. Online they have a very nice explanatory video which looks just specific enough as to make one think they might actually, truly be doing what they claim to be: recycling the aluminum and composting the coffee grounds.

Of course there are plenty of ways to make filtered coffee that don't require recycling pods at all. At our house, because my husband is a certified coffee fanatic, we have many of them: the French press coffee pot, the stovetop espresso pot that is popular in Italy, the glass pour-over Chemex, and of course the good old electric drip coffee maker. The good news is that all of these are available in all or mostly nonplastic options, and coffee filters are made of paper and thus home compostable, along with your coffee grounds.

On the tea front, during this year I was determined to avoid the plastic tea bags, as well as much of the heat seal shrink-wrap and plastic overwrap that is used in so much tea packaging by buying loose tea and using a tea strainer or "brewing basket." (For folks who want their tea on the go, there are quite a few brands of plastic-free tea infuser travel mugs available.)

We had used a set of two Finum brewing baskets—which are made of a rigid plastic frame (yeah, I know) and stainless-steel micro mesh—for perhaps twenty years now and they show no signs of wear. It's a mesh cup that sits inside your teacup or mug and holds the loose tea while it steeps; when done brewing you just lift it out. According to their website they even have baskets designed to fit an entire teapot.

But, bearing in mind the relationship between heat and nanoplastics, I was thinking there must be a version of this product that avoids plastic entirely, right? And there is. The Vahdam "Classic Tea Infuser" is made entirely of stainless steel, no plastic. I was delighted to order one and try it out, only to be confronted when it arrived with a whole bunch of crinkly plastic packaging protecting my metal tea infuser from . . . what? Alien mind-reading devices?

> Dear Vahdam: Your Classic Tea Infuser is pretty, functional, PBA free and even dishwasher safe. A thought: would you please consider omitting the entirely unnecessary plastic overwrap? Because, and not to put too fine a point on it, avoiding plastic is the WHOLE REASON I PURCHASED YOUR PRODUCT. Yours sincerely, Eve

Giant Egyptian cucumbers

I cook a lot, ergo, I do a lot of dishes. I get very opinionated about which dish sponge I buy because as we all know, the right sponge can make the difference between struggling to clean a stubborn pan and being done with the dishes so one can go have a glass of wine and knit. Up until now my favorite sponges were ocelo sponges, which are made of cellulose (wood pulp) but also incorporate a tougher, "scrubby" component, which I now realized was made of nylon, not to mention being sold encased in plastic packaging overwrap. How on earth, I wondered, was I going to find a truly efficient sponge that didn't contain any plastic?

I found a Scotch-Brite product at my supermarket marketed as providing "greener clean" sponges "made with natural wood pulp."

Nice! But wait . . . "*with* natural wood pulp"? This sounded suspiciously like "tested *with* plumbers"! When I called the 800 number on the package I spoke with Gina who explained that unfortunately the scrubber portion of the sponge used not only agave fiber, but also recycled polyester, rendering it unable to be composted. She pointed me to other sponges in their line that did not have a scrubber component and which would be *industrially* compostable at end of life. So I'd be taking my nasty worn-out sponges to . . . the industrial compost bin at the bagel shop. But at this point I'd have to wear a clever disguise involving a beret and a mustache so as to avoid being recognized as the woman in the large WANTED poster, "for the crime of creepily over-visiting the trash sorting area." Even so, in the end I still had the crinkly plastic overwrap to deal with, didn't I? Back to square one.

Searching online for answers, I found a slew of sponges marketed as "biodegradable," some of which even had recyclable packaging. In the comments I found dozens of consumers who were all like me: trying to figure out what was greenwashing-speak and what was real. What do you really mean when you say "will biodegrade naturally"? People were doing paranoid things like burning their sponge scrubbers to see if they turned to ash (coconut fiber) or goo (plastic) and reporting a suspicious "distinct plastic burning smell."[13]

Just as we had experienced in our family's Year of No Sugar, I was realizing that there was a point at which this all became just, well, *silly*. In restaurants, at a certain point we had to accept: if they say there's no sugar in this, we have to believe them, right? Like, at what point are you wandering into the restaurant kitchen and getting arrested for trying to read the ingredients on a Sisco packet of gravy? Similarly, if you have an entire industry playing cat and mouse with the truth about plastics in order to appear like they're implementing change when they are not, well, *they're going to win* aren't they? Because this is their whole job, what they do all day every day, whereas the consumers, the public, have lives to live and presumably do not have unlimited time budgets for exhaustively researching sponge materials. If we as consumers really care about what materials are in the products we buy—in much the same way that we have come to increasingly pay attention to the ingredients that are in the foods that we buy—then, it was beginning to dawn on me, it requires the same strategy: legislation. Correction: legislation with enforcement. Because when the fox watches the henhouse, what do you end up with? An empty coop.

More on that point in a little bit.

I turned away from the dubious roster of green*ish* products online and I went eco-trendy. I splurged and ordered a cake of solid dish soap with a dish brush and dish scrubber from The Earthling Co., pairing these with a gleaming white porcelain ceramic sink caddy. Maybe this was the solution to my sponge conundrum after all! It wasn't.

Although I love my gleaming white porcelain sink caddy, the first drawback I encountered is that it is one more thing that requires regular cleaning (surprise!) lest it starts to look like a white porcelain caddy for pond sludge and toast crumbs. On it there is a cute little square area perfect for my soap cake, but after about five minutes the soap cake stopped looking ready for the Instagram and instead resembled a waxy Superfund site. Plus the "untreated German beechwood" dish brush and scrubber with "Mexican Tampico fiber" bristles were pretty to look at but completely nonfunctional for a confirmed sponge addict like myself. Some habits refuse to be broken. I went back to the drawing board.

I tried coupling copper scouring pads with fabric dishcloths, and then with small cloths I had handknit from cotton. The copper turned green and scummy, and the dishcloths took so long to dry they smelled of mildew. I toyed with the idea of knitting something from jute twine, which again, I realized was getting perilously close to Amish candle-making territory. Like, who is even going to ever *do* this?

Then I had a stroke of luck. Online I came across "Heirloom Mayan Loofah Scrubbers" which are made from one plant, giant Egyptian cucumber to be exact, which is officially the coolest name for a plant I have ever heard. According to the package, when you are done with it, you can toss it in your home compost or bury it in your garden and it will degrade in thirty days. Also, according to the paper wrapper, these loofahs are grown by a single Mayan family in Guatemala. I was so grateful I wanted to fly to Guatemala and go meet these amazing people.

Instead, I ordered a package, feeling sure I'd probably have to sacrifice some degree of effectiveness in exchange for this degree of biodegradability. I was wrong. The loofah sponge works noticeably better than my old ocelo favorite. No, I can't buy them at my local supermarket, and yes, at six for twenty dollars (rather than ocelo at six for fourteen dollars) you are paying about a dollar more per sponge.

That's not nothing, but it felt like the price of admission for keeping my dishes clean, my sink unsludgy, and the fox out of my chicken coop.

PETS

Cat litter

I've never gone terribly long without owning a cat. Or two. Three at most—I swear.

We had said a tearful goodbye to our last kitty a year before we began No Garbage, and with all the staying at home we were doing as a result of the pandemic, we felt like we were at last ready for a new furry addition. On one of the days when Ilsa was looking particularly down I decided she was in the market for an emotional support animal, and that afternoon Steve and I took her to the local humane society to find a new cat to adopt.

We came home with two.

Immediately I was faced with a dilemma I had been studiously avoiding thinking about up until that very moment: *what will we use in the litter box?*

In the past I had been, admittedly, the worst kind of cat-owner in the environmental department; when it came to cat poop and pee, I just did NOT want to deal. In the interest of minimum effort and maximum cleanliness, I had bought the most high-tech (read:

expensive) litter I could find: silica gel–based litter.* Every week, when it was time to change the litter, I wrapped it all up neatly in the plastic disposable litter pan liner before sending it on its way to live in the landfill for the next several thousand years.

I shudder to think of it now.

Several years ago my brother had suggested trying a newspaper-based litter that sounded super environmentally friendly, but it also sounded messy, smelly, dusty, *and* difficult to find. At that long-ago time in my life, in addition to two small cats I also had two small children, so generally speaking if it wasn't at my supermarket, I wasn't buying it. Period.

Fortunately, times have changed, and environmentally friendly litter is now a lot less messy, more effective, and more available. But I still didn't want to have to make a separate trip to the pet supply store, especially while we were trying to limit our germ exposure. While at the humane society I had noticed that their litter boxes contained an unfamiliar pellet mixture.

"That? Oh, those are wood pellets," the shelter worker said through her paper mask. "They work great and they're biodegradable. You can buy them packaged as cat litter but it's cheaper to just use pellet stove pellets."

Cat litter I can put in my compost?

"You can also use chicken feed."

When I looked into it I was surprised to realize that these days there are actually quite a few litter options which are both biodegradable and flushable (for those without access to compost). They are made from corn, soybeans, or even grass. The bad news is that all of them come in bags made of plastic (many of which are eligible for the plastic film bin at the supermarket) or a paper-plastic amalgam (which are eligible for nowhere but the landfill).

---

* I used to think silica gel was somehow dangerous, on account of the fact that the tiny little packets of it that come with some products or foods always say DO NOT EAT all over them. It turns out that the warning is primarily intended to prevent choking. Silica gel is actually nontoxic and a natural occurring component of sand.

But I was excited that we could use something that we already were using around the house: not only did we already have chickens, we also already had a pellet stove. We already had biodegradable cat litter in our house and we didn't even know it. If we went with the wood pellets we'd also save money, because buying large bags of pellets for our stove meant we were paying twenty cents per pound, whereas those same wood pellets being sold for cat litter were priced at about a dollar a pound, so about one fifth the cost. (We just had to be sure to get the *soft* wood pellets, because hard wood pellets don't absorb as well.)*

There was just one catch. Although these cat litters were natural and biodegradable, if we put them in our compost we couldn't use that compost on our garden down the road. The consensus is that bacteria from cat poop can cause toxoplasmosis, which is really, really dangerous for pregnant women, babies, and immunocompromised people.

When I was pregnant I was delighted to have a legit reason to put my husband in charge of litter box patrol. Now, though, I wasn't so happy, and I kept trying to find a way around it: *none of us are currently pregnant or babies or immunocompromised! Our cats live indoors only so the chances of them acquiring this bacteria, which often comes from eating raw meat, are very remote!* However I had to admit that our cats do occasionally catch the stray mouse and devour it like it's a pepperoni pizza and although we aren't super susceptible, getting toxoplasmosis does mean you run a slight risk of infections that can cause blindness.

Blindness.

I conceded: we would have two composts, one would be for kitty litter and shredded paper (which I still wasn't entirely convinced was free of nasty chemicals I didn't want in my garden/food) and the other for food scraps and the like, and eventual use in the garden. The kitty litter would break down naturally and avoid the landfill.

---

* I have heard tell that the same material is also packaged as "equine pellet bedding" at even less expensive rates.

Although more complicated than I liked, it still seemed quite a bit easier than teaching the cats to use the toilet.

Pet food

Like many cat and dog owners I feed our animals a combination of both wet and dry food. Because the wet food comes in cans, I can wash these and put them directly into metal recycling with no worries; they are either steel or aluminum, both of which have value in the recycling market and excellent recyclability as a result. The problem comes with the dry food.

Just like staples such as flour and sugar, a few short decades ago dry pet food used to be widely available in paper bags at the store, the way our chicken feed still comes now. Then came the Inexorable Plastic Creep, the result of the plastic industry lobbying for more markets, and thus more items in our supermarket to be packaged in plastic.

When I called up customer care listed on the website for Rachael Ray Nutrish pet foods I got ahold of Chris who was able to inform me that my suspicion was correct that none of their dry cat food bags are recyclable, being an amalgam of paper and plastic. She did say they were "working on it."

After searching the internet in vain for "dry cat food recyclable packaging" I called up Chewy.com customer service and got the same answer from Alex: as far as she could tell, no dry cat food they sell is currently packaged without plastic, most of the time fused with paper, and therefore in no manner recyclable.

By this time my cats were periodically sending me small, handwritten notes imploring me to give up this fool's errand. Perhaps they were afraid I'd ask them to give up dry food altogether, but they were safe since my vet recommended against that. I would just have to keep looking till I found a solution, or wait for Rachael Ray to call me back, whichever came first.

CLEANING PRODUCTS

I grew up in a house where we had a slick plastic bottle for every possible cleaning task. Cleaning grout? Removing mildew? Polishing the coffee table? There was sink cleaner and shower cleaner, and never the twain should meet. When I got a home of my own, I continued this practice, although I tried many different cleaning products which are marketed as nontoxic and earth friendly, or at least earth friend-*lier*. Products from Seventh Generation, Mrs. Meyer, Method: What I often found was that they either don't work well, are too expensive, or both. Plus, most of them still come in disposable plastic bottles.

It took me a while to wrap my head around the idea that these cleaners we buy at the store were not holy formulas handed down by the gods, but rather pricey combinations of industrial chemicals and ingredients that way-back-when people used to mix up themselves. Over the years I had accumulated a small collection of books containing recipes for various kinds of homemade cleansers, but always ended up stymied by too many options (forty-seven ways to clean glass!) or ingredients that sounded mysterious and intimidating. *Vegetable glycerin? Washing soda?* No, I did not have these things "hanging around my kitchen," actually.

It wasn't until this year that, in the interest of avoiding still more plastic bottles, I went back to the drawing board. I googled "make your own glass cleaner" and "make your own toilet bowl cleaner" and looked for the simplest solutions I could find, using ingredients and bottles I already had on hand. Of course, to buy these ingredients, it still usually entails buying a plastic bottle, but stay with me here, because my logic is threefold. When you make your own cleaning supplies:

1. You're saving money
2. You're avoiding any unknown scary chemically shit you don't want in your body or on your household surfaces
3. You're able to use a lot *less* plastic, buying common ingredients like vinegar in larger, gallon containers, *and* reusing the spray bottles over and over

Please note that I use a lot of vinegar in my cleaning. Vinegar by itself makes a good cleanser but does not kill as many germs or disinfect surfaces as well as, say, rubbing alcohol, hydrogen peroxide, or bleach. Also, because it is acidic, it is probably not a good choice for porous surfaces such as wood floors or stone countertops.

The biggest rule in making your own cleaning products is this:

Just as you should never mix bleach and ammonia, never, ever combine vinegar and bleach, because this creates chlorine gas, which is poisonous.

Got it? Okay, scary warning dispensed. Now let's get to cleaning:

All Purpose Cleaner

In a spray bottle combine 50 percent water and 50 percent distilled white vinegar

That's it. That's the whole recipe.

Glass Cleaner

¼ cup rubbing alcohol

¼ cup distilled white vinegar

1 tbsp cornstarch (this little bit of abrasiveness can help remove dirt and streaks, but can be left out)

2 cups warm water

Toilet Bowl Cleaner

Sprinkle baking soda in the bowl, scrub with toilet brush

Pour distilled white vinegar around the bowl, let sit a while, and then flush.

(This works best, by the way, if you clean regularly. For stubborn stains I use a pumice stick that I buy from the Vermont Country Store. It used to come with a wood handle, but you'll never guess what they've unfortunately switched to! Plastic. But you can find them without handles, so buy those instead.)

Sink Cleaner

Combine dish soap and baking soda to make a paste. Scrub around sink surface with a bristle brush and then wipe off with damp towel.

Grout Cleaner

½ cup baking soda
¼ cup hydrogen peroxide
1 tsp liquid dish soap
Scrub into grout with a bristle brush, let sit for 5 to 10 minutes, and then rinse off.

(Note: When it comes to dish soap, be aware that brands like Dawn are approximately one-seventh petroleum,[14] and containing petroleum can mean heavy metal residue is in your dish soap, which can be linked to everything from cancer to infertility. Instead, look for a nontoxic, organic dish soap such as Dr. Bronner's Castile Soap.)

For my spray bottles I used plastic ones I already had on hand. I have a shoebox with old toothbrushes that I use for scrubbing, and instead of paper towels I use rags made from old bath towels, cut up with pinking shears (to discourage shedding). I collect all the rags in a bucket after using, and before the day is out, I run them through the washing machine all at once. I bought a small jar of lavender oil and add a few drops of it to my all-purpose cleanser whenever I want to feel like a fancy lady.

I'm still figuring it out as I go, but I am quite unreasonably proud of the fact that I can clean my house now without having to buy all the expensive, harsh chemicals in landfill-destined plastic bottles.

OTHER

Reusable bags—shopping, produce and foldable totes

Of all the eco-friendly efforts one might make, bringing your own reusable bag to the supermarket seems like the most obvious no-brainer. Like many folks, this was one of the first changes I made, years ago, in an effort to reduce household waste. The first thing I bought was a bunch of cloth bags from a local supermarket. And they were simply *awful*. I know, I'm sorry, but most cloth bags, in my opinion, super suck.

WHAT I HATE ABOUT CLOTH BAGS

- Cloth bags do not stand up on their own, allowing easy access. Instead they flop around like angry fish while you are trying to load them with your oatmeal and broccoli
- Often cloth bags use a separate plastic bottom to stabilize and distribute the weight of the contents, which works great except when it falls out and gets lost *all the time*
- Cloth bags show dirt FAST. Silk chiffon has nothing on cloth bags
- Once you wash them they get wrinkled and crumply looking, and forever after look like they belong to a hobo

---

The cloth bags did not win my undying love. Then, somewhat reluctantly, I purchased plasticized bags with handles from a different supermarket, and more than fifteen years later I am still using them. Yes, they're plastic, but over the years this plastic has allowed me to save literally thousands of disposable bags; this is a good example in which purchasing a durable plastic item to replace a disposable plastic item can actually be a really decent, functional solution.

When it came to bringing my own produce bags to the store, I discovered a similar situation: one day I woke up and found myself with a collection of both cotton mesh (made by Tiblue) and nylon drawstring bags (made by 3B Bags) and, sad to say, I invariably preferred the nylon. This is because the cotton ones get stuck on each other more easily, and make it harder to see what is inside when it comes time to check out. Invariably, I, or the cashier, has to open the bag and pull the produce out far enough to read the PLU code, whereas in the plastic bags the contents are readily visible through the nylon mesh. It's a matter of a few seconds, but as with any chore or task that you do every week, efficiency does make a difference. The upshot for me is that I have both and I don't really worry about which ones are which: I grab a handful of six or seven of them randomly every week when I head to the store. After removing the produce at home they go into the wash with my dishcloths and cloth napkins. If I felt like I needed to buy more of them I'd be sorely tempted to buy the nylon mesh, but probably give in to my newly burgeoning plastic-phobia and buy cloth instead.*

The last bag in my reusable arsenal is my just-in-case foldable Baggu that has its own little pocket carrying case. And yes, it is made of nylon, albeit recycled. Although there seem to be a million reusable nylon bags out there, many of them are boring, ugly, and use stuff-bags or no container at all, which means they look permanently wrinkly and/or dirty.† Baggu, instead, is a bag you fold up and put into its own little neat square pocket. And they come in bright colors with whimsical designs. (I am *all* about the whimsical designs.) I have two Baggus—a large and a small—that I just leave in my purse all the time. That way if I make an unexpected trip to the store, I'm never without a bag. When I get home, I fold it neatly back up and return it to my purse.

But because we were in a pandemic, remembering to bring them wasn't the biggest problem with bringing my own bags. Instead, sometimes it was being allowed to bring them in the first place.

In the early months of our Year of No Garbage I was delighted to find my supermarket pushing the "bring your own bag!" message pretty hard, due to the impending March 1, 2020, implementation

---

* I should also point out that our health food store features "biodegradable" produce bags that feel like plastic, but are home compostable. Sadly, I don't love them: they have a clingy, gummy texture that makes you suspicious that the moisture from your Swiss chard might cause it to spontaneously degrade in the back of your car before you even get home.

† I should also point out that our health food store features "biodegradable" produce bags that feel like plastic, but are home compostable. Sadly, I don't love them: they have a clingy, gummy texture that makes you suspicious that the moisture from your Swiss chard might cause it to spontaneously degrade in the back of your car before you even get home.

of a plastic bag ban in all of New York State (I live in Vermont, but my closest supermarket is just over the border in New York. Vermont enacted its own plastic bag ban on July 1, 2020.) I have to admit that the anti-plastic nerd in me was quietly ecstatic the day that, after much preparation and multiple warnings, the evil rolls of plastic bags had disappeared *for good*.

Except it *wasn't* for good. The triumphant moment was as short lived as a perfectly ripe avocado. As quick as you can say "COVID-19" we were now abruptly encountering the same response from *every* store when it came to "bringing your own" reusables and containers, which is to say: OMIGOD DON'T.

The truth is that the plastics industry has long been trying to plant the seeds of doubt about the safety of reusable bags. Back in 2010 a study funded by the American Chemistry Council (funded by plastics producers!), looked for salmonella, listeria, and E. coli on reusable bags and ooo—you know what?

They didn't find any.

But they could have! Seriously, after the study was released, *that* was the headline.

In response, here's what Michael Hansen, senior staff scientist at Consumers Union, which publishes *Consumer Reports*, had to say about it back then: "A person eating an average bag of salad greens gets more exposure to these bacteria than if they had licked the insides of the dirtiest bag from this study."[15]

Not that I'm planning on licking my shopping bags any time soon, mind you, but what I think is important to notice is a recurring tactic of using fear to get folks to consume more plastic: reusable bags could make you sick—*better use plastic!* Tap water could be unclean—*better buy bottled!* Someone might have touched that sandwich bread—*better put a sealed plastic bag inside the* other *plastic bag!*

Yes, keeping everyone safe and healthy is, and should be, a paramount concern. But we don't need to fabricate problems where they do not exist just to keep the plastic people in business. With the discovery that reusable bags did not spread COVID-19, or any other horrible bacteria, the plastic bags bans were, ultimately, back in business. As of this writing eight out of the fifty United States now have plastic bag bans in place.

It's a start. I anxiously look forward to the extinction of the disposable plastic bag, and the day when to see one, you have to seek out the diorama at the Museum of Natural History titled: Crazy, Self-Destructive Things Humans Used To Do. (The figures in it will be not only carrying single-use plastic bags, but will also be drinking soda and wearing parachute pants.)

Hankies

As far back as I can remember my family has always been a Kleenex family. You just don't go to the grocery store and come home without a box or two, and I never, ever went anywhere without a small travel packet in my purse.

With the advent of No Garbage I learned quickly that all used paper tissues needed to be either flushed down the toilet or put in the compost (same for hair from hairbrushes and clipped toenails).

But I was in search of a better option. In this day and age, it can be as tricky to find cloth handkerchiefs as it is to find a snood or sock garters, but I did manage to find them at the Vermont Country Store, very plain, plaid cotton squares in sets of three. Then a friend sent me a thoughtful birthday gift: a lovely set of delicate ladies' hankies she purchased from an antiques seller, embroidered with flowers and assorted frippery.

It took me awhile to get into the habit of washing the hankies and always having them on hand. A decorative tissue box in our living room was repurposed into a hankie container, the assorted colorful squares rolled up and inserted in the holder in the manner of a bouquet. Whenever I think of it, I replace the hankie in my coat pocket with a fresh one, tossing the other into the laundry. Keeping hankies in my purse proved harder, because keeping the kind of overstuffed and chaotic purse that I do, they always ended up at the very bottom of my bag, scrunched up, and, if not exactly dirty, less than appealing to bury my face in.

The solution was to follow the lead of the portable shopping bags I carry in my purse: to keep them neat, clean, and separated I decided I needed a designated pouch. Could I make one myself? I'm crafty, so probably. But out of curiosity I decided to see what other options I had.

I googled "handkerchief holder" and found a Montreal-based company named Tshu (which, okay, is adorable), and whose website demonstrates that they are a tiny company equally obsessed with zero waste and noses. Their hankies have *names* (Gilbert. Louise. Elvis.) AND they include instructions for how to blow your nose on an organic cotton hankie: "Don't be afraid. Sit back and put on a nice, relaxing song. Jazz perhaps." *It goes on from there.*

They make a point of paying their employees fairly *and* planting a tree for every hankie purchased, so you know it isn't going to be cheap. A pack of four lovely handmade hankies cost eighty-six dollars, single ones ran eighteen to twenty-two dollars. This is *not* Kleenex, folks.

I loved everything about this business, but the cost definitely gave me pause. After considerable hesitation, I purchased a set of "orphans": five imperfect "seconds" hankies for a reduced total rate of twenty-five dollars, plus a holder for twelve dollars. With shipping I was paying forty-one for what amounted to reusable nose towels.

On the other hand, for the cost of ten boxes of disposable tissues—or perhaps three months' worth—I was going to have a lifetime supply of tissues in my purse. When they arrived I was delighted—an adorable set of orphans it was, and most importantly the cute little hankie holder worked as promised keeping my tissues neat and clean till needed. Could I have made my own? Absolutely. Was I ever gonna get around to it? Nope.

So. Guess what everyone I know is getting for Christmas this year?

Lint removers

Since I've always had cats I always have a very nice collection of cat hair. My solution to getting it off my clothing has long been to use a refillable adhesive strip lint roller, whose plastic, sticky layers peel off after use and are discarded. If you've ever used these before then you know that they are annoying and wasteful, with the added bonus of coming in different size rollers so that you inevitably purchase the wrong refill for your handle. But what other option was there? Only buy clothing that coordinated with my cats? For a while I wondered if committing to zero waste meant I'd have to walk around looking vaguely furry for the rest of my life.

Then at some point I stumbled across an advertisement for the Uproot Cleaner. It has a handle, to which a triangular metal head is attached. This wonder tool promised to get rid of pet hair, lint and pilling on clothing, merely by swiping the flat metal head across the surface.

I ordered one hopefully and was exasperated when it arrived swaddled in umpteen layers of utterly unnecessary plastic, not to mention being made with a plastic handle, which could easily have been bamboo. Like the tea strainer, I was annoyed at the thoughtless use of plastic packaging in a product which in many circles has been marketed as a zero waste solution.

But I will say: it works, and surprisingly well. So I'm going to grudgingly recommend it, all the while hoping that they start using some more environmentally friendly materials.

(Shouldn't be long. Customer Service got some pointed email feedback from me which I'm sure has entirely changed their business model.)

THE UPSHOT

One day the toothbrush Greta had bought made me do a double take. Made by Woo Bamboo who advertises themselves as "Plastic Negative," the toothbrush itself looked okay but . . . the package contained plastic. Huh? On the website they go on to proudly proclaim "the entirety of this packaging is safe for disposal in landfills, or in home compost bins; leaving no toxic trace behind!"

Whoa, back up a minute. Safe for disposal in landfills? You're shitting me, right? So Woo Bamboo is proud that their packaging is supposedly safer for the environment than . . . leaking car batteries and untreated medical waste?

Honestly, though, I think we're not supposed to really read that part. We're supposed to get all caught up in "Bamboo's Hot, Plastic's Not!" and ignore the fact that the packaging is *the very thing* they are purporting to avoid: single use disposable plastic.

There's something about being told that you're Doing the Right Thing—the healthy thing, the environmental thing—that seems to give us license to turn off our normal healthy skepticism. When that happens, we can end up doing precisely the opposite of what we wanted to do in the first place.

When it comes to being more planet friendly: the health food store, the farmers' market, the gift shop, and the supermarket all have products to sell you in the name of being less wasteful and supporting a circular economy, but how often do we see things like that toothbrush that *just don't make sense?* The recycled paper that is packaged in cellophane? Or the reusable glass travel mug you ordered that arrives in a box full of Styrofoam?

It's important to bear in mind that even the most truly virtuous product still has an environmental footprint. That doesn't mean we need to give up and lock ourselves in the basement in the name of a better environment; it means keeping your brain plugged in and rethinking what you really need as well as distinguishing between the good guys and the greenwashers. It's not easy, because we live in a culture that encourages us to define ourselves by what we buy, believes that more is always better, and that uses half-truths and deception at every conceivable turn. We shouldn't have to work this hard to figure out what is truly compostable, or whether a plastic made from sand is better than a plastic made from petroleum, but as a society, this is where we are currently at.*

The good news is that hopefully this book presents you with a whole bunch of that information already parsed out. The bad news

---

* I hereby apologize to my sixth grade English teacher for ending that sentence with a preposition.

is that the industry keeps coming up with better, more ingenious ways to greenwash us all the time. So be vigilant. Don't take things at face value. Don't take that free tote bag if you already have fourteen at home. Don't buy glass or metal straws if you really don't have to use a straw in the first place. And for crying out loud don't buy an avocado-hugger, because you should really send that money to the giant Egyptian cucumber farmers instead.

Try This, Not That

I'm not a huge fan of "Zero Waste Kits," which often include items that are, in fact, wasteful, (if one metal straw is good, fourteen must be better!) as well as being surprisingly unimaginative, or confused with self-care (bath bombs are nice but kind of beside the point.)

Instead of Buying	Try
Another fabric tote bag	Foldable nylon tote to keep in your purse or car
Another reusable water bottle	Ceramic travel mug with metal tea infuser
A metal straw cleaning kit	Toothpaste tablets
Portable bamboo flatware set	Reusable hankies (cut up old flannel sheets or other cloth)
Silicone food storage bags	Pyrex with glass lids (find in antique shops or Goodwill)

CHAPTER NINE

BUT DO I *HAVE* TO BUY A BIDET? BIG-TICKET ITEMS

It's one thing to purchase a new kind of dental floss, and another thing entirely to buy a full-fledged machine. In the world of being more sustainable, big-ticket items are probably the most daunting change, because they're an actual investment. They also usually entail more challenges to your life than figuring out how to get rid of the packing material it came in and a bigger learning curve than switching from liquid to solid shampoo.

Because it is daunting, it can be helpful to know someone who has already taken the plunge and lived to tell the tale. Bidets? Home composters? Ozone laundry systems? Gather round and I will tell you what I have learned.

BIDETS

Like many Americans, I always found bidets a little bit intimidating. They were a weird European thing. When I was a teenager, we moved into a newly built house and it came with a bidet in the master bathroom: an entirely separate toilet-like apparatus that sat next to the actual toilet, for some completely unknown reason. In the twenty-some years my mother owned that house, no one ever used it.

Fast-forward to pandemic-era 2020, when a surprise toilet paper shortage meant people online could suddenly *not stop* talking about bidets. Bidet attachments for your toilet, specifically, and the pros and cons of different models, whether you really had to spend hundreds of dollars or not, whether a bidet eliminated the need for toilet paper entirely, and so on.

After initial reluctance, I began to be intrigued, although still kind of terrified. We did a whole bunch of online research, reading reviews, ratings, and comments. It was Steve, mercifully, who made phone calls to talk to the customer service representatives who apparently were available all day long to talk about things like what kind of water temperature and pressure you might prefer on your hindquarters. Would you like a nice enema feature? If I ever had to talk about such things with a complete stranger I would, most certainly, expire on the spot.

We settled on a Bio Bidet with some, but not all, of the possible bells and whistles. When it arrived, it was composed of a seat and lid to replace our existing ordinary seat and lid, as well as a remote control (our toilet needs a *remote?*); a plug provided electricity.

Ilsa was horrified.

"I am pretending the bidet thing is not happening," she said, while Steve was hooking it up.

"Want to try it out?" Steve asked me.

"Um." I replied. Did he really intend to stay for this? "Not with you *here*."

So he left the room, at which point I was officially traumatized by my first bidet experience.

First of all, it acts like it's haunted. If one so much as enters the bathroom doorway, sensors cause the lid to open, as if in ghostly welcome. Upon sitting down, one finds that the seat is noticeably warm—oh, *hello there!*—which takes a little while to get used to.

As I sat down for the very first time and regarded the myriad of buttons on the remote, I thought, "Well, how bad could it be?" and pressed the button politely marked "rear."

YOW!

A hot poker had jumped into my private area so, of course, I leapt up from the toilet seat. Which fixed the problem except that now A STREAM OF HOT WATER WAS SPRAYING EVERYWHERE.

From outside the bathroom door Ilsa and Steve called, "*What?* What happened?"

"*I'm being PEED ON*," I yelled.

Today, I am happy to report that our bidet and I are on much better terms. I continue to be a little disconcerted by features like the automatic lid, which sometimes will open when I sneeze in another part of the house, but not when I stand next to it waving my hand emphatically over the sensor. I have to admit that once I got used to cleaning my tush with a spray of water rather than a wad of paper, I preferred it.

We still use some toilet paper, because, despite the fact that the Bio Bidet has a special drying feature (of course it does), it kind of takes forever. Nevertheless, I quickly discovered that not only were we using less toilet paper, we were quite literally using *half as much.* Given that, according to my math we were essentially paying double for our super sustainable toilet paper, this meant the math worked out, right?

Except for the cost of our bidet, which was a pretty penny: around six hundred dollars. Between my anxiety about the entire enterprise and Steve's love of extreme gadgetry, I do think we ended up spending more than we absolutely needed to. Mind you, there are models out there for around a hundred dollars that don't do any of the spooky things ours can do, and for a while I campaigned for us to buy one of these budget models to install on our downstairs toilet for comparison purposes. I was roundly voted down by my family members. Apparently one tush-shower in our house was enough.

However, a good friend told me that they love their more economical version. I concluded that it really comes down to how many features you care about, and in hindsight (oh dear) I would say in our house we could have just as well have done with fewer bells and whistles. I mean, do you need the water temperature to be adjustable? Do you want the drying feature? Do you want the nozzle to be "self-cleaning" (this means it self-sanitizes between uses, but you still do have to clean it when you clean your toilet) or offer a "feminine wash" as well?

So many choices. But I'm not sure if the potty poltergeist comes standard.

OZONE LAUNDRY SYSTEMS

Pods. You know them: those cube-like little packets that are supposed to save us from the arduous and soul-destroying task of having to actually measure liquid detergent. The horror.

Lately quite a few ads had been trying to persuade me to switch from liquid laundry detergent to pods, purportedly "eco-friendly" because they weigh less and therefore use less energy to get where they're going. On the other hand, my environmentally minded friends recommended laundry "tablets," "strips," or "sheets," which dissolve in water and have an even lighter environmental footprint. For example Greta likes Blueland laundry tablets. But be careful! Whatever product you choose, make sure it doesn't contain polyvinyl alcohol (PVA or PVOH) which is derived from petrochemicals and—debatably—a source of ocean microplastics.[1]

But we are lucky, because in our house we don't have to worry about any of this because these days we don't use laundry detergent at all.

Instead, we have a system called an EcoWasher.* Essentially, this is an appliance the size of supermarket sheet cake. It attaches to the wall above your washing machine and magically makes your clothes clean.

At least this is how it was explained to me at the appliance store. What I *heard* was *You don't have to buy laundry detergent anymore!* It also didn't hurt that this supernatural contraption would pay for itself pretty quickly: the average American family spends $180 per year on laundry detergent; an EcoWasher costs $400. On top of that it only washes in cold, so you save the cost of heating the water; and depending who you ask that can amount to another $150–$300 savings per year.

---

* EcoWasher is just one of a variety of different "Ozone laundry systems" on the market today.

We particularly liked the fact that we could get away from traditional detergents that can contain harmful chemicals and fragrances—better for us, better for the environment. After all, if the average American household uses 5,600 gallons of water per year washing clothes, and there are roughly 130 million American households, this means that we have something like 728 billion gallons per year of petrochemical-filled water flooding back into our waterways.

We were convinced. We got it home and hooked the panel up to our washing machine and were amazed to find that it was true: our clothes somehow came out clean, using *only* cold water. How was this possible? I had no idea.

So I started to look into it. On EcoWasher's website they explain that inside the flat panel our water goes through "ozone infusion" creating something called "hydroxyl radicals." From the hydroxyl radicals, ozone is formed.

A little bit of knowledge is a dangerous thing. Up until now, I had just kind of blissfully accepted that my EcoWasher knew what it was doing, and we left each other alone, but now that I had this modicum of information, complete with chemically sounding words? I had a billion questions:

> *Ozone infusion*—is that okay?
> Does ozone get released? Is that good or bad?
> And *hydroxyl radicals*—are those like *free* radicals?
> Aren't free radicals *bad*?

All of this brought me to the Big Kahuna Question: does infusing ozone and creating hydroxyl radicals in my washing machine do any damage to me, my family, or to the environment?

As I wondered this, a rational angel appeared on my shoulder whispering "Oh, Eve—don't you think if your washing machine technology was creating a dangerous rip in the time-space continuum we'd have *heard* about it by now?" Not surprisingly, the conspiracy theorist angel on my other shoulder wasn't convinced.

In an attempt to get to the bottom of such questions I called EcoWasher. While I waited for them to call me back, I watched a whole bunch of YouTube videos and read articles explaining ozone laundry science. I found out that the EcoWasher is based on technology that has been used in hospitals and resorts for decades. I also found out that hydroxyl radicals are famous in the world of chemistry for acting like "nature's detergent," decomposing pollutants, and neutralizing viruses and bacteria. All this sounded pretty good.

But reputable sources agree: Hydroxyl radicals *are* free radicals and are bad—at least when they are in our bodies. In the atmosphere, however, they turn into *good* guys, scouring the stratosphere like a scrub brush on your grandmother's linoleum floor. Chemistry is confusing this way: because it's almost impossible to keep the good guys and bad guys straight when they keep shape-shifting depending upon their context. On top of their Dr. Jekyll/Mr. Hyde personality, I learned that hydroxyl radicals have a life span of *less than one second.*

I concluded that hydroxyl radicals sounded a lot scarier than they really were. I figured as long as the little suckers stay out of my body and in my washing machine for their short little one-second lives, I probably didn't need to freak out about them very much.

But what about the ozone? Where did it go? Did it have to do with the ozone layer? *Could I be destroying the ozone layer with my washing machine?*

Well, no. As for where it comes from and where it goes, you probably won't be surprised to learn that once again the answer is "it depends!" Of course, when ozone is in the stratosphere, or upper atmosphere, it protects the earth from damaging UV rays. Most of us came to know this back in the 1980s when it was revealed that chlorofluorocarbons were creating a dangerous hole in this protective layer. So far: ozone=good guy!

But put ozone in another context and everything changes. When ozone is present in the *troposphere*, or lower atmosphere, it becomes a greenhouse gas, trapping heat and warming the planet, not to mention causing problems for people with breathing disorders. Plus—and this blew my mind a little bit—did you know that ozone is just another kind of oxygen? It's called an allotrope, meaning an element that takes different physical forms.

To recap: ozone laundry systems take oxygen (two oxygen atoms) from the air and charge it with electricity, the unstable hydroxyl radicals (one oxygen and one hydrogen atom) are then formed as a result of the reaction.[2] There they begin the good work of killing the bacteria that makes our clothes smell, before dying a graceful death at the ripe old age of one second. I don't think your clothes are entirely clean yet, but that's okay because this reaction also leads to the creation of the slightly more stable ozone (three oxygen atoms) which has an approximate half-life of thirty minutes (depending on what it encounters in your washer) before it turns back into regular old oxygen in the water. During that time it continues the excellent work of killing microorganisms such as viruses and bacteria in your laundry.[3]

The reason you need to use cold water? Is because it helps extend the life of the ozone.

Phew.

I'm not sure at this moment if my eleventh grade chemistry teacher would be proud of me, or sobbing softly into a hankie, but at least I could rest easy that my magical detergent-free washing machine lived up to its billing, even under scrutiny. I breathed a sigh of relief well aware that, this year, arriving at a conclusion like that was definitely turning out to be the exception, not the rule.

HOME COMPOSTERS

Living in rural Vermont means that composting our food scraps is relatively easy. I know some folks who—no kidding—just have a *pile* in the backyard, no cover, no chicken wire, nothing. Others try harder to keep it contained and to deter the inevitable interest from various members of the local animal population.

Years ago, we had experimented with a "turning barrel" composter, but I quickly discovered that I have the arm strength of a gummy bear, and so once anything was actually in it, the darn thing never got turned at all. Then our friend and handyman Lucas suggested what amounted to a wood box with planks that can be removed from the front when it was time to turn or empty it. Now this, requiring zero muscles on my part, I could do.

I loved my wood box composter, but when the rats found it, it had to be moved much farther from the house.

Today the rats are gone (sorry, rats, my husband is a prize-winning sharpshooter) and although the occasional opossum, stray cat, or skunk occasionally tries to take up residence amongst the warm piles of decaying organic matter, it does work pretty well.

This is important, because depending on who you ask, our landfills are made up of anywhere between 20 and 60 percent organic material, which is to say, material that could have been composted.[4] No matter what figure you come up with, when you consider the fact that in the sealed environment of the landfill the environment does not allow the material to biodegrade, it's far too much.

For city dwellers the compost question is more complicated. While some urban communities now have compost collection alongside trash and recycling collection, in Greta's Brooklyn neighborhood at this time the only option would have been for her and her boyfriend Steven to make weekly trips to "drop-off sites."

Right. My nineteen-year-old was going to collect all her decaying food and once a week bring it—on the subway perhaps? Or in the car of a particularly understanding Uber driver?—to a compost collection site. Oh, and don't forget! They won't accept meat, fish, or dairy scraps! So for those . . . I dunno, find a nice stray cat, I guess?

Then again, I could always recommend they try the super low-tech "worms in a box in the closet!" model, which I understand works very well for some eco-minded city dwellers, but, honestly, I knew that Greta, in her Brooklyn apartment the size of an extra-large box of Wheaties, would never go for this.

In an attempt at more realistic solutions, and after a bit of research, early in 2020 we purchased a Vitamix "Food Cycler" home composter for Greta and Steven's apartment. I figured since we were asking them to eschew trash while living in a New York City apartment for a year, it was the least we could do. At four hundred dollars, it was certainly an investment, which they promptly left behind in the city on March 13th when they fled the end of the world that was apparently commencing. I think they used it once?

A few months later, we retrieved the home composter, and I tried it out for myself.

This is probably a good time to admit to you that I am not good about composting rules. I like to put everything in the compost pile. I put meat, fish, and dairy in. As we've already seen, I put in paper napkins, paper towels. I've put in bits of wool, yarn, and hair. For a while I was adding dryer lint too, until I realized that a good portion of dryer lint probably contains microplastics shed from our clothing.

My feeling is always: hey, it's better than going to the landfill.*

So why would I even bother with a home composter at all? Well, for one thing I was simply curious: would it really break down our food scraps into actual compost that we could spread around our plants within mere hours, as advertised? Then there was the fantastical claim that it would even break down meat bones . . . this I had to see. Keeping meat out of the compost pile would certainly be a good thing to do if we could, given the fact that bones take much longer to break down than other scraps, and the presence of meat and bones attracts more critters.

And it was all true, pretty much. In this contraption the size of a bread maker and the weight of an anvil, all our banana peels and carrot tops somehow turned to rich brown dirt overnight. Chicken bones in particular could be counted upon to degrade entirely, and although it did use electricity, it only produced a mild hum when running.

The problem came when I tried to *use* this lovely fragrant compost. Inside, sprinkled in the pots of our house plants, the cats found the aroma intoxicating, and immediately proceeded to dig up all our plants. Outside, the chickens made a similar discovery, as if we had sprayed our flower beds with a perfume called *L'Eau d'Meat*. Both inside and out I frantically tried scraping the compost away but the

---

* And as already mentioned, for safety reasons we don't apply the kitty litter compost to our garden.

smell was *everywhere* and all our animals were desperately trying to murder all our plants in an effort to find the food that must be buried underneath them.

After this, for a while I decided to abandon the Food Cycler. It was small, took a long time to run the full cycle, and frankly, it was getting me into too much trouble. Not long after that, though, I found that the outdoor wood compost bin had one night been pulled apart at the seams, and although we never saw it, there was evidence that a bear was the culprit. Putting meat in the compost was effectively establishing a Bear Buffet fifty feet from our house, and twenty feet from the chicken coop, so perhaps it was not the very best idea. Today, the Food Cycler is our meat-and-bones solution, and the resulting soil material gets thrown in with the food compost—destined one day for the garden—outside (but separate from where we put the kitty litter). Yes, it's a little complicated, but at last I think we have arrived at the nicest and most bear-free scenario.

And although he has not expressly informed me, I'm sure the opossum is pleased with this arrangement as well.

CHAPTER TEN

....

SINGLE STREAM IS A LIE AND OTHER FUN RECYCLING FACTS

Way back in January 2020, when people still did crazy things like gather in groups, I was faced with the first of many No Garbage social conundrums: I was offered wine in a plastic cup.

I was at an art opening. The director of our local art center, Anne, is a friend and was aware of our No Garbage project. So, when I hesitated, trying to find the right response, Anne kindly jumped to the rescue and said she'd see if she could find an actual *glass* glass in the kitchen.

After Anne disappeared, the catering fellow did some research, which is to say he looked at the bottom of one of the disposable cups. He informed me that I need have no fear, because the plastic was indeed recyclable.

Me: Hooray! I will take the cup home and add it to our single-stream recycling!

Problem officially solved—the end.

Oh dear. Remember, this was January and consequently it was at the very baby steps beginning of our project, before I learned so many things, simply by asking question after question after question. But sometimes, often in fact, no matter how far I followed the trail, no one I could get ahold of *really* knew. Sometimes there were dead ends. Then, at one point or another during the summer I heard about an online college course being offered, a class unlike any other I'd ever heard of.

The class was Beyond Plastics Pollution. Offered by nearby Bennington College, it was to be taught by visiting professor Judith Enck, formerly a regional administrator for the EPA under the Obama administration. Enck has made it her mission in life to make a difference on the issue of plastics, which she calls, without hyperbole, "The greatest moral threat of our time." I had never taken an online college class before, and despite the fact that the pandemic made our house feel like a castle fortified with an invisible moat, the newfound ubiquity of Zoom gave us a new, surprisingly safe way to interact with the world outside.

Wow, I thought, *maybe I can at last get to the bottom of some of these questions:* is TerraCycle for real? What happens to our plastics #1–7 when they leave our single-stream recycling bins? Is removing stickers really that important?

I was in good company: eighty students had signed up for this Zoom seminar, most of whom were long past college age. I was excited to finally get down to business with not only an expert teacher, but a group of folks from all over the country who, like me, thought talking about plastic and recycling and single-use disposability was a perfectly charming way to spend a Thursday evening.

I was hoping for good news, of course, affirmation that all our efforts as eco-conscious citizens were not in vain. That somehow, some way, if we all just contort our lives enough and in just the right ways, we could make that individual difference everyone talks about.

Instead of that, I got the truth.

Coupled with some of the depressing information I had already been able to glean up to this point, everything was starting to make more sense, but not in a good way. Instead, it was like a poster for a low budget horror movie.

"It *can't* be killed!"

"It will *never* go away!"

"*Beware the savage lies and shocking deception of the . . . PLASTIPOCALYPSE!*"

So, without further ado, let me introduce you to the very, *very* bad news about plastic that took me months of investigation, and a college course, to finally get to the bottom of:

Top Ten Terrible Truths About Plastic:
1. Plastic is not *really* recyclable.
2. "Single-stream" recycling is a lie.
3. "Compostable" plastics are pretty much a total lie (with one notable exception).
4. "Extreme Recycling" Programs are pretty much a total lie too.
5. Forget *one* giant ocean garbage patch; there are *five*.
6. Plastic drives climate change.
7. Plastic is racist.
8. Plastics do not break down—or go away—ever.
9. Plastics are in our water, air, and food. Also our bloodstream, poop, and the placenta of newborn babies.
10. There *aren't* seven kinds of plastic as recycling symbols indicate; there are *tens of thousands*, all largely untested for effects on human health.

Got it? Between invading our bodies, killing the environment, and the fact that we're being aggressively lied to about what to do with it and where it goes when we're done with it, this list can be a little overwhelming, and maybe even hard to believe. So let's take a few moments to break it down:

1. Plastic is not really recyclable

How do we define *recyclable*? Anyone who talks about the "circular economy," in which materials go around and around in an eco-friendly cycle of reforming and reuse, is not—cannot be—talking about plastic. Ever. Even the very best, most adaptable plastics are ultimately irredeemable garbage.

This is because unlike glass and metal, which can be recycled infinitely, even genuinely "recyclable" plastics can only be re-formed one or maybe two times before the chemical composition degrades to the point of being utterly unusable. They will just fall apart. Then what?

I bet you can guess! They go to sit in the landfill for eternity or create toxic fumes and ash as they are burned up in an incinerator. When I learned this I realized that, when we talk about plastic, we really shouldn't even use the word *recyclable*, because it does not apply.

But let's say you're a "glass half full" type of person and you think being able to melt down and re-form plastic once is better than nothing at all, so you go to the store and try to buy your food in recycled plastic containers to support this recycling effort.

For the most part, you can't. And there's a reason for that. *Most recycled plastic is too dangerous to put food in.* According to a report from Environment and Climate Change Canada (a department of the Canadian government): "The vast majority of plastic products and packaging produced each year and placed on the market is *not suitable for processing into food grade PCR*"* (PCR is "Post Consumer Resin," i.e., used plastic).[1] In other words, as Jan Dell, chemical engineer and founder of the Last Beach Cleanup, put it when she spoke to our Beyond Plastics group, "It will *kill people.*"

Think about it: plastics don't just contain food, they can contain all kinds of things: motor oil, drain cleaner, mouse poison . . . many of them things you really wouldn't want to put in your body. And unlike glass or metal, plastic absorbs some percentage of those toxic substances and brings them along for the next application. (More on the absorbency of plastics in chapter 11).

But I hope you haven't forgotten about all those ten thousand synthetic chemicals, some combination of which went into the creation of those plastics in the first place, because those are there too. Put them all together in a nice chemical stew in which, well, who knows what reactions could occur, what additional new chemicals could be formed? Given these facts, perhaps it's not actually all that

---

* Emphasis mine.

surprising that a recent study of recycled plastic children's toys concluded that they contained high levels of toxic chemicals—such as flame retardants and dioxins. Some "were found to be *as contaminated as hazardous waste*,"[2] emphasis mine.

Still want to buy recycled plastics?

Nearly half of the new plastics generated each year go to create packaging.[3] No one seems to be able to tell me what percentage of packaging plastics go specifically to *food* packaging, but, after studying the orgy of plastic that is my local supermarket for the last year, I think it is very safe to say that it is a freaking *lot*. The Canadian government concludes that most plastic *which has been recycled only one time* isn't safe enough to contain food without possibly poisoning people, this strikes me as one more significant blow to the idea that plastics are recyclable.

What this also means is that when we reuse or repurpose plastic, again unlike other truly recyclable materials, it does not reduce or replace the production of new products from plastic. Those products keep right on being made at the same rate, regardless. It's the difference between "Hey, let's make this into something we need!" and "Can we make this into anything? 'Cause we've gotta do something with it."

Plus, when we hear about plastics being "recycled," what they are almost always talking about is *down*cycling. If this term sounds uncomplimentary, it's meant to. Downcycling, as we've alluded to earlier, is the process of taking a material and making it into something not as durable or functional or valuable as it was in its first life. Although a plastic picnic bench *sounds* durable, functional, and even more valuable than say, the bunch of plastic chip bags that provided the material to make it, one reason that process is termed *downcycling* is that it also requires *the addition of new, virgin plastic, and/or a bunch more toxic chemicals,* in order to hold the whole thing together. Because old, repurposed plastic is fragile, and its uses are severely limited. (Not to mention the concern about chemical contamination from the previous lives of all those plastics.)

Maybe you've seen advertising for fleece jackets or parkas or shoes that incorporate recycled plastic material. Is *that* downcycling? What's important to remember is that whether it is destined to be outdoor decking or a new pullover, the material integrity of the plastic is *compromised* in the process of being made into new things. Whether it's construction materials or garments that are made with "recycled" plastic, they will inevitably: 1. shed plastic microfibers, 2. degrade faster than those made with virgin plastic, and 3. emit any number of synthetic chemicals—including endocrine disrupting POPs and toxic heavy metals, as well as anything weird those chemicals have inadvertently combined and formed along the way. According to Dr. Jenny Davies of Cafeteria Culture, the older a plastic, the greater a tendency it has to "leak" this cocktail of toxic chemistry.[4]

I don't know about you, but suddenly I'm not anxious to wear a pullover made of recycled plastic bottles anymore, much less drink water from a container made from them.

Bear in mind also that "recycling" plastics doesn't have to mean turning them into picnic benches or a snazzy new T-shirt. It also could mean grinding them up into flakes and using it as concrete filler, or drainage gravel, or "infill" for synthetic turf sports fields.

So when you hear about "plastics recycling," we probably shouldn't picture shiny new food containers. Instead, maybe we should picture plastic being melted, ground up into chips and then reinserted into our environments *to degrade further*, shedding toxic, chemical-laden microplastics that flow into our ground and water supply.

Writer and sociologist Rebecca Altman recently wrote that "[plastic] recycling is a flailing, failing system."[5] Our instructor Judith Enck told our class flatly, "Plastic recycling has been a failure," and makes no bones about it: "Plastics, as a material, is not recyclable." In Jenny Davies's presentation one of the first slides is titled: "Plastic is not recyclable."

That's not even the worst part. The very worst part is that the plastics industry has *known this all along*. Yup. In the *Frontline* documentary *Plastic Wars*, they cite industry documents from as far back as the early seventies describing large-scale plastic recycling as unfeasible. Former vice president of the Society of the Plastics Industry (1978–2001) Lewis Freeman says, "There was never an enthusiastic belief that (plastics) recycling was ultimately going to work in a significant way."

This is deeply important, so let it sink in for a moment: despite touting recycling as the solution to the ever-growing plastic pollution problem for decades now, and spending millions upon millions of dollars to promote plastic's image, (Keep America Beautiful! Plastics Make it Possible! Give Your Garbage Another Life!) *they never believed it.*

2. "Single-Stream" recycling is a lie

I've mentioned previously the oft-cited statistic that, once discarded, plastic only gets recycled between 8 and 9 percent of the time, as well as the fact that while finalizing the manuscript for this book a new report showed that in 2021 the recycling rate of postconsumer plastics in the United States had actually fallen to between 5 and 6 percent.[6] Now that we know what happens in the recycling process, and how potentially toxic that product can be, maybe we should be glad most plastic doesn't get "recycled."

Still, this statistic is puzzling, isn't it? So many garbage service providers now accept plastics #1–7 in single-stream recycling, and although this doesn't account for all plastics, it certainly seems like it should account for a lot more than 6 or 8 percent. If they're collecting all these plastics under the name of "recycling" *where are they all going?*

The statistic makes a little more sense when you learn that, no matter what RIC numbers you're putting into your recycling container by the curb, *plastics numbers 1 and 2 are the only varieties that are* maybe *getting "recycled."* This is because these are the only plastics which are not incredibly difficult to "recycle" (which is to say, re-form once with the addition of lots more virgin plastic and chemicals) and therefore have some actual market/monetary value.

Yet even looking exclusively at the recycling for numbers 1 and 2, the statistics aren't terribly impressive. According to the EPA, in

2018 the rate of recycling for PETE (plastic #1) was 29.1 percent, and for HDPE (plastic #2) it was 29.3 percent.[7] Compare that to the same year's rate of recycling for, say, lead-acid batteries (99 percent) or corrugated boxes (96.5 percent). Plastics #1 and 2, the most usable and thus most valuable of all the possible plastics, are *still much more likely to end up in the landfill or incinerator than to get recycled.*

And the other five categories of plastic that you have so carefully washed and dried and separated and placed in blue bins by the curb every week to be carted away under the guise of "recycling"? Are not getting recycled at all.

I found this fact hard to wrap my mind around at first, so let me repeat: *No matter what your garbage service provider is telling you, numbers 3, 4, 6, and 7 are not getting recycled.* Number 5 is a veeeery dubious maybe. As I learned in my Beyond Plastics class, in the recycling industry it's a bit of an open secret that single-stream recycling collects far more than can legitimately ever be recycled. As you can imagine, if those other RIC number plastics aren't being recycled, they can end up being landfilled or incinerated, just as if you hadn't bothered to separate them in the first place, and that's the *best* case scenario. (We'll talk about the worst case scenario in a minute.)

Now, I know this sounds a little like the old joke about the restaurant where the food is terrible *and* the portions are too small. If "recycling" of plastic is really just toxic downcycling, why complain that more plastics aren't being recycled?

Well, firstly, because I don't like being lied to. Secondly, if people mistakenly think that all these different types of plastic are being recycled in a responsible way, they're much less likely to change their behavior, or buy products in a different container, or look for alternative solutions. I mean, say I am in a life-or-death grocery shopping situation where someone is pointing a gun at my head telling me I *have* to choose a plastic container, what would I do? I would make it a point to choose the package with a RIC number 1 or 2 over any other, because I know this at least will legitimately be collected and have a *chance* at being at least downcycled. It may not end up being a stylish backpack from Everlane, but a plastic can always dream, can't it?

I'm not saying not to recycle, or even not to recycle plastic. Definitely recycle, *especially* everything else: Glass! Cardboard! Metal! Paper! What I am saying is that, when it comes to plastic, be keenly aware of the game of deception that is being played on us as consumers. Remember how I said even if we aren't in a position to do much, we can change the way we think about plastic? Davies articulated this important shift in perspective during the course of her talk.

"Plastic is a hazardous substance," she said. "Plastic is *not your friend*."[8]

As much as possible, try to avoid plastic, but when you find yourself with plastic to dispose of, my advice is to put plastic RIC numbers 1 and 2 in your recycling bin, because at least they've got a chance. Anything higher than RIC #2 can only go one place so we might as well be honest with ourselves about it and put it in the actual trash.

And then we need to try to do better.

3. "Compostable" plastics are pretty much a total lie. (With one notable exception)

They're made from plants! And they cost about four times as much as petroleum-based plastics! They *must* be better, right?

As you'll recall, I had learned that most "compostable" plastic products are, in fact, not compostable, at least not in the back-yard compost sense, not recyclable (Polylactic Acid—PLA—is classified under "other" or plastic #7, which as we now know, when put in "recycling" bins, gets trashed), and do not degrade in a landfill.

Unfortunately, PLA—the "bioplastic" made from plants such as corn, sugarcane, or wheat—can be as problematic as plastic itself. Conventional, petroleum-based plastic is a synthetic, carbon chain polymer most often made up of carbon, hydrogen, and oxygen. PLA, it turns out, is a synthetic, carbon chain polymer made up of

. . . carbon, hydrogen, and oxygen. And here's an important detail: often PLA incorporates the addition of *petroleum-based binding ingredients*.

You can argue *most* of the resources used to create PLA (plants) are more renewable than regular plastics (fossil fuels). You could argue that at least *some* of the PLA will make its way to an industrial composting facility, where the temperatures will be high enough to actually break it down, but is this really good enough? Are we willing to pay quadruple for this quasi-solution?

My takeaway: PLA is largely a pipe dream intended to mollify those of us who have seen the video of the turtle with a straw in its nose, or otherwise been awakened on some level to the fact that too much plastic exists. We are supposed to accept "it's made from plants!" and not realize that bioplastics are *more* likely to end up sitting in a landfill forever, not less.

But let's say, for the sake of argument, that you live in an urban area that collects compostable material for the elusive "industrial composting" at the proper pressure and temperatures. At least *then* compostable ware is great, right?

Nope. Because it turns out that even many industrial composting facilities do not want this material for one simple reason: there is currently no easy way to distinguish between bioplastics and regular plastics, and this similarity leads to problems with contamination. One industry article called this the "Trojan Horse" effect.[9] Imagine: machines can be programmed to remove all the hard plastic-y stuff, but now, with the introduction of compost ware how do they know which to remove from the compost and which to leave?

Just when I was beginning to think all was lost in the compostable department, I listened to a webinar on bio-based plastics that are made from mushrooms and seaweed. (Hemp is also being used as a compostable option for fabric and packaging.) Sway, Ecovative, and Loliware: These were companies talking about *home* composting, and about what happens when their product ends up where it shouldn't: like in the ocean. And yes, you could take a bite out of their packaging and eat it, but honestly it wouldn't be very tasty.

Sway is working to replace the 180 billion plastic film bags used per year in the fashion industry with thin film bags made from seaweed that grows abundantly in the ocean and degrades within four to six weeks in a home compost. Ecovative makes Styrofoam-like packaging material from fungus that you can literally break up and put in your garden as a soil amendment straight out of the box. Loliware makes their "Blue Carbon Straw" from seaweed, and their motto is "Designed to Disappear." All three described their products as extremely stable, not subject to degrading until exposed to the microbes in compost, and comparable in cost to PLA products. Their processes were all designed to be scalable and to work on existing infrastructure.

Am I skeptical? After being on the zero waste roller coaster this long, I'd be foolish not to be. But I really liked what I was hearing, and unlike PLA and other so-called "bioplastics," it didn't feel like another false solution. It felt like maybe, at last, we might be on to something that could truly be one solution to the big fat mess we've made. Maybe.

PLA, which is the current go-to for non-petroleum-based plastic, currently occupies 1 percent of the overall market,[10] but it is definitely poised to grow. Mainly this is because of a misperception: people are trying to do the right thing, yet only being fed half-truths. It will be key for the makers of regenerative alternatives to plastic, like mushrooms and seaweed, to use terms that quickly, easily differentiate themselves from the PLA market. (Loliware uses the term *hypercompostable*, which I love.)

Towards the end of the hour-long presentation, Julia Marsh, the cofounder and CEO of Sway, said this: "Compostability is an inevitability."

You hear that, plastic? They're coming for you.

BIODEGRADABLE VS. DEGRADABLE VS. COMPOSTABLE

Raise your hand if you are getting tired of the word salad involved in describing the environmental credentials of packaging for everything from organic strawberries to foot powder.

What's important to understand is that some of these words actually, legally, mean something, while others mean nothing at all. In particular the terms for biodegradable, degradable, and compostable are often confused for one another, when in fact they have very distinct meanings.

Here's a quick primer:

Biodegradable Microorganisms recognize biodegradable material as food, and when they "eat" it they break it down into water, carbon dioxide, and natural materials like dirt. The EPA says biodegradable items should decompose within "a reasonably short period of time," but definitely less than a year.

Degradable when used to describe plastic simply means that the item can be broken down into tiny fragments, i.e. microplastics. Oh, yay. Some products are labeled "oxo degradable" (degrades in the presence of oxygen) or "photodegradable" (degrades in the presence of sunlight), but they all amount to the same thing: more microplastics. So even though it is touted as a positive attribute, when it comes to plastic, being merely *degradable* is actually a bad thing.

Compostable means that this item will decompose into elements found in nature *within a timely manner.* So what constitutes a timely manner, exactly? According to the Federal Trade Commission, "in approximately the same time as the materials with which it is composted." Sooooo helpful. By itself this term is too vague to mean much, which is why you need to know what conditions are necessary for this decomposition to take place: industrial or home compost?

INDUSTRIALLY COMPOSTABLE VS. HOME COMPOSTABLE

Industrially compostable (also known as commercially compostable) items are those that will likely not break down in your home compost, but *will* break down under specifically controlled temperatures and pressures designed to create compost at a large scale. This can take between a few weeks and a few months. If a plastic-resembling item is labeled "compostable," it is probably *industrially compostable* only.

Home compostable items are those that will break down in a few months under ordinary home compost pile or bin conditions, which are much more variable.

To Sum Up
Best!	Home compostable
Good	Biodegradable
Meh	Industrially compostable*
Mostly Terrible	Degradable

Fluff words that, by themselves, mean nothing:
Green
Bio†
Natural
Eco
Clean
Eco-friendly
Environmentally friendly
Environmentally safe
Environmentally preferable
Sustainable

---

* If an item is just labeled "compostable," assume they mean industrially.

† In the European Union, use of the term *bio* indicates produce was grown using organic farming guidelines. In America it means nothing.

4. "Extreme Recycling" Programs are pretty much a total lie too

When my super-eco-friendly shampoo bar arrived its packaging was marked, "82% compostable," with the helpful direction to *Contact your local municipality for instructions.*

Oh, *right.* I live in a town that has persistent problems with things like runaway livestock and whether or not the main road is about to fall into the local slate quarry. I'm sure our town officials would be just delighted to discuss my concerns with industrially compostable shampoo bar packaging.

Mind you, I love and admire the shampoo bar people, and they are far from the only folks using "check with your local whatever" strategy. It's essentially a conceptual get-out-of-jail-free card. Is this recyclable? *Gosh—maybe!* Most people will accept that as an absolution of the company. And perhaps one out of a hundred folks will actually take it upon themselves to truly find out more.

This is a self-selecting group. This is the group who actually collect their plastic bags to bring to the supermarket plastic film recycling bin or who really pays attention to the How2Recycle label that is now on thousands of products. They find out more about TerraCycle, and their programs for recycling difficult-to-recycle materials, or maybe they wash and collect their aseptic and gable-top cartons for mailing in to one of the four locations listed on the Carton Council website.[11]

Their intentions are good. In making such changes, these people will feel they've done something to help. In the absence of being able to throw things away, I had come to rely heavily on such extreme recycling, both in practical "what the heck do I do with this" terms, as well as conceptually: "I'm not alone! Someone out there will help me with this!"

Unfortunately, as we rounded the corner of our No Garbage year into fall time and my Beyond Plastics class unfolded, I was learning that all of the programs cited above have come under varying degrees of suspicion for misrepresenting what they do and for taking advantage of people's genuine desire to do the right thing for our environment—aka: "greenwashing."

How2Recycle, it turns out, is an entity created by the packaging industry that "certifies" recyclability for a fee, which is kind of like a mouse certifying himself to guard the cheese board. You've probably encountered their very official-looking symbol that appears on more than 2,600 brands, and maybe you didn't find it confusing. Unfortunately, a lot of people do. Just like the RIC codes, when people encounter symbols on their products that make *any* mention of recycling, they tend to assume it means "YES! PLEASE RECYCLE ME!" Even among those one-out-of-a-hundred folks who are paying actual attention, it can seem like each and every product package featuring How2Recycle labels requires a magnifying glass and a forensic investigation to decode.

"Ah, *yes*, Watson." (Draws heavily on pipe, looking contemplative.) "You see it says right here that the plastic canister is *traditionally* recyclable, whereas the plastic overwrap—which, as any cretin knows must be *removed* (hand me that shrub trimmer, would you, good fellow?)—cannot. HOWEVER, in fact, it may be recycled in the store-drop off bin for *plastic film* recycling. Which leaves us only with the plastic pump. In this matter the label is crystal clear. It is helpfully recommending that we 'check locally,' which of course means bugger-all."

How2Recycle purports to make recycling product packaging simpler and easier, make consumers feel "empowered" and to help companies to "increase the recyclability of their packaging." Yet a review of the statistics they post on their own website[12] shows that roughly half of their labeling is on plastic packaging and out of all that plastic packaging labeling, *82.2 percent is either not recyclable at all or not "optimally recyclable," (i.e., "check locally").*

What this means is that the biggest part of How2Recycle's business is plastic products that are not recyclable. Ironic, right?

But it makes sense, if you look at it from the industry point of view. In fact, it's a bargain! Companies pay an annual fee to use the How2Recycle labels on their products. According to their website, a company with revenue exceeding $1 billion can join for a measly six thousand dollars. Compare this to what it might actually cost to reengineer their product's packaging to make it more environmentally friendly, and you can see that it makes economic sense not to change. Rather, just throw a few thousand at it and your products too can enjoy the shiny veneer of recyclability and caring.

One of the recycling methods you often see promoted on How2Recycle labels is "store drop off," which refers to the plastic film recycling, which you may recall I spend some time tracking back to Trex and the outdoor decking they manufacture.

A few months after I made these phone calls, Greenpeace filed a lawsuit against Walmart over this very issue, arguing that Walmart is knowingly promoting a recycling system that is deceptive and not available to most consumers. As of this writing that lawsuit is ongoing.

As I mentioned previously, much as I want to believe in a program like Trex's plastic film recycling, more often than not when I take my plastic bags to the supermarket bin someone has mistaken the bin for a garbage can and dumped trash in it. Does that then mean the whole thing gets trashed? It's very likely. I am having a very hard time imagining the supermarket employees, underpaid and overworked as they are, carefully removing takeout containers and soda bottles from the plastic film bin so they can make sure that my Ziploc® bags and Bubble Wrap gets to Trex to be made into a park bench.

Currently, the United States only has the capacity to process less than 5 percent of the plastic films for recycling, and most of what does get recycled apparently comes from "back-of-store sources" like pallet wraps because they are cleaner (i.e., no take-out containers and soda bottles).[13] Jan Dell, the founder of the Last Beach Cleanup, explains that Trex "has capacity for less than 3% of our plastic film . . . so this whole store drop-off program, in my opinion, is just hollow."

Which brings us back to TerraCycle. Like it or not, one of the biggest lessons of our Year of No Garbage was turning out to be: if all else fails, send it to TerraCycle. I had a special bin I was accumulating for the Zero Waste "Everything" box, which you may recall is the most expensive box type by far, because you can put anything short of reactor-grade plutonium in it. For that box I had been saving fun things like a pair of fleece slippers with giant holes in the soles, used-up makeup containers, and old ballpoint pens.

But as you can imagine, my unease with the whole TerraCycle system persisted, which was not helped by the fact that I continued to receive a new email from them every damn day encouraging me to buy more crap because I could eventually *send it all to them*! I wasn't alone in my discomfort. Although some in my Beyond Plastics class used the free or paid programs too, everyone was wondering what I was wondering: was it a mirage? Was it just too good to be true? Keep in mind this group was TerraCycle's core audience: the people who looked forward to watching a PowerPoint presentation on the evils of plastic. Who read articles about biopolymers for fun and already knew what "anthropogenic" meant. If *these* people doubted the legitimacy of the enterprise, then TerraCycle had a serious credibility problem.

Our teacher Judith's comment was that, it really didn't matter, because TerraCycle's model was not "scalable," which was probably true, but deeply unsatisfying.

And finally there was the Carton Council, who you'll recall told me I could mail in all my clean, rinsed cartons. Well again, this is another *industry organization*. I don't know about you, but whenever one puts the words "voluntary" next to "large corporation," I get nervous. In a YouTube video[14] on their website, the Carton Council shows chopped-up cartons being made into paper products and construction materials such as drywall. As with TerraCycle's video, it was hard to watch these generic industrial videos and know that this was, in fact, happening.

Or was I just being paranoid?

Even if we accept that, indeed, we are watching the reincarnation of all the cartons eco-conscious consumers have carefully washed, collected, and paid to mail to collection centers in Colorado or Nebraska or Michigan, you then have to ask the next logical question: do mail-in programs make ecological sense? All the resources used to clean, pack up, and mail our trash around the country of course result in lots of water use, additional carbon emissions, and packaging waste. Dell's organization, The Last Beach Cleanup, did the math and found that if 60 percent of plastic cups created were mailed in for recycling it could create the equivalent CO2 emissions of over 25,000 additional cars on the road.[15]

I want to believe. I really, *really* do. I want it all to make sense. I want to believe Walmart when they essentially say (through their attorneys) "*Of course* we're recycling! We don't need to provide any pesky documentation! Just trust us!" I want to believe because, despite all evidence to the contrary, it would mean that as individual consumers we really do have some measure of control. The truth is much more depressing. The closer you look at any of these programs the more you have to admit: a whole lot of it just doesn't add up.

But here's a different question: is it *intended* to work?

Stay with me, because I have a theory about this.

Plastic Free July is an annual worldwide initiative, founded and based in Australia, that invites people to reduce their plastic consumption for just one month every year. They estimate that in 2020, 326 million people participated in Plastic Free July,[16] just over 4 percent of the planet, which is a truly phenomenal achievement.

But this same survey also found that eight out of ten people are concerned about the environmental impact of plastics, which is even more astounding. Eight out of ten![17] What these two statistics together suggest is a huge gap between the people who say they care and the people who actually change their behavior as a result.

Although it is hard to quantify exactly, I think it's safe to say that for every person participating in an environmental initiative, any environmental initiative—from mailing your recycling around the world to bringing your own cup to the coffee shop—there are many times more people who are aware of the plastic problem and believe it is important, but for whatever reason have not changed their behavior as a result of that belief. The behavioral economist Colin Aston-Graham calls this the "attitude-behavior disconnect."[18]

My theory is that not only do most existing Extreme Recycling initiatives not work, they are not intended to actually work. Rather they are intended to make consumers think that something is being done, to mollify not only the 4 percent of consumers who are actually changing their behavior, but also the other 80 percent, who know there is a problem.

This playbook has a long history. Remember the Keep America Beautiful campaign and the commercials featuring a misty Iron Eyes Cody? Not only was the actor not a Native American (he was Italian American) but Keep America Beautiful the nonprofit organization was founded in 1953 by a combination of corporations, government agencies, and nonprofits. Corporations, you say? Why yes, several can and glass bottle producers, as a matter of fact, who had been starting to get some heat about what happened to their packaging at end of life. A 2005 documentary film and book[19] accused this group of perpetrating one of the first greenwashing efforts, because its narrow focus on litter and personal responsibility diverts attention away from the idea that product packaging should be made in more sustainable ways.

Gosh, everything's fine kids, if we just don't litter! Pay no attention to that nasty effort to legislate refillable glass bottles and expensive aluminum can redemption. Gee whiz!

What's happening today with many Extreme Recycling initiatives reminds me an awful lot of this same strategy. Give people the sense that the problem is being solved, by someone! Somewhere! And they'll believe you because most people have short attention spans and busy schedules. Remember the article that told me when it came to toothpaste tubes that "TerraCycle's got you covered"? I guarantee you that the author of that article looked into TerraCycle for about 3.5 seconds before moving onto the next zero waste "tip." The majority of the readers of that article didn't immediately go create TerraCycle accounts. What they did do instead, I imagine, was think, "Oh, good! Someone's *doing* something about that! Good for them."

But what if we all woke up one day and realized that no one was really doing anything about any of it? That we are being played, manipulated by enormous forces who are trashing our planet and our bodies in the name of economic gain? What if even the supposed good guys are wolves in sheep's clothing?

Then what?

5. Forget one giant ocean garbage patch: there are five

I hereby suggest that the Great Pacific Garbage Patch should henceforth be called the Great Pacific *Plastic* Patch, because what we're talking about floating around persistently in the ocean is not wood, paper, or metal—it's plastic. Also, it isn't an island of trash as so many people imagine, but more like a giant plastic soup, swirling around in the water both above and below the surface: big plastic, little plastic, microplastic, nanoplastic.

Although the Great Pacific Garbage Patch was the first one to be discovered, accidentally, back in 1997 by sailor and researcher Charles Moore, it makes perfect sense to realize that of course, there can't only be one. After all, the phenomenon of the *Plastic* Garbage Patch (as I'm stubbornly going to call it from now on) is created by the spiraling currents of major ocean gyres, of which the world has five: the North Atlantic Gyre, the South Atlantic Gyre, the North Pacific Gyre, the South Pacific Gyre, and the Indian Ocean Gyre. All of them now have Plastic Garbage Patches.

Pulitzer Prize–winning author Edward Humes explains in his book *Garbology*, "These are vast, constantly shifting areas of deep water that together encompass about 40 percent of the global ocean surface—which means the gyres cover more of the earth than all the dry land put together. . . . Researchers have found all five of the major gyres have higher concentrations of plastic than other parts of the ocean."[20]

So what portion of those gyres are considered "garbage patches"? Well, if a garbage patch is defined as "a collection of debris, mostly consisting of plastic, which moves about in the sea,"[21] then it is certainly conceivable that all of the five gyres may be considered Plastic Garbage Patches. Which would mean that, together, Plastic Garbage Patches take up a greater expanse than all the land on earth. While you consider that mind-boggling idea, let me gently remind you that

that's just the *surface* area. That's not even counting the millions of cubic miles of plastic-filled waters below the surface. Depending on who you ask, the Great Pacific Plastic Garbage Patch, located midway between Hawaii and California, covers a surface area anywhere between twice the size of Texas and the entire continent of North America. According to Humes it covers 20 million square miles, making it the largest ecosystem on earth.[22]

Even in the Mariana Trench, the deepest, most remote ocean location on earth? They've found plastics. A plastic bag found at 36,000 feet below sea level is officially the deepest found plastic item.[23] (To give an idea of how far down that is, if you turned Mount Everest upside down in the ocean it *still* wouldn't reach where that plastic bag was.)

This is gross and unappealing, but can feel very far away, especially if you are like me and live in a state that has no ocean view. One way this hits home more personally, is remembering that this troubling ocean landscape we are increasingly creating is related directly to our food chain.

I didn't know the term *biomagnification*, but I was familiar with the principle that toxicity works its way up the food chain. When tiny fish eat microplastics and then bigger fish come along and eat *them*, and so on, until finally a human comes along and gets a concentrated package of what is both fish and plastic. And remember what we said in the conversation about recycling plastics for food packaging? Not only are the plastics themselves created in combination with tens of thousands of chemicals that determine their different particular properties, plastics are also dangerous because they absorb chemicals from other contexts. Floating around in the ocean, plastic acts as a toxin sponge for whatever might be floating by. The person who comes along to eat that fish isn't just getting some free plastic in the deal, not only getting whatever chemicals went into making that plastic, but they're also getting whatever else has hitchhiked along *with* the plastic. Seeing fish in the supermarket case advertised as "wild-caught" doesn't sound quite so appealing once you know this.

On top of serving contaminated fish for dinner, we are messing with the very mechanisms that keep life on this planet humming along. Humes points out that "half the oxygen we breathe emanates from microscopic phytoplankton sloshing around the surface of the ocean."[24] A study done by Moore found water off the coast of California to have more plastic than plankton.[25]

Essential though they are, plankton are hard to empathize with. For a lot of people watching a video of the turtle having a plastic straw extracted from its nose is far more impactful. Pictures of dead albatrosses with stomachs full of colorful plastic skimmed from the ocean's surface are also pretty horrifying, as is the knowledge that they are carrying all that plastic back to the nest to feed to their babies, who are dying too. Whales are washing up on shore all over the world dying from the fact that they're consumed the weight of a full-grown person in plastic.[26]

Even if not for the obvious suffering our plastics are inflicting on our fellow creatures, doesn't this still seem deeply wrong? The ocean is more than a resource, it's a breathtakingly beautiful and powerful natural wonder. What's next? Dumping our trash plastics into the Grand Canyon, or on the Moon?

Plastic pollution is now present in *every* marine habitat. Both inadvertently and on purpose, we are dumping 8.8 million metric tons of plastic waste in the ocean each year. That's a full garbage truck of plastic waste every minute.[27]

Imagine the moment when we have more plastic in our waters than fish. It's on the horizon: the documentary *The Story of Plastic* (2019) features an interview with a fisherman in the Philippines who reports his catch is usually 60 percent fish and 40 percent plastic. It has been projected that by 2050 the ocean will contain one pound of plastic for every three pounds of fish.[28]

Or imagine the day when there are no more whales because they've swallowed all our old bouncy houses and flip-flops, beach umbrellas and trampolines. In 2016 scientists found "marine debris" (read: garbage, mostly plastic) in the bellies of nine out of twenty-two beached whales.[29]

Once we thought the oceans were so vast that nothing humanity did could truly affect them. Plastic has changed all that.

6. Plastic drives climate change

Despite all the corporate sustainability pledges that are so in fashion now, plastic production is nevertheless expected to triple in the next twenty-five years. Imagine three times as much disposable plastic as we have now—still not getting recycled. And if this happens, emissions from the plastic life cycle are projected to equal fifty times the emissions of all the coal power plants in the United States.

But why? Don't we have enough plastic currently being produced? In fact, the reason plastics are projected to triple by 2050 isn't because we *need* more plastic. It's because the fossil fuel industry sees the writing on the wall: electric cars, renewable energy sources. As the demand for fossil fuel falls, what will these enormous petrochemical companies focus on in order to make up the shortfall?

Plastic.

This is why so many products which used to come in glass, cardboard, and paper now come in plastic. You've noticed it right? Dog food, flour, sugar, pasta sauce, birdseed, cornstarch, spices, egg cartons. Even the organic chicken feed at our local Tractor Supply comes in a plastic bag (although if I shop at the local general store I can still buy it in paper.) Does it seem ironic to anyone else that an organic product comes swaddled in plastic? I've stopped even looking at the organic produce section of my supermarket because the entire thing is like a riotous plastic bacchanal. My local health food store presents another example of this weird disconnect: organic, recycled, dye-free, hormone-free products are, almost without exception, offered for sale there wrapped in all manner and variety of hermetically sealed plastic.

You could blame it on concerns for safety or durability, but I have a pretty clear memory of the everyone being just fine when their cornstarch came wrapped in nothing but a paper bag.*

---

* Worried about someone tampering with your food? Occasionally you can still find jars with a *paper tab* that must be ripped to expose the contents.

It's all part of a concerted effort on the part of big petroleum to lobby on behalf of their product. Plastic is now boldly going where it never has gone before, and for no other reason than the desperation of fossil fuel industry looking for what Judith Enck terms "Big Petroleum's Plan B."

Speaking of irony, there's more. This ramp-up of plastic production will work directly against the climate emissions gains made by the switch to electric cars and alternative, sustainable energy sources.

We learned in Enck's Beyond Plastics class that when plastics are made from a combination of chemicals and fossil fuels, they produce greenhouse gas emissions every step along the way. From fracking to refining and producing, to transport, use, and disposal, greenhouse gases and toxic emissions are present at every stage of the plastics life cycle.

We don't have to wait until 2050 to see the impact of this. According to a report put out by the nonprofit think tank Beyond Plastics in 2021, the amount of "carbon dioxide-equivalent gas (CO_2e)" emitted per year by the plastics industry in the United States is 232 million tons, roughly equivalent to the emissions of 116 coal-fired power plants. "To provide context," the report explains, "If plastic were a country, it would be the world's fifth largest greenhouse gas emitter, beating out all but China, the United States, India and Russia."[30]

That is *now*. And by their own reports the plastics industry plans to triple production, and thereby triple those numbers.

This is why the headlines generated by this report have concluded: "Plastics Are the New Coal."

7. Plastic is racist

Maybe you've heard of "Cancer Alley." This is the eighty-five-mile stretch of land in Louisiana between New Orleans and Baton Rouge that is characterized by both "a high percentage of black residents, [and] low socioeconomic indicators."[31] Not coincidentally it is also home to nearly 150 oil refineries, plastics plants, and chemical facilities that have spilled over 140 million pounds of chemicals into the surrounding environment between 1997 and 2012 alone.[32]

A color-coded map that illustrates risk of cancer from air toxins throughout the entire United States was issued in 2014 by the EPA's National Air Toxics Assessment.[33] On this map, where I live, Vermont, is a lovely butter yellow, which puts it in the lowest cancer-from-air-toxins risk category of between 6 and 25 cases per million people. Louisiana, by contrast, is mostly bright green, indicating a risk of between 25 and 50 cases per million. However, spreading like a tiny bruise on the foot of the state's boot shape is a very small but defined midnight blue.

This is Cancer Alley, where the risk of cancer from air toxins is higher than 100 in a million. Which is to say that if you moved from Vermont to Cancer Alley you'd be quadrupling your risk of cancers like leukemia or non-Hodgkin's lymphoma from air toxins such as formaldehyde, benzene, or 1,3-butadiene.

According to Louisiana journalist Tammy C. Barney, "You only have to smell 'Cancer Alley' to know how toxic it is."[34]

Cancer Alley is notable enough to be the subject of a 2021 UN report condemning the situation, as well as decrying plans approved in recent years to build a *new* complex in the area that would be one of the largest plastics facilities in the world. It's an extreme and horrific example of environmental racism via plastic, but it's definitely not the only one.

In her book *A Terrible Thing to Waste: Environmental Racism and Its Assault on the American Mind*, author Harriet A. Washington explains that "African Americans and other people of color are 79 percent more likely than white US residents to live in neighborhoods" of toxic environmental chemicals emitted from sources such as "petrochemical plants, refineries, garbage dumps, [and] incinerators."[35] These are the poisonous places where we source, make, and dispose of our plastics.

All the processes involved with plastic—from fracking to incineration—are not *just* toxic, they also disproportionately end up in low-income communities and communities of color.

That's here in the United States. But plastic discriminates around the world.

Remember all those "recyclable" plastics that are being collected but definitely *not* recycled? It wasn't so long ago that plastics intended for recycling would be shipped off to places like China that handled the dirty work of sorting, melting, and chipping. Then, as now, the only plastics actually worth the effort were RIC numbers 1 and 2. It's just that we didn't *see* the ugly process of sorting, discarding, dumping, and burning that took place. Author Adam Minter gives a haunting description of the global plastics recycling center in Wen'an, China, and the scrap plastics trade in his 2013 book *Junkyard Planet*. At the time this "shadowy trade" often involved burning unusable plastics in the streets and dumping unusable plastics and plastic cleaning fluids into a giant pit on the outskirts of town. The people of the city were suffering strange new ailments involving strokes, paralysis, and lung scarring. "Wen'an is the most polluted place I've ever visited," Minter writes.[36]

At the same time, in the United States pressure was mounting from the packaging industry for garbage service providers to collect more plastics, in order to present a facade of sustainability. "Look! Everything is fine! You can recycle *all* the plastics #1 through 7!" In no universe could one ever recycle all those different kinds of plastic, but who would suspect that, when it was all being faithfully collected in those big blue bins that read: RECYCLING! Instead of the truth which instead would read: DESTINED TO BE SHIPPED TO ANOTHER COUNTRY AND BURNED IN THE STREET! CHILDREN WILL PLAY IN ITS TOXIC ASH AND BREATHE ITS POISONOUS CANCER-CAUSING FUMES! HAVE A NICE DAY!

Eventually, China's situation became untenable. With the National Sword Policy they stopped accepting our "recyclables" in 2018.

And yet the collection of plastics, often all the RIC numbers 1 through 7, continued. Which raises the question: if all this stuff wasn't going to China anymore, and no one can even pretend to recycle most of it, where is it going? What I found out from Judith's class is that—in the very *best* case scenario—this plastic "recycling" is thrown in with garbage and ends up in the landfill or the incinerator.

Worst case? Our plastic is being dumped on impoverished countries around the world, in the name of "recycling."

The documentary *The Story of Plastic* shows devastating footage of countries around the world whose residents and officials are often bribed to allow illegal dumping of plastics. Thailand, Malaysia, Vietnam . . . often these countries have little or no infrastructure to deal with this problem and the piles of other country's plastics are dumped unceremoniously into their landscape, accumulating in their streets, fields, and waterways.

When you see the footage you will realize that it is no exaggeration to say that there are residents of these countries who live, work, and play in piles of our trash, our plastics, which we naively believe have gone off on a magical journey to be turned into some new product.

Then, when the elements wash our nondegradable plastic garbage into waterways and ultimately into the ocean, we blame them, these developing countries, for being dirty and not managing *their waste* properly. A 2021 study found that Asia accounts for 80 percent of global "plastic inputs" to the ocean, which often gets misconstrued to mean that the United States is not the one causing the ocean plastics problem. But in fact, an awful lot of that plastic originated in the United States.[37]

Wow. Just—wow.

8. Plastics do not break down—or go away—ever

Think about a potato chip bag you used in third grade. The foam insert from some shoes you bought ten years ago. Cellophane heat seals from every jar of peanut butter, salsa, or cough medicine you've ever opened. I could easily fill a whole separate book with every plastic item I've personally used and discarded over my lifetime, and it's like your own personal horror movie to realize that, unless it made its way to an incinerator, all of it is still out there, in the world. Somewhere.

That's because plastic does not degrade. According to a report from the National Academy of Sciences: "the vast majority of plastics are carbon-carbon backbone polymers and have *strong resistance to biodegradation*," (emphasis mine).[38]

As the Australian anti-plastic activist and founder of Plastic Free July, Rebecca Prince-Ruiz, puts it: "Unlike organic material such as paper, food scraps or plant matter, plastic doesn't break *down*. In the environment, when it's exposed to sunlight and the elements, it instead breaks *up* into smaller and smaller pieces."[39] Plastics don't biodegrade because they aren't recognized by microorganisms as food. So instead of disappearing biologically, by changing into something else, plastics disappear only to the human eye, becoming microplastics and eventually microscopic nanoplastics, even as they remain resolutely themselves.

Asking how long it takes a plastic bag to "break down"—a hundred years, three hundred years, a thousand years, never—is the wrong question. Instead, what we should ask is how long it will take that plastic to break down into microscopic granules. And those stubborn carbon-carbon polymers are still holding on for dear life, no matter where they travel.

And as it turns out, they're traveling *everywhere*.

9. Microscopic plastics are in our water, air, and food. Also our bloodstream, poop, and the placenta of newborn babies

Just as our No Garbage Year was beginning, and before the pandemic exploded onto the world's consciousness, for a brief moment in February of 2020 the public was transfixed by a completely different health threat: at a press conference, Senator Tom Udall (D-NM) held up a small, wallet-size rectangle.

"This credit card here," he said, "this is how much plastic you are consuming every week."[40] The credit card represented the five grams of plastic on average we are all consuming in things like bottled water, beer, table salt, and shellfish,[41] as well as fruit, vegetables,[42] and meat.

Microplastics have been found in 90 percent of table salt,[43] 90 percent of bottled water,[44] and 83 percent of tap water.[45] It's not only in our food and water, however. As Dr. Jenny Davies points out that in the course of her lecture, we all breathe in about a million nanoparticles of plastic per hour.[46]

It shouldn't have been that surprising. In 2018 an Austrian study studied poop samples of eight people from a variety of locations in Europe and Asia and found microplastics in *all* of them.[47] A more recent study found that baby poop contains even higher concentrations of microplastics than that of adults.[48]

I found this new information astonishing. World-altering. Let me just stop for a moment and point out that I didn't let my kids get sealants in their molars because I was afraid of the microscopic amounts of plastic they'd inevitably ingest. According to the American Dental Association, dental sealants are made of a plastic resin composite that does contain BPA, but you get more exposure to this chemical by touching a grocery store receipt.[49] It was like I was trying to avoid a drop of rain while swimming in the ocean.

Microplastics are generally defined as any plastic particle measuring smaller than five millimeters, so think somewhere between a grain of rice and a grain of salt. When they get smaller than that, so small that they are no longer perceptible to the human eye, many people redefine them as nanoplastics, although scientific researchers tend to use the term micronanoplastics (MNPs) to include both visible and nonvisible plastics under 5mm. After hearing a Zoom presentation from Lyda Harris, PhD, Microplastic Postdoctoral Fellow of the Seattle Aquarium, I learned that microplastics come in all kinds of quantifiable shapes and textures: fibers, films, fragments, and spheres, also known as "nurdles." They can be so small as to be able to be carried by the wind, becoming "atmospheric plastics," and are being found even in remote and supposedly pristine places like the French Pyrenees,[50] the peak of Mount Everest, and the Arctic Circle.

Researchers recently found "plastic particles" in the blood of 77 percent of study participants.[51] However, the story I nominate for most likely to completely freak you out? The one that found microplastics in four out of six human placentas.[52] Oh, and breast milk. Did I mention they found microplastics in breast milk?[53]

In fact, in every food, in every part of the human body, when researchers have gone looking for micronanoplastics? They have found them.

No one knows exactly what the effect of these tiny plastics accumulating in all our bodies really is. I mean, besides our bloodstream and our poop and our breast milk, where is this plastic going? Does it accumulate in certain organs?

According to Dr. Davies, the largest nanoplastics are one-eighth the size of our red blood cells, which means that they can penetrate our cells, causing inflammatory response, cell malfunction, and death.[54]

Here's a question: do micronanoplastics pass the blood-brain barrier? Well, studies show they do in mice.[55]

I may never get a gold star in biology, but I know enough to know that these facts about plastic particles invading our organs, our bloodstream, our cells, and quite possibly even our brains are all extremely troubling for the future of human health, and that's *before* you have factored in the toxic chemicals, the poisons, that are being carried along with them.

Which brings us to the final lie and accompanying uncomfortable truth:

10. There aren't seven kinds of plastic as recycling symbols indicate; there are tens of thousands, all largely untested for effects on human health

Scientists have found microplastics every single place they have looked for them. This is something we know, and this should scare us.

But maybe even more than this, we should be scared of the things we *don't* know, because what we don't know is a lot. As we've mentioned, in the United States chemicals are presumed safe until proven harmful. According to environmental author Harriet Washington, there are approximately six hundred thousand industrial chemicals in use in the United States today that have never been tested for their effects on humans.[56] According to Enck, there are 1,606 chemicals associated with fracking, and 906 chemicals used in the manufacture of plastic packaging alone, including PFOA and PFOS, which are known carcinogens; BPA, which is an established endocrine disruptor; and PBDEs (flame retardants), which are both.

In 2001 Bill Moyers introduced the concept of body burden—the man-made chemicals we hold in our bodies—to his horrified PBS audience in his documentary *Trade Secrets*. Moyers agreed to have his blood tested for man-made, synthetic chemicals, chemicals that did not exist a hundred years ago. Many of these come from the creation of different plastics. Would they find any?

They found eighty-four.

And we've come a long way since 2001. How many would appear in his blood today? We are all walking chemical repositories now. In fact, it occurs to me that *we* are the real recycling bins. All the materials, *everything* we have put into the environment, we are unwittingly taking into our bodies as well. And just like in single-stream recycling, everything does not go where it is supposed to. Ninety-two percent of urine samples show BPA. According to annual studies conducted by the CDC, we *all* have PFAs and PFOSs in our blood.* These are all well known and heavily used plastic additives.

The scariest movie I ever saw as a kid wasn't a horror movie. It was a comedy. In *The Incredible Shrinking Woman*, Lily Tomlin stars as a woman whose body starts to mysteriously shrink because of the random cocktail of chemicals her ordinary modern life has exposed her to. At one point towards the end of the film she becomes so small that she is about to disappear entirely, and she gives a speech from somewhere in the drain of the kitchen sink in which she says goodbye to her family. I was abjectly terrified by this brand-new idea: the idea that we modern humans were playing with chemistry and don't fully know what we are doing, or understand the potential ramifications.

---

* According to annual reports from the National Health and Nutrition Examination Survey (NHANES). They began testing blood for PFAs and PFOSs in 1999.

This film may as well have been written about the plastics industry. Tens of thousands of chemicals, never tested for effects on human health? Which are now being unconsciously ingested by, it seems, every life-form on the planet? We are playing with fireworks in a cardboard house, wearing clothes made of tissue paper. What could possibly go wrong?

These days many scientists are frantically engaged in the process of trying to find out what we've done to human health by allowing our entire society to live submerged in a chemical soup every day, breathing, eating, drinking, and absorbing chemicals from plastics. It's difficult work, in part because in this field of research, there is no such thing as a control: there are no humans who have not been exposed to these chemicals, so there's nothing to compare our exposed modern-day selves to. Except the past.

So let's look at the past. Here are some of the things scientists suspect are due to exposure to classes of endocrine-disrupting chemicals like phthalates (chemical additives that make plastics soft), bisphenols (chemical additives that make plastics hard), and perchlorate (a chemical used to make plastic have less static):

- In the United States in 1975, breast cancer affected one in eleven women; nearly fifty years later it affects one in eight.[57]
- The age of first menses has been steadily dropping in young girls for decades. One study of Danish girls showed average age for first periods dropping from age 11 to 9.9 over the course of fifteen years.[58]
- Other signs of puberty in girls have been showing up even earlier. Although a landmark study from 1960 found that puberty started on average for girls at age eleven, in 1997 a study published in *Pediatrics* found the average age for puberty had fallen to 9.96 for white girls and 8.87 among Black girls.[59]
- The average sperm count for a Western man in 1960 was 99 million per millimeter; in 2013 it was 47 million per

> millimeter. This represents a 50 percent drop in semen quality in about fifty years.[60]
> - The miscarriage rate has risen by 1 percent per year over the last twenty years.[61]

In experiments scientists have discovered that they can prevent tadpoles from ever turning into frogs, simply by adding a high dose of perchlorate to their water.[62] This is a chemical that is commonly used in plastic food packaging for things like cereal, flour, and spices.

Just in case you don't find that unsettling enough, even the chemicals that are harmless in small doses on their own, when combined with other chemicals in "safe" doses have been shown to tamper with sexual development, for example producing feminine physical characteristics in male rats. In some cases even the scientists have trouble telling them apart.[63]

In the lecture I watched by Dr. Davies, she pulled no punches when it came to the extent of the problem of plastic and its related toxic chemistry. "We are faced with a near permanent contamination of our water, our air and our soil," she explained.[64] As prominent biologist and endocrinologist Barbara Demeneix puts it in the documentary *We the Guinea Pigs*, "We are undergoing the most vast experiment on the human population because we *do not know* the consequences."

One of the most alarming facts I learned during our Year of No Sugar is that today's generation of children is the first in modern history predicted to have shorter life spans than their parents.

Coincidence?

It feels like one of those Agatha Christie novels where it turns out that *all* the characters have been lying and *everyone* is the murderer, doesn't it? The more I learned, the more naive I felt. While I had been obsessing about the Right Answers to proper sticker removal and whether or not the little cellophane windows on pasta boxes interfered with paperboard recycling, companies and governments were turning a blind eye to mountains' and oceans' worth of permanent, toxic garbage being dumped around the world—often quite inten-tionally—on the very people who had no recourse to deal with it and didn't generate it in the first place. And none of it was going to go away. Lies, obfuscation, and misdirection are not new strategies by global corporations: Big Oil and Gas are phenomenally powerful and they are taking a page from a tried-and-true playbook written by the tobacco industry.

More than 380 million tons of plastic are currently being pro-duced every year. And by their own admission, the plastics indus-try is just getting started, enthusiastically hailing the beginning of a "New Plastics Economy."[65] At its current rate of expansion, plastic production is projected to double by 2040. Depending who you ask, it is projected to either triple or quadruple by 2050.[66]

Or, in Enck's words: "We have to stop making plastic if we don't want to be *buried* in it."

Fortunately there is some good news to be had, starting with the fact that the Beyond Plastics online course continues to be taught every semester with an ever-growing enrollment. All of my fellow classmates struck me as highly motivated people who planned to immediately take the Beyond Plastics message out into the world. Enck and her compatriots have already been instrumental in several pivotal initiatives to date including:

- The New York State Plastic Bag Ban, which became fully effective late in 2020.
- New Jersey's recent passing of the strongest anti-plastic law in the country: banning polystyrene, plastic bags, and paper *and* plastic bags, effective May 2022.
- Most significant of all, there is a serious, credible effort underway to address the plastic problem at a national level. When Sen. Tom Udall (D-NM) gave that press conference revealing that we all eat one credit card's worth of plastic a week, it was because he was announcing that he and Rep. Alan Lowenthal (D-CA) were introducing to Congress the *Break Free From Plastic Pollution Act* which includes

> *national* bans on polystyrene, plastic straws and plastic
> bags, a *national* container deposit program, banning the
> shipping of plastic waste to other countries, *and* a three-
> year freeze on new plastic facilities in the United States.*

Now *that's* exciting.

Have you forgotten all about that wineglass at the art opening?
Because there's a little bit more to that story.

After Anne kindly went off to find me a *glass* glass, a few minutes
went by. I started to feel self-conscious, hanging out there by the
refreshments like a cheese plate stalker. As the head of the art center I
imagined her getting interrupted seventeen times and ultimately forgetting all about my glass, for which I certainly wouldn't blame her.

So I took the "recyclable" cup of wine, misplacing all my confidence in that sneaky little "chasing arrow" triangle. Two seconds later
who should return but Anne, holding a *glass* wineglass and looking
confused as to why I was drinking from a plastic cup after she had
gone to all that trouble for me.

Oh, I was embarrassed. But worse than that, I was disappointed
in myself. I realized what a short little window of patience I had. God
forbid I have to walk around and look at art for ten minutes without
an adult beverage in hand!

I've thought about that moment many times since. We can be
aware of the terrifying facts about plastic and our environment, but
even so—can we be counted upon to act upon this knowledge? Even
when it isn't convenient?

I think the key to making positive change on plastic is two-
pronged. First, people need to be informed not once, but repeatedly,
armed with facts and horrified by the imagery too (sadly, the plastic
straw turtle will not be the last). They need to watch movies like *The
Story of Plastic*, to find out what is really happening as opposed to

---

* Since then Udall has left office. The new bill sponsor is Sen. Jeff Merkley
(D-OR).

what we are told by everyone from the packaging industry to your garbage service provider.

Second, we need to use this information to make actual legislative change, like the Break Free from Plastic Pollution Act, so that the rules are fair, consistent for everyone and reflect the truths we know.

After that? Maybe then we can celebrate with a nice glass of wine. And I do mean a *glass*.

CHAPTER ELEVEN

....

ALL THE RIDICULOUS
TERMS TRANSLATED

One way to obfuscate the plastic issue is with big, complicated science words that, when used, make the average person think one of two things: Wow! I couldn't possibly understand the complexities of this issue, but I'll trust the people who know this vocabulary! Or, who wants wine?

But, if you know some of the jargon being thrown at you, you don't have to choose between blind trust and feeling stupid. Instead, you can cut through the bullshit and realize that *energy recovery* is code for *burning garbage* and that a product being *degradable* sounds good but isn't.

And then there are other not-so-familiar words that are used to talk about the problem by the good folks genuinely trying to do something about it. For example, I think it's not entirely self-evident what *extended producer responsibility* is, or whether *environmental consumerism* is a good or a bad thing, but I think we'll be hearing these words more and more in the years to come.

Anthropogenic

Means "man-made." It's not a compliment

As in: "The Great Pacific Garbage Patch is an *anthropogenic* phenomenon." "*Anthropocene*," which has been used to describe the era during which humans began to significantly impact their environment, although it is not at this point an officially recognized scientific epoch.

Advanced recycling/chemical recycling/energy recovery/gasification/ pyrolisis/repolymerization/ resource recovery/waste to energy

Don't all these terms sound lovely? *Chemical recycling* is surely what they do on the Starship Enterprise, and *waste to energy* could be a Greenpeace initiative.

In fact, all these terms are more or less euphemisms for one thing: *burning garbage*. And specifically burning *plastics*, which, being made from fossil fuels, burn extremely well. The problem is that this burning results in Really Bad Stuff: toxic fumes, toxic ash, and greenhouse gases.

On top of this, burning plastic only reduces the overall volume by two thirds; what are we supposed to do with the one-third of material that is left over at the end and filled with toxic heavy metals and furans? (See *furans* definition, below.)

It is important to recognize these terms, because the packaging and plastics industries are trying to divert our attention from the fact that we all have microplastics in our lungs by promising to invest in something that sounds environmentally responsible, when in fact "resource recovery" will just make our air still more toxic, especially for the communities where the incinerators are located.

At the same time, it becomes a de facto license for the manufacturers to keep right on making plastics, and even amp it up as planned by tripling production by 2050. *Plastic problem? No, no! . . . we took care of that! Pay no attention to the man behind the curtain with the giant flamethrower . . .*

Biomagnification/bioamplification/bioaccumulation/ bioconcentration /biological magnification/ biopersistence

All of these terms are referring to the fact that toxins accumulate in the food chain, which can amplify their effect. You may not care whether a microscopic zooplankton has heavy metal—a by-product of burning certain plastics—in their food, but if a sardine eats a steady diet of such zooplankton, and then a mackerel eats a steady diet of these sardines, by the time that mackerel lands on your plate for dinner you now potentially have a not-so-insignificant amount of heavy metals in your food. Biomagnification is why people worry about too much mercury—a neurotoxin—in our seafood, for example, which is in the environment largely as a result of centuries of humans burning coal. (Bioaccumulation, by contrast, refers to what happens over time as toxins build up in one organism.)

Just as coal did (and does), microplastics and toxins from plastic production and disposal all enter the environment and thus the food chain. These may start out invisibly small, but this does not mean they can't hurt us. On top of the fact that plastics often have toxic chemical additives, when they break down in our environment it has been established that they act as sponges for other toxins floating around in the environment. (See *hydrophobic* below.)

Bioplastics

Doesn't a name like bioplastic sound inherently good? Like its probably biodegradable, right? Alas, not so. In fact, not all bioplastics are bio-based. I literally had to go lie down when I found that out.

Okay. Deep breath.

WHAT EVEN ARE BIOPLASTICS IF NOT BIO-BASED? you might reasonably ~~shriek~~ ask. Remember the show *Newhart*, the one where Bob Newhart's character ran an inn in Vermont? In one of the very first episodes he calls a service named "Anything for a Buck," and when three guys show up, one of them famously says "Hi. I'm Larry. This is my brother Darryl. And that's my other brother Darryl."

This is kind of like that. The term *bioplastics* can mean two related, but entirely separate things.

Bioplastics (first kind) are plastics made from—or partially made from—plant polymers, instead of petroleum. If a bioplastic is made from plants such as corn, potatoes or sugarcane than it is indeed bio-based. Although it seems counterintuitive, being made from plants is no guarantee that they are any more biodegradable than regular plastics. Bioplastics made from plant polymers are often labeled "PLA," which stands for polylactic acid, but probably reads to a lot of consumers like "PLA-nts"!

Bioplastics (second kind) are plastics that are made *to* biodegrade, even though they might not biodegrade in every environment, what's known as "conditionally compostable," which brings us back to the industrial composting facility we've been talking so much about. They might be plant-based, but they don't have to be; they could also be fossil fuel–based.

The upshot here is much the same as compostables: if it's confusing, that's by design, and if it's misleading, all the better. In the end there's a lot of greenwashing going on and very little good.

Types of Plastic

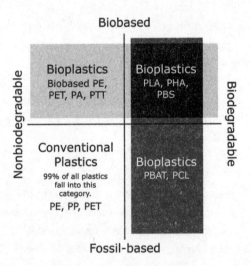

NOTE: This chart is a little misleading, scale-wise. No matter how they are defined, bio-plastics are currently only a drop in the bucket: non-degradable conventional plastics currently make up 99 percent of the 404 million tons of new plastic made every year. So imagine one enormous white square representing conventional plastics and the three shades of grey represented by little teeny-tiny, pin-prick size dots.[1]

Cost externalization

This is the policy of most product and packaging manufacturers today: we make it! You figure out what to do with it! According to Jim Puckett of the Basel Action Network,* cost externalization is what he calls "an unpaid bill" that ultimately gets paid for by the health of our bodies and the health of the planet in the form of pollution and an exploitative, black-market waste trade. Cost externalization is essentially the opposite of extended producer responsibility (see below).

Environmental consumerism

Our capitalist society is based on buying stuff—and lately a lot of terms have been bandied about to describe consumers who are conscious of the environmental impact of their purchases, and making an effort to put their dollars into conscious consumerism, environmental consumerism, ethical consumerism, and green materialism, all of which more or less come down to the same thing—influencing culture with the power of your pocketbook.

I'd make the argument that, although putting your money where your conscience is should be a good thing, there are two things wrong with relying on environmental consumerism to solve our problems with waste: first, the onus is put on the individual consumer. At this point in our history, our problems of waste, and plastic waste in particular, are driven by a complex system of interlocking parts on an industrial scale. Trying to solve a systemic cultural problem on the scale of the individual is a woefully incomplete solution. What we need is a combination of individual *and* legislative changes.

The case of the plastic bag is a good example. You can bring your reusable bags to the store until you are blue in the face, but that doesn't change the fact that New York State was sending 23 billion plastic bags to the landfill every year.[2] That is until the New York State plastic bag ban was enacted late in 2020.

---

* More about the Basel Action Network in a bit.

The second problem with environmental consumerism is that it has the danger of encouraging continued consumerism, *now with a shiny green veneer!* It's tempting to buy all the items for sale in the eco-friendly boutique, replacing my plastic Tupperware with pretty enamelware and my ordinary plastic dust broom with a handmade straw broom, but then aren't I just wasting the items I already have in the name of a superficial "environmentalism"? I'm not against buying something that will make you happy and serve the purpose of eliminating waste/avoiding plastic, but we should be careful not to replace one wasteful practice with another one.

As the Zero Wasters like to say, the most environmental purchase is the one you didn't make.

Extended producer responsibility (EPR), aka "packaging reduction"

You already probably use EPR in some part of your life: aluminum can redemption, or maybe battery, paint, and e-waste collection programs. EPR is essentially a program for end-of-life product takeback. It is a recognition on the part of the government that this material is potentially problematic, toxic, or dangerous if not disposed of properly, which means that the company producing it needs to participate (read: pay for) at the end of that product's life. ("Potentially problematic, toxic, or dangerous." Huh. Does this sound like any popular material we know, I wonder?)

EPR is the opposite of Cost Externalization.

HOWEVER: Something to be aware of is that Big Oil is on to EPR as the next big conversation, and so they are getting in on the ground floor, supporting legislation at both the state and federal level to define "chemical recycling"—which is burning plastic—as an acceptable component of EPR. Which is ridiculous. We wouldn't allow companies to burn house paint or batteries, because of obvious toxicity, and we shouldn't allow them to burn plastics either, for just the same reason.

Let me repeat: *Not every EPR bill is a good one, and burning plastic is not recycling.* There is no place for so-called "chemical recycling" in any legit extended producer responsibility bill, period. Don't be fooled. (For an excellent list of the "Ten Requirements for Effective Extended Producer Responsibility" you can visit the website of Beyond Plastics.)[3]

Fracking/hydrofracking/hydraulic fracturing

This is a process for mining the fossil fuel natural gas: pressurized liquid (composed of water, sand, and chemicals) is injected into the ground in order to fracture shale and thereby release raw natural gas, which is primarily methane, but also usually contains other things too, such as ethane, butane, and propane. Once upon a time no one bothered to strip out the flammable gas called ethane. Today, however, it is a valuable by-product of the process, because it the feedstock for—you guessed it!—plastic. This is why the plan to dramatically ramp up plastic production in the coming years had been called "Big Oil's Plan B."[4]

Free-market environmentalism

This is the theory that companies will be motivated to work in an environmentally friendly way in order to meet consumer demand for environmentally friendly products. Yes, this is a real theory: that companies will act responsibly when it is profitable to do so. Waiting for this to happen unfortunately ignores A.) greenwashing or the practice of giving the appearance of environmentalism without the actuality, and B.) the fact that there is far more money to be made catering to the many customers who don't particularly care about the environment or who are not able to prioritize environmental choices.

Let's not hold our breath waiting for the free market to take care of the environment, shall we?

Furans, heavy metals, and dioxins

The first thing you need to know about these is that they are all very, very bad. Toxic. Carcinogenic. Producing birth defects. Am I getting my message across? Poison. Lead, mercury, and PCBs all belong to this category.

The second thing you need to know is that these all result from burning plastic. When plastic is burning, these poisonous chemicals and pollutants are floating into the air, remaining in the ash left behind, getting collected by any water that happens by.

Remember this next time you make s'mores and please don't burn the chocolate wrappers or the marshmallow bag in the campfire. More importantly remember this when people try to sell you on *chemical recycling* or *waste to energy* (see above) because I promise you: this is the next move on the part of Big Oil to support their plan to ramp up plastic production.

They're gonna try their best to make it sound awesome. Don't buy it.

Greenwashing

"Green is the new black," explained associate professor of advertising Sigal Segev in an interview with the BBC.[5] According to a 2017 study by Unilever, 30 percent of consumers prefer to buy brands they believe are more sustainable or environmentally sound.[6] Which is great news until you realize that most corporations prefer to take advantage of this tendency not by redesigning their product, but by making false or misleading claims. As mentioned above, there's unfortunately virtually no regulation in place determining legal definitions for all those lovely-sounding buzzwords that show up over and over: "green," "bio," "natural," "eco," "clean," "environmentally friendly," and so on.

In fact, when the BBC investigated, they found that 42 percent of online product environmental claims were "exaggerated, false and potentially illegal." Greenwashing is very real and it is everywhere.

Hydrophobic

Literally, this means "afraid of water" and, surprisingly, we're not talking about eleven-year-old me looking at the frigid waters of Lake Saint Catherine at my camp's 8 a.m. swim class. In fact, we're referring to a property of chemicals that makes them want to avoid water, so instead they jump on the nearest solid. In the ocean, this means hydrophobic chemicals will enthusiastically hitch a ride on a micro-plastic, because, ew! water. Because of this tendency, microplastics act as toxic sponges in ocean environments, absorbing chemicals that are biopersistent (or tend to hang around and not break down), such as PCBs (industrial chemicals now outlawed due to links to birth defects and cancer), PDBEs (flame retardants linked to hormone disruption and reproductive harm), DDT (pesticide now outlawed due to links to endocrine disruption, liver damage, and cancer) and mercury (so poisonous it causes both long- and short-term effects, including neu-rological damage, reproductive harm, and heart disease).

Nurdles

Although it sounds like it should be the name for a new pup-pet-driven children's television show, in fact, nurdles are "the worst toxic waste you've probably never heard of."[7] Nurdles are the raw materials of the plastics industry, tiny plastic pellets from which most plastic products are made, allowing for easy transportation between factories. Perhaps the biggest problem with nurdles is that they are easily spilled at every stage of plastic's production, inadvertently released into the environment before they've even been used or made into anything.

Worse still, major spill events of nurdles seem to take place on a regular basis. In 2021 a container ship caught fire and sank in the Indian Ocean while carrying eighty-seven containers of nurdles, or 75 billion of them. For weeks, dead turtles, whales, and dolphins washed to shore with nurdles riddling their systems. Sri Lankan fishermen reported they couldn't even swim without getting the lentil-size pellets in their ears.

Waste broker

When you call your trash service provider and ask where the recy-cling goes, they will tell you it ultimately goes to a waste broker. They have no idea what happens after that, because it is through waste brokers that an almost impossible-to-trace journey occurs, shipping our trash around the world. This leads us nicely to:

Waste trade colonialism

Ever since China stopped taking our "recyclables" in 2018, the musical chairs game of waste from broker to broker inevitably leads to illegalities, bribes, and black-market importation. This is how our "recycling" comes to be dumped on developing countries lacking infrastructure to address it in Asia, Africa, and Latin America.

Remember Jim Puckett of the Basel Action Network talking about cost externalization? On the subject of waste trade colonialism, he had this to say: *Export creates the delusion of circularity for a material which is inherently linear.*

Translation? Plastic isn't recyclable, and we shouldn't exploit the world's poorest residents in the process of trying to fool ourselves that it is.

CHAPTER TWELVE

IS LIFE WITHOUT PLASTIC
EVEN POSSIBLE?

Have you ever had a three-week-old bag of pumpkin guts in your fridge, and wondered what the statute of limitations was on keeping it? Of course, you have.

When this happened to me in late November the situation was of course complicated by the fact that I couldn't just do what any sane twenty-first century American would do and throw it away. Instead, there I was, covered in pumpkin goo washing out a white plastic garbage bag with the garden hose. In the rain.

Who said life without garbage isn't glamorous?

The pumpkin guts had been sent home in a plastic kitchen garbage bag by a well-intentioned parent after my daughter Ilsa had been pumpkin carving at a friend's house and mentioned that she wanted to roast the seeds. But when the bag of pumpkin innards had been sitting in the back of the fridge for three weeks, I knew that ship had sailed.

I didn't want to clean out this plastic bag of slimy goo. I wanted to toss the whole thing in the garbage can. Only I didn't have a garbage can anymore.

I looked this perfectly ordinary kitchen garbage bag in the eye and understood that neither snow nor rain nor gloom of night could prevent me from having to deal with its existence, a plastic bag that will be around much longer than I, or my kids, or even my grandkids will be.

The guts were deposited in my compost pile, to happily decompose over the coming months, and after rinsing it with the garden hose, the plastic bag enjoyed a place of privilege on my clothes drying line. And it really wasn't *so* bad, cold slime and all.

But then what? That plastic bag stared at me and I knew the odds were not good that it had anywhere good to go after its stay at my house. Sooner or later, recycled or not, one day it was destined to break up into tiny bits of plastic, invisible to the human eye. It would be absorbed into the world's ecosystem, and contribute to the toxic, never-ending fallout that poisons our world and every form of life in it.

And for what? Some unwanted pumpkin slime?

Although the burden of *what to do with this?* often fell to me (or was handed to me) everyone else did have to deal with it, too.

Sometimes the girl's friends understood, but mostly they seemed mystified. When the project began, Ilsa's birthday brought in a flurry of unplanned-for packaging and gift wrap, but one friend thoughtfully placed snacks in glass jars as a gift, so Ilsa wouldn't have to deal with crinkly plastic snack wrappers. Which was lovely, even though the glass jars were festooned with colorful thin plastic "curling" ribbon . . . which we now know is made of 100 percent polypropylene. What was harder to forget was that all those wrappers were still out there, somewhere.

At Halloween Ilsa meticulously planned a COVID-19-safe outdoor movie night for a handful of friends that included measuring precise six-foot distances between lawn chairs and candy dishes with spoons to prevent cross-contamination. When more candy arrived unbidden in her friends' pockets, she asked them to take their wrappers home. (I agreed with her entirely. Being a good host is one thing but washing and sorting everyone's extra wrappers? Is another.)

Once while in Brooklyn, Greta was waiting in line for a COVID-19 test outside in the cold, and a woman offered to get them both a cup of hot coffee if she'd hold her place in line. The woman returned and handed Greta a cup of to-go coffee, but without being able to throw it away, Greta had to ferry that plastic-lined paper cup around for the rest of the day.

"Now it sits on my kitchen counter. *Forever*," Greta said with exasperation.

The book *Garbology* by Edward Humes begins with the premise that Americans are addicted to garbage, but it's not *just* individuals who are addicted, but society as a whole, which has evolved to accommodate this addiction so completely that swimming against the tide of disposability is incompatible with normal day-to-day functioning.

Americans are addicted to garbage, but it's worse than that: it's like we're all alcoholics living inside a bar. Even if we want to get away from our addiction, the surrounding environment actively encourages failure. *Enforces* failure.

It's enough to cause one to feel a little desperate sometimes.

"I just want you to know that when this is over, *we are not going to be doing this forever.*"

That was Steve. It was late on a Saturday morning in December, the final month of our Year of No Garbage, and we were standing in the driveway, arguing.

It had all started because of a beanbag chair. I had made it a few years ago for our daughters. After picking a pretty fabric and sewing the pieces together with a zipper, I realized that stuffing it was . . . *problematic*. At least, if I didn't want to use plastic. I desperately tried to find some eco-friendly stuffing.

Straw was too prickly. Rice or dried beans, even if I could get enough of them, were both too heavy and too appetizing to mice. Old blankets or clothing were too deflated.

I ultimately bought what I thought was the next best thing: a bag of "recycled" beanbag filler. When it showed up, though, I was horrified: "recycled" beanbag material is basically shredded-up chunks of spongy Styrofoam tossed festively with staticky plastic micro beads. Even though this preceded the Year of No Garbage, I was aware that this was perhaps the worst thing I'd ever bought.

But I *had* bought it, so I figured it would go into the beanbags, be zipped shut, and I'd *never have to deal with it again.*

That was all true, until in September 2020, when we adopted our two cats from the local shelter. As it turned out, the cats loved the beanbag, but at first were also not entirely clear on the distinction between it and the litter box.

So the peed-on beanbag went into a storage closet to await the day when I felt brave enough to deal with a sack of used pee-scented Styrofoam.

And this was that day.

Steve was trying to help me transfer the beanbag filler from the festively patterned fabric shell to our long-neglected garbage bin outside and all the while he was getting more and more agitated.

I'd had two bad options. One was, to categorize the filler under "Health and Safety" garbage, our one exemption, and feel justified tossing it. I mean keeping old cat pee could definitely be considered a kind of health violation. The other choice was to wait until January 2021 to dispose of it. Both options felt like failures.

"You can *never* write about this on your blog. You know that, right? I mean, how do you justify throwing something like this away?"

As we tried to dump the contents of the fabric bag, plastic beads and fluff were getting everywhere, floating in the air, sticking to our clothing, falling like snow onto our driveway.

"They will *crucify* you." Steve said simply.

When he said "they," I knew what he meant. Yes, he meant my blog readers, but also the world at large in a more general way. If I ever wanted to talk or write about this project in the future, I'd have to answer for *this*. Did it matter that I had purchased it not really knowing what it was? Before this project had even started?

"Well . . . If they do, they do," I said, uncomfortably. "I mean, I *have* to talk about this, right? This is what the whole thing is about. I mean: *look at this.* Things like this should not exist."

"Things like this should be *illegal*," Steve said, walking away in disgust.

All that fluff and springiness I had so wanted for the beanbags was now working utterly against us. Styrofoam and pellets had completely filled the entire ninety-six-gallon trash bin and were resistant to being packed down in any way, bouncing right back up after every attempt. Flecks of plastic were stuck in my hair, my clothing . . . bits were drifting by on the ground. It was a plastic fucking nightmare.

"Where are you going?"

"To get a shovel."

Steve somehow managed to scrape up most of the bits that had fallen onto the ground, along with some gravel and dirt that helped weigh it down in the bin somewhat. From the garage he grabbed an old Foamcore lawn sign to pack on top and help keep it contained. The sign was from the climate strike in September of last year.

"Well *that's* ironic." I said.

We bickered some more about what would happen if the wind blew our bin over (clearly, we would have to move) or whether I should take any pictures of the hideous blob. It was beyond lunchtime, and we were both getting hungry. Arguing on an empty stomach was a specialty of ours.

That's when he said enough was enough.

"These projects? They *change* us, change our lives," he said. "And all this garbage everywhere? All over the house? With nowhere to go? We can't keep doing this. It's killing our family."

I just looked at him. I was still trying to process how we had come to a place in our culture where people were making and purchasing stuff like immortal beanbag filler. It's beyond maddening when you are forced to really look at it—it's . . . obscene. Steve clearly did not want to look any more. Yet, how could we possibly go back to life as before, knowing what we knew now? Knowing that our "recyclables" end up littering the landscapes of countries halfway around the world? Or floating in the ocean? Knowing the chemical-saturated, planet-destroying path we are on?

How can you ever put the genie back in the bottle?

It scared me, this fight, because it had veered into territory that touched on the fear that I am doing something horrible to my family in the selfish interest of my work. Each one of the three times we've embarked on a "family project" I've considered the questions:

Is this okay to ask of my family?

Will it cause pain to or harm my children?

Will this do harm to my marriage?

I know I'm lucky. Very lucky. Not many families would have been willing to go along with such schemes. But now, in the home-stretch, in the last month of what has turned out to be, all told, a three-project, ten-year enterprise, Steve might now be coming to the conclusion that I *had* done some harm to our family.

But Steve doesn't believe in a "no-win scenario."

What was making him crazy was the realization that I'd been coming to lately: that there is no real solution here: there is no good place in the universe for the vat of horrible plastic crap that was before us. Being a truly eco-friendly consumer in today's world of plastic everywhere in tens of thousands of variations is almost impossible because the game has been rigged: plastic is just too darn profitable for too many people. Want to eat? Drive a car? Want to live in today's world? Whatever you do or consume, it involves plastic.

So we make deals with ourselves. We do the "best we can." We are encouraged to think we can make a difference by doing good things like recycling, and that such efforts are enough. We absolve ourselves. When you step outside the system however, as a Year of No Garbage had allowed us to do, you see the lie plain as day: the current system isn't set up to actually work.

After we had secured the treacherous bin and headed inside, the argument blew over. I understood that the little pieces of sticky plastic everywhere had triggered Steve into wanting to pitch the baby of our whole year-long project out with the Styrofoam bathwater. If only for a few moments.

But that disgusting, landfill-ready mess was all the more reason for us to persevere. I think Steve hit the nail on the head when he was trying to scrape the driveway clean, when he said this stuff should be illegal. And then he said something else that I felt in my gut to be true.

He said, "This stuff is a *sin*."

Remember that documentary by Bill Moyers, *Trade Secrets*? The first time I ever really thought about plastic was when Steve and I watched it, not long after Greta was born. It wasn't just about the impacts of industrial chemicals on our health, it was also about the cover-up conducted by chemical companies to hide this information from the public. Documents showed *they knew* how bad these chemicals were, even as, for years, they publicly denied it. (Remind you of any other historically similar scenarios? Cigarettes? Sugar?)

Being horrified by this documentary was the very moment I resolved to eliminate plastic from my life. I began a mental list of every place that plastic showed up in my life and within minutes I realized, with dismay, that plastic was far more pervasive than I had ever realized. Eliminating plastic from everyday life as we knew it would be *impossible*. As quickly as I had made the resolution, I had abandoned it. That was twenty years ago.

Now, in the universe of zero waste, I'd come to realize once again that plastic is Public Enemy Number One, but now it was even worse than PBS had led me to believe. Not only was it doing all kinds of bad things in our bodies and in our environment, it also doesn't degrade, it often can't—or won't—be recycled. We have invented a monster, and the monster is everywhere.

So it was one day in December 2020 that it occurred to me again to wonder: How long could a person today avoid plastic? For example, how hard would it be to avoid plastic ENTIRELY for . . . *a single day?*

I decided to try it. With a new wave of COVID-19, Greta and Steven had returned to Vermont, so we had a full house again. After reassuring my family I would attempt this particular challenge solo, I laid out a quick set of rules. It would be very literal: *I couldn't touch plastic.* It would last from the moment I got up until the moment I went to bed. And no obvious cheats, such as wearing gloves.

Leading up to this Day of No Plastic I was super excited: weird experiments, obviously, being my idea of a good time.

But every day I realized more and more things I wouldn't be able to use. Not only could I not touch ballpoint pens, my alarm clock, my hairbrush, the computer keyboard or mouse, or food packaging, I also couldn't touch key items such as the toilet seat, my cell phone, or even medication bottles. Most of my clothes were off limits because they contained synthetic fibers, including all tights, socks, and bras.

I couldn't drive anywhere, because cars are 50 percent plastic. This was probably just as well, because I also couldn't wear my glasses.

Still, I was not prepared. I woke up on the morning of the appointed day and after carefully hovering over the toilet seat, automatically touched the plastic top of our glass soap dispenser to wash my hands. I was barely awake and already I had made mistake #1.

At breakfast my family exclaimed over realizations of all the things I wouldn't be able to touch that day.

You can't answer the phone!

Hey Mom, you may not be able to turn on a light switch . . . but you can use an oil lamp!

I couldn't do any of my normal exercise routine, because my yoga mat was plastic. I couldn't even take a walk because I had no shoes without plastic. Or a coat without polyester fiber, plastic zipper, or plastic buttons. Greta helpfully pointed out I couldn't even get out of my own pajamas since the buttons are plastic.

There was an extended discussion over whether I would even be allowed to *walk on our floor*, which is painted—thankfully resolved when Steve recalled that the latex paint is covered by a natural finish made of whey protein.

So I wouldn't have to learn how to fly. That was good.

On a normal day, I'd write or do research, but of course the computer is all plastic. Magazines and books were off-limits, since I couldn't be sure if there was plastic (many contain polyethylene coatings) in the glossy pages and covers. Doing laundry was verboten, since all the washing machine dials are plastic. I also couldn't clean, because even my homemade cleaning solutions are in plastic bottles, the dishwasher is plastic, and the vacuum cleaner is plastic.

I found myself moving in slow motion, in an attempt to think before automatically touching something. Maybe I could veeeeeeeery carefully get ingredients out for making dinner later . . .

But the cap of a glass spice container was plastic.

A welcome diversion was the arrival of the mail, which gave me the chance to realize that I couldn't even open a package without touching plastic tape.

At lunch, Ilsa had to feed me chips so I wouldn't have to touch the plastic bag trying to extract them. I felt like a toddler.

By this point I was walking through the house like a ghost with no power to affect the physical world: leaving lights on, leaving dishes in the sink, leaving laundry with all its covert synthetic materials unfolded. And without my glasses nothing was sharp so I walked around in a kind of a fog.

I couldn't do anything I normally do. Exercise, cooking, cleaning, writing, research, reading emails . . . it was kind of like having a vacation day, but the worst, most frustrating vacation day ever.

My only solace was an embroidery project I'd been making for a Christmas gift. My needle was metal, and I'd checked the thread and confirmed it was 100 percent cotton. The towel, I knew, was cotton. Then I chanced upon the tag on the towel itself and read with dismay: *57% cotton, 32% polyester, 11% rayon.*

Was it too early to go to bed? It was 2:30 p.m.

"You could knit!" Ilsa suggested. "I could open the knitting book for you!" I slumped. Having people do so many menial things for me was unfamiliar and exhausting. It felt like a weird new kind of meditation retreat: I just sat in my (wool) armchair and watched other people do things: wrap Christmas presents, make coffee, scroll on their phones, do homework, open mail . . .

I tried to help prep dinner and automatically touched the kitchen timer. Plastic. Reached for the colander handle. Plastic. Cheese grater. Plastic.

By the end of the day I had resorted to averting extreme boredom by reading the classifieds in the free newspaper circular that comes every week with our mail. I read an article entitled *The Various Types of Glaucoma and Their Symptoms* four times.

When I headed to bed, my hand stopped by the lamp on the nightstand, hovering by the plastic switch—HA!—it almost got me.

I still hate plastic and everything it is doing to us, but this impossible day gave me a newfound understanding of what we are really up against. Who knew that in only a few short decades our society could have so thoroughly encased ourselves in mysterious plastic chemicals, to the point that doing without them immobilizes us?

Recently I had happened upon an article in the *New York Times*, "Life Without Plastic Is Possible. It's Just Very Hard."

I beg to differ—and I speak from experience.[1]

Some twenty years ago, Steve's brother Chris gave me a book for Christmas titled *The Good Life*. It was written by radical self-sufficiency proponents Helen and Scott Nearing, who are credited with birthing the back-to-the-land movement of the 1960s and were heralded as having written "a Walden for our times."[2]

The Nearings moved to Vermont in 1932 during the height of the Great Depression and for the next few decades proceeded to build by hand and from scratch a homestead that gave them everything they needed for life. (After that, Vermont was getting too crowded so they moved to Maine where they started the process all over again.) They built their home and a series of outbuildings from native stone and concrete. They grew crops for most of their food, chopped wood for heat, and made and sold maple syrup as their "cash crop." Vegetarians, the Nearings ate fruit for breakfast, soup for lunch, and salads for dinner.

What I thought twenty years ago when I first read *The Good Life* was that the Nearings were crazy, of course, but also profoundly driven as only true believers can be. Although I admired their total commitment to an extreme idea, I also wasn't sold on it: their writing style was just so serious, both in tone and subject matter. There were entire passages devoted to articulating the five reasons why they chose to turn a cement mixer by hand rather than with a motor. I mean, I know homesteading is serious business. But I came away wondering, was there any *fun* in "the Good Life"? What makes the Good Life worth living?

It seemed like everything in my Year of No Garbage boiled down to just one question: *How does one avoid plastic in contemporary society*? And I had to wonder if that question is paradoxical: can one only avoid the use of plastic by opting out of contemporary society, à la the Nearings's Good Life model? Because that's just how entrenched we are.

Do you recall the iconic cocktail party scene in the movie *The Graduate*, the one where Dustin Hoffman's character, Benjamin, is given career advice by a family friend? "*I just want to say one word to you,*" Mr. Maguire says gravely, eager to offer a priceless pearl of wisdom. "*Plastics.*" The scene was meant as a joke, a stark contrast between the soul-deadening concerns of corporate life—and the compromises we make to grow up—and Benjamin's desperate search for personal meaning in his life. The executive might just as well have said "soybeans" or "pork bellies."

But he didn't. And now, when we watch this movie today, that scene takes on a whole new meaning. That executive doesn't just represent the soulless machine of capitalism, he is proffering a vision of the American future that today has come to pass. He doesn't know it, but he is an oracle. That deal Mr. Maguire was offering? We took it. We live in that compromise, knowingly or not, having bargained away not just our souls but our bodies and the planet in the deal, in the name of ease, convenience and profit.

Many times throughout this year I had thought to myself, *This would all be so much easier if we just became Amish. Or hermits.* If we just ditched everything we owned and started over the way Helen and Scott Nearing did with a hammer and a wheelbarrow full of cement. But are those our only two choices: the glittering superficiality of a cocktail party with ominous undertones, or the stern asceticism of the recluse?

I'd like to think a middle way is possible. One that doesn't require us to give up and start over, but neither does it pretend everything is fine, *just fine!*, when the whole world is on fire and every time we blow our noses plastic comes out. *The Graduate* asks us the question: can you grow up without selling out? And I want to say yes.

How do we get to that place?

CHAPTER THIRTEEN

....

BREAKING UP WITH GARBAGE

I had officially fallen out of love with garbage. Our relationship had been based on a series of lies and half-truths, and, at times, downright fantasy. It's been unhealthy not only for me, but also devastating for society, the environment, and the planet as a whole. I wanted to break up.

We had been able to end the year without having thrown a single thing away, excepting only our anemic "health and safety" trash, which I estimated had amounted to about two kitchen size (thirteen-gallon) garbage bags for the whole family in an entire year, as well as the horrendous pee-soaked Styrofoam. Everything had gone somewhere: what wasn't recycled or composted was donated, offered up online, sent hopefully on to TerraCycle or Trex, made into a craft project, or repurposed in other ways. Although I stopped short of anything as exciting as milk-tab jewelry, I found it fun to find new lives for plastic containers as yarn bins, or as a way to give extra eggs to our neighbors. On particularly creative days I made things: I cut up a laminated calendar and wove it into a basket and repurposed old Altoid tins as tiny family-photo holders for gifts. Ilsa made a nifty pencil case out of a small gift box, but don't tell her I told you.

Plus, I found ways not to buy things, especially things I knew would contain more plastic. When my tights or corduroy pants got holes, instead of buying new ones I put my sewing machine to work. Instead of buying a whiteboard for notes I used card stock instead. I knew buying light hand weights for a new workout meant they'd all be coated with plastic, so I held cans of chickpeas and artichokes instead.

In 2019 our family produced 4,992 gallons of garbage; in 2020 we produced ninety-five.

According to my math, that meant we had saved an amount of material equivalent to what would fill up a twenty- to thirty-cu-bic-yard dumpster—the large kind you see on construction sites or renovation jobs.

I was proud of that.

As we began the new year, it was with relief, but also apprehension: how were we to proceed now?

My first New Year's resolution was to cancel my garbage service. You'd think we might have done this already, since we'd spent the entire year not throwing anything away, but while our garbage bin had spent the entire year sitting in the garage, the big blue bin for recycling collection had been putting in some overtime. It seemed silly to pay for garbage removal we weren't using, but there was no way to separate the garbage collection from the recycling service. I asked.

After learning in my Beyond Plastics class that only RIC numbers 1 and 2 were actually being recycled, we had stopped putting plastics numbers 3–7 in the blue bin, so our use of the curbside service we were paying for shrank still further.

Instead, we will take our recycling to the local transfer station. It not only saves money, it feels more honest: my local dump accepts only #1 and #2.*

For the few things we actually *want* to throw away we could bring these to the dump on a pay-by-the-bag system too, which I calculated would save us about five hundred dollars per year.

And I had made up my mind to stop being so paranoid and accept TerraCycle as legit. I had no concrete evidence to the contrary. I would be a real zero-waster with virtually no garbage at all, and we'd all live happily ever after; *the end.*

---

* Not long after this, early in 2021 the ownership of the transfer station changed and they went to "single stream," accepting all plastics #1–7. Argh. We still only place plastics numbers 1 and 2 in the recycling.

It would've worked too. (Insert ominous foreshadowing here . . .)

But by March 2021, TerraCycle was being sued by The Last Beach Cleanup for deceptive labeling and failure to provide any proof of actual recycling.[1] (Later in the year the case would be settled, and TerraCycle would agree to pay all legal fees and make changes to their labeling.)

After the filing of the lawsuit, I waffled for several months more. A Zero Waste Box I still had in the basement just sat there. I wasn't sending it in, but I hadn't quite given up either. Such is the power of wishful thinking.

Then, through my Beyond Plastics connections, which by now had turned into an alumni group which met regularly, I had the chance to see a startling new documentary by investigative journalists entitled *The Recycling Myth* in which some thirty bales of "recycling" that had been carefully collected and sent to TerraCycle played a starring role. That's because they ended up exactly where they were not supposed to be: waiting to be burned in a cement kiln in Bulgaria. The film makes the assertion that this is all part of a billion-dollar international "plastic black market" in which plastic intended for recycling is "burned, hidden, smuggled, and dumped." TerraCycle founder Tom Szaky says these plastics ending up at an incinerator was a simple "mistake."

Seeing that film, including footage of Szaky telling the filmmakers to turn off their cameras, was what finally did it. My stubborn optimism had suffered a catastrophic blow. I had wanted so badly to believe that TerraCycle and Santa Claus and the Easter Bunny were real, that I had been willing to overlook the fact that Santa's handwriting looks suspiciously like Mom's.

Without mail-in programs like TerraCycle or Carton Recycling, I was forced to admit that an object might really, truly have nowhere to go but the landfill.

So maybe technically it's not a breakup with garbage, since we still have to see each other occasionally.

But that doesn't mean I'm giving up. What I *am* giving up on is the myth of personal responsibility.

It's taken a lot to get me to this point, because as you have perhaps guessed by now, I am a both a very obstinate and a very optimistic person at heart. The idea of personal responsibility, and the assertion that individual actions and choices matter is tailor-made for a person like me. When faced with a conundrum, I have long felt that, if one just looks hard enough, solutions reveal themselves. *There will be a way.* So, it took me an entire year of looking and asking and researching to finally accept what so many have long suspected. To recap:

- Plastic recycling does not work.
- Extreme "recycling" programs are not trustworthy. (Yet.)

Additionally:
- One cannot—in this day, age and culture—entirely avoid disposable packaging.

Yes, I know there are dozens of zero wasters on the internet at this very moment holding up their mason jars full of their waste for the entire year in protest of this statement.

"It *IS* possible!" they say, "Just look!"

But the number of people who are both willing and able to *genuinely* go full bore zero waste under our existing system is so small as to be statistically insignificant.

Which means, effectively, that even though it is technically possible, it is not realistic. And it's not going to fix anything.

The *New York Times* recently ran an article titled "Trash or Recycling? Why Plastic Keeps Us Guessing," in which it described our current system as "a secret language."[2] In fact it's even worse than that. After spending an entire year making it my job to avoid making garbage, I can now confirm that there *is* no secret language, because that would imply that if you just worked hard enough, it would finally make sense.

It never makes sense.

Zero waste is a lovely idea. But for 99.99 percent of the people living zero waste in our current culture—like mail-in recycling, like pay-to-play recycling, like single-stream recycling—it is a false solution. It's a lie born of our own self-blame—if we try hard enough, we can make a difference. A lie that industry is happy to let us believe. *Yes*, they agree. *It really is up to you!* They promote the principles:

> *Learn the recycling bin dos and DON'Ts!*
> *Check with your local waste disposal services!*
> *Contact your local municipality for instructions!*
> *Bring to a drop-off location for special recycling!*
> *When in doubt, throw it out!*

These are not "recycling principles." These are cop-outs.

I'm not suggesting that just because personal responsibility will not solve the problems of garbage and plastic and climate change, we should all just throw in the towel.

Forget it! Hand me that plastic straw! Turtles be damned!

No. What I'm saying is that personal behavior changes are never going to be enough all on their own, because the forces at work are so enormous. The Sunrise environmental movement likes to point out that "the biggest driver of emissions is the political power of the fossil-fuel industry, not individual behavior."[3] If BP, Chevron, Exxon, and Shell have their way, it will become impossible to live in modern society without using more and more disposable plastics. It will be the offer we have no option to refuse.

Whaddya gonna do? They say. *Stop buying things? Stop eating food? I didn't think so.*

But what if, instead of having the fossil fuel and plastic packaging folks hand us a product and say, "good luck with that!" we required *them* to take responsibility for what they make? This means a legislative will that currently doesn't exist. But it could.

The time for pledges and promises has come and gone. Take for instance the Coca-Cola Company. Did you know that today Coca-Cola is the number one plastic polluter in the world? That's pretty impressive since they didn't even start putting Coke in plastic bottles until 1978. I'm just old enough to remember getting soda from a vending machine in glass bottles, after which you'd put the bottle back in a crate that sat next to the machine. Today Coca-Cola produces 3.3 million tons of plastic packaging each year.[4] And although they are uniquely positioned to change the whole conversation about plastic and plastic pollution by finding genuine solutions, they don't.

Instead, Coke relies on the fact that people have short memories. An article in *The Intercept* put it this way: "Since at least 1990, Coca-Cola has made repeated promises on the plastics front, including commitments to use more recycled plastic, recover and refill more of its bottles, and incorporate more plant-based materials. The company, which has fought against effort that would reduce plastic waste . . . regularly rolls out these goals with much fanfare and rarely, if ever meets them."[5] There's even a whole documentary about it, *Coca-Cola's Plastic Promises.*

So the Coca-Cola Company obfuscates. They hire Bill Nye the Science Guy, who has been a noted voice on climate change, to voice an animated version of himself with a Coke bottle for a head and a Coke label for his signature bow tie and have him saying that "the good people at Coca-Cola are dedicating themselves to addressing our plastic waste problem!" instead of, you know, *actually* addressing our plastic waste problem.[6]

(Side rant: SERIOUSLY, BILL NYE?)

An investigation by the German media organization DW found that "two-thirds of [corporate] pledges to go greener on plastic fail or are dropped."

"When companies fail to meet their pledges, they usually don't mention this openly. Instead, they silently drop the goal or shift its scope or target year."[7]

Nope. No more pledges and promises. Instead, lets return to an idea we've discussed earlier: extended producer responsibility (EPR). This is a system by which companies are required to manage the waste generated by their product, rather than pawning that job off on their customers. It already exists in some industries. Think: tire, car battery, and paint take-back programs. Taxpayers need to understand that when companies aren't responsible for "end-of-life" for their product and packaging, *we* foot the bill instead, through land-fill and incineration costs, or cleanup costs to remove it from the landscape and the ocean. We pay with the environment, and we pay with our bodies.

So here's my *Wild Idea Number One*: If you *make* toxic pieces of shit, you should have to *deal* with those toxic pieces of shit. By law.

Wild Idea Number Two: Make anything that is not *genuinely* recyclable or compostable in all fifty states illegal to make or sell.

Not possible, you say? Again, this is a phenomenon that already exists regarding some materials and products. Bans are popping up in states throughout the United States and in countries around the world on plastic's worst offenders: Styrofoam, plastic bags, plastic straws, plastic-lined coffee cups, and plastic cutlery. People are amazingly adaptable. After our local supermarket finally took away the plastic bags once and for all late in 2020, do you know what happened? Nothing. One day we were poisoning the environment with plastic bags in the name of ultra-convenience and the next? We weren't. Nobody died or even got a nasty hangnail.

Perhaps you're wondering: but what about the people who *need* plastic, medically? Medical plastics represent a tiny fraction of the overall plastic produced. Forty percent of new plastics are used for packaging.[8] As a society I am confident we can draw a legislative line and say, yes, we need plastic ventilators that save lives, but no, we don't need more Bubble Wrap.

Wild Idea Number Three: Supermarkets need to invent the plastic-free aisle.

If my supermarket can have a gluten-free aisle, a health food aisle, or an organic produce section, why not a plastic-free aisle?

Wild Idea Number Four: Somebody needs to invent the Anti-Replicator. And then give me credit for it.

You know how the replicator on board the Star Trek *Enterprise* makes pretty much everything its crewmates need or want by synthesizing it from "pure energy"?[9] One thing the world could really use right now is the opposite of that: an anti-replicator that could break down materials into their constituent parts.* For instance, it could break plastic down into little piles of hydrogen, oxygen, and carbon, which could then be put toward other applications.

Imagine it: some of the least desirable places on the planet—landfills—would suddenly become the most sought-after real estate, virtual gold mines of materials of every conceivable variety. Need some water? Just go buy some hydrogen and oxygen from Howard's Landfill and Material and he'll fix you right up!

Wild Idea Number Five: The world needs more free tables.

Thanks in part to the heroic efforts of online activists like the Trashwalker (look her up on Instagram), I've been awakened to the concept of the free table and the free store. Back in the day when we first encountered the town dump, they used to have a version of this: a designated area off to the side where people put things and took things as they wanted, all free. Sadly, at least at our facility, this practice has now been banned. Sure, you can take things to Goodwill or the local charity shop, but often these places are overflowing and consequently choosy about what they accept, often throwing huge volumes of perfectly good items away for lack of room or storage.

The online version of the free table is Freecycle, a nonprofit network you can join whose express purpose is diverting reusable items from landfills. You receive email messages whenever someone in your area is looking for something, or whenever someone is trying to get rid of something, the only stipulation being that it must be free. Front Porch Forum, local message boards, and Facebook groups are also all great resources for this kind of activity. Feel embarrassed to post things most folks today would throw away without a thought? Don't. The *Wall Street Journal* article "Free Stuff is All Over Craigslist and Facebook and It's Getting Weirder" describes people posting free items such as cracked bowling balls, twenty-three empty beer bottles, and five single-serving packets of Arby's sauce. Although no one took

---

* For those of you Trekkies out there who are pointing out that they already have a Bio Matter Resequencing Converter, this seems only to work for bio-matter. An anti-replicator could break down abiotic materials too.

me up on the four nearly full bottles of aloe vera gel I offered on Freecycle, no one weird-shamed me for it either, so I took it as a win.[10]

And don't forget the Break Free from Plastic Pollution Act. This would be an enormous step forward, uniting the diverse, scattershot state and town-level initiatives around the United States into a comprehensive plan at the federal level. This bill represents the best of what we know works, and an attempt to address the most egregious problems through extended producer responsibility/packaging reduction, with a ban on polystyrene, plastic straws, and plastic bags, a national container deposit program, banning the shipping of plastic waste to other countries, and pausing construction of new plastic production facilities.

Feeling cynical? Don't think it can happen? A 2022 study found that eight out of ten American voters support laws to reduce single-use plastic.[11] As I write this, Canada has just passed a ban on single-use plastics effective December 2022.[12] Early in 2022 France banned all plastic packaging on fruits and vegetables, and Spain is implementing a similar measure in 2023.[13] Australia has had a plastic bag ban in place since 2018, and India has banned single-use plastic food ware beginning July 2022.[14] This is happening; we can do this.

To bastardize a famous quote from the author L. P. Hartley:

"The future is a foreign country. We will do things differently there."

Although I started this Year of No Garbage without really knowing where we'd end up, I've arrived at a place of conviction: garbage—in the conventional sense—is both harmful and unnecessary. But far and away the biggest offender is a material that didn't even exist until the beginning of the last century: *plastic*. I never want to use a garbage can again. My family, on the other hand, isn't so sure. It was much the same with our previous family projects. I'm always the biggest zealot in the room. Just because I've become a fanatic doesn't mean they have.

It was one day late in December of 2020, when we were all in the kitchen—cleaning, making food, chatting—the conversation turned to the impending end of the No Garbage year. Greta was very much looking forward to it. Steve was talking about bringing a garbage can back to the kitchen. Ilsa just seemed relieved that the third and final official project would be behind us.

Every once in a while, during such conversations, I felt an unspoken question in the air: *Can't we just be a normal family?* I felt bad about that. I hope I haven't traumatized my children *too* much in the last decade, asking our family to interrogate the things everyone else around us takes for granted as part of "normal" life . . . sugar, clutter, garbage: the things we eat, the things we keep, the things we throw away.

As it turns out—and I'm as surprised as anyone about this—living No Sugar, No Clutter and No Garbage all led to the same place: *living thoughtfully.* When people are nostalgic for the "good old days" they're not pining for beef shortages and the whooping cough. I'm pretty sure what they're captivated by, when it comes down to it, is the pace. Even the Little Rascals sat down for breakfast together. Being thoughtful about your space, your resources, your food, where the objects of our life come from and where they all go; devoting the time to put those ideals into practice: getting objects to people who will love and use them, recycling and reusing, cooking as much as possible from basic ingredients.

If the unexamined life isn't worth living, it follows that living mindfully gives us purpose. I hope my kids will live life with a sense of curiosity about the world and our place in it. I hope that if something doesn't seem right, they'll know that blind acceptance is not their only option; that even if one person might not be able to solve the problems of the environment, global warming, racial and environmental injustice, we can *start the conversation*, change minds, reveal a wrong, by the simple act of slowing down and taking a closer look.

Or, as one member of my Beyond Plastics class quoted the Jewish maxim: *It's not for us to finish the work, but neither should we desist.**

As for "normal"? I guess they've figured it out by now: I'm just not that mom.

---

* This is from Pirkei Avot, a compilation of ethical teachings and maxims from Rabbinic Jewish tradition.

EPILOGUE

....

THE PLASTIC FAIRY
AND THE HONEY BADGER

I t was the year after the Year of No Garbage had officially ended, and I was waiting. Waiting for the Plastic Fairy to come and make four, enormous, fifty-five-gallon black plastic garbage bags disappear, so I could have my basement back.

She was coming, right?

As I'd learned with our other two projects, even when you are supposedly "done," you are *not done at all*. In fact, in some ways, that is when the hardest work begins.

After all, the whole point of the crazy year-long project is to change how we do things so dramatically that it changes *us*. We come to see the world differently, behave in it differently; in one way or another it becomes a yes/no, black-and-white world. And that's difficult, but once you become accustomed to it, it eventually becomes an unthinking part of your behavior. What's significantly harder is when the project comes to its conclusion, and you have to decide what's next.

No more black-and-white world. Instead, it's "What shade of gray would you prefer? Here are four million to choose from."

Getting to the new normal was a struggle. I am often accused by my family, quite rightly, of clinging to the rules of a project that is no longer in effect. Meanwhile, I often find my family so anxious to soften the harsh rules that I fear we will lose all the new, good habits we worked so hard to establish. And then, what was it all for?

There are discussions, arguments, and usually some tears (mine) before compromises are reached.

So I shouldn't have been surprised that, over a year after our Year of No Garbage had officially concluded, it was *still* messing with me.

Denial is always an option! Reader, I just kept right on washing those plastic packages. There had to be another answer, there just *had* to. I was determined to sit tight until I found it.

Steve kept asking, where was all this plastic gonna go? I didn't know. I still had one TerraCycle box left and yet knew there was a good chance that box probably wasn't going to go anywhere good.

So, after canceling our curbside service and deciding TerraCycle was too sketchy, I couldn't bear the thought that after all we had been through, and all we had learned, we were just going to go back to where we had started: throwing plastic away.

Consequently by December, a year after our project had officially concluded, entering our house from the basement garage was getting increasingly difficult because of this Plastic Gauntlet. Even though I had consolidated it all into four enormous black plastic bags, Steve pointed out that this still did not solve the fundamental problem. Which is to say, we were keeping what at this point could only be considered . . . garbage.

Gasp! He used the "G" word. After a year of not throwing anything away, characterizing something as "garbage" was obviously just a failure of the imagination. Wasn't it? Yet, as the months rolled by, it was dawning on me that society *still did* not agree with me, and that was a problem. No one was going to take these enormous bags of clean plastic off my hands.

The Plastic Fairy was not coming.

So I made Steve a promise: I would concede. I would take these big terrible bags to the dump and pay for them to be classified as trash, hauled off for landfilling or burning. *After* January first 2022. Because that way I could see how much we had accumulated in the months since we had stopped sending it to Terracycle.

And so that is what we did. It was not easy for me to part with those big ugly body bags of plastic. Probably it is the hoarder in me, that gets attached to the very weirdest things and can't let go. But, I'd like to think it is also because I was resisting doing what we are all supposed to do: *Pitch it and forget it.* I can't forget it. I don't want to. Because those black bags full of my single-use plastic will be out there in some landfill for the next several hundred years, at least. Unless they get incinerated, in which case they will be reborn as toxic fumes and a pile of toxic ash which will *then* sit in a landfill, for the next several hundred years.

But at last we came to a level of compromise and gingerly installed a new system in our kitchen that consists of one recycling bin and one—I have a hard time even saying it—garbage. (Steve has jokingly labeled it *The Bin of Shame.*) It is a measure of how much we'd changed, I think, that we entirely forgot to put an actual "garbage bag" liner in the bin, because we are so used to everything being washed and clean, including the Saran Wrap.*

As I write this, the pandemic has become more or less endemic and our days of trying not to ever throw *anything* away are now behind us.

Instead of that ninety-six-gallon trash bin we used to fill each and every week, today we fill one-half of a kitchen-sized garbage bag every week, *always* composed pretty much entirely of single-use plastic food packaging that I couldn't figure out how to avoid.

We have gone from 96 gallons of trash per week to 9.

What had been 4,500 gallons of trash per year had become 450, achieved mostly by paying close attention and making a host of incremental changes: eliminating paper towels, instituting a burn pile for small and unrecyclable paper, collecting wine corks and plastic caps to donate for school craft projects, composting *all* food scraps (not just some), collecting *all* plastic film for the Trex bin at the supermarket (yes, it's a question mark, but it's free, so we limit our plastic film

---

* Which, these days, never enters our house unless a well-meaning soul brings us food wrapped in it. I have yet to reach the zealot level of refusing gifts.

as much as we can and then take that gamble), washing and recycling aluminum foil, avoiding as much as possible buying things that are made with the express purpose of being thrown away.

Here's another technique for reducing garbage: after forgetting that first time, now I don't line the garbage can with a disposable plastic garbage bag anymore. Garbage bags are black holes, I realized. They encourage things to be thrown in them, things we'd rather not think about or deal with. Not having a bag in the bin means no messy organic material (which should really all be going into the compost anyway) but it also means, when I empty it, that's one more time I think about my garbage and what it is composed of. I use chicken or cat food bags to ferry my garbage to the dump.

Do you recall that in the movie adaptation of *The Lorax*, the town of Thneedville is made entirely of plastic, down to the inflatable trees and the flowers? I'd focused an awful lot on food packaging in this year but, as my ill-fated Day of No Plastic amply demonstrated, plastic is not just a problem in the kitchen. It is literally everywhere in our lives: our televisions, cars, phones, clothes, bike seats, and picture frames, not to mention the mountains of it in commercial or industrial settings: hangers, shopping carts, computers, and cash registers . . . hospitals! Day care centers! Construction sites! I've obsessed for a year and written an entire book and yet we haven't even begun to talk about the horrors of plastic in things like synthetic turf: plastic grass playing fields that poison our children and the environment on a scale that is truly daunting.[1]

Heck, I used plastic to create *this book*—from the computer keyboard I typed on, to the spiral binding on the draft copies, to the ballpoint pen I took notes with. And don't forget that the final book you hold in your hands right now, like most modern books, incorporates plastic in both the binding and the cover! I certainly haven't. Although I'd hoped for low-plastic options for printing, there still is plastic in here to hold it all together, and this is my official apology to the universe for that. My hope is that in the process a greater good can be achieved. There is some plastic we need. But what we also need is a more complete comprehension of the problems we've created.

Every bit of plastic we don't buy is a tiny revolution against the status quo.

In our house these days "trash" consists of nonrecyclable plastics, which is to say RIC numbers 3–7 and unnumbered, virtually all of it food packaging, as well as "Health and Safety" items such as Band-Aids and dryer lint. And sometimes I really do have to break down and admit that no one in the world has a good use for a broken plastic coat hanger.

You could say going from ninety-six gallons to nine is a significant improvement, and it is. But this seems to me to be the limit of how far we can go with personal responsibility, and I want more. In the absence of the magical Plastic Fairy I've realized what we really need is the Legislation Honey Badger.

Through legislation, we can put the onus squarely on the producers of plastic to change their ways. If the pandemic has taught me anything, it is that people have the power to change quickly when the need arises. *We could eliminate unnecessary single-use plastic tomorrow*, and the environment, animals, and people everywhere would all be immeasurably better off for it.

We don't have to struggle through a year of no anything to get there either. All we really have to do is think differently (plastic is a hazardous substance, plastic is not our friend), and then decide what's next.

I feel the frustration of folks who want answers. Like, *now* answers. "Tell me what to do" answers. But when it comes to garbage and plastic and recycling, incontrovertible answers are in rather short supply. My advice, if people want advice, is to do the very best they can given everything they know and everything they've learned. And then call your political representatives and tell them we want a world where we are protected from the harmful effects of plastic.

If you want to dress up like a giraffe and play dead in front of Trader Joe's corporate headquarters to protest the fact that single-use plastics are killing us and the planet, like my friend Eileen? Go right ahead. For that you get extra credit.

We can't rely on half measures—such as recycled paper wrapped in plastic—and false solutions—like mailing our plastic away to be repurposed or buying PLA non-compostable "compostables." We have to go the source.

When it comes to plastic, the failure of personal responsibility is that we live in the world. Even if we become such amazing recyclers and bring-your-own-container-ers, we still live in a world that is running full-tilt in the other direction, all day long, every day. Even if we, personally, achieve Zero Waste Perfection Nirvana, it still does nothing about the enormous amount of plastic that is being used in our name, behind the scenes: the volumes of plastic wrap wound around grocery store pallets, the piles of wet wipes cleaning the public bathrooms we use, the Styrofoam packaging you never asked for that shows up on products you mail-ordered. For fear of chemical contamination you may never let plastic touch a single food in your home, or microwave a food in plastic, but can every restaurant you eat in say the same thing?

In an article about the declining age of puberty, author Sandra Steingraber puts it this way: "This idea that we, as parents should be scrutinizing labels and vetting birthday party bags—the idea that all of us in our homes should be acting as our own Environmental Protection Agencies and Departments of Interior—is just nuts. Even if we could read every label and scrutinize every product, our kids are in schools and running in and out of other people's homes where there are brominated flame retardants on the furniture and pesticides used in the backyard."[2]

So we're surrounded, and it's tempting to come out with our hands up. It's bad, yes. Worse than most people imagine. But that doesn't mean it's hopeless or that we should give up, quite the opposite. It means we have work to do. That's the part that no one wants to hear. But it's the truth. We've spent a hundred years, give or take, putting a system and a culture in place that relies on a material that is toxic in our everyday lives, and it is now catching up to us. We now have to dismantle that culture and rebuild it in another way.

Fortunately, there is some precedent for this.

Think of lead:

By 1980, uses for lead, which was known to be toxic since the days when Rome was built, had so expanded that Americans used nearly ten times the amount per person that even an ancient Roman did. Americans were also suffering from lead exposure on unprecedented levels. By the time leaded automobile gasoline was finally outlawed in the United States in 1986, it was estimated that lead-related heart disease was killing five thousand Americans per year and that between 1927 and 1987 about 68 million young children had "toxic exposures to lead from gasoline."[3] Toxic exposure can mean anything from kidney disease or cancer to developmental delays and reproductive disorders.

Today in the United States you can no longer add lead to paint or automotive fuel and you can't install water pipes made of it. But we still live with the legacy of lead everywhere in our air, our water, our bodies, and our environment because "lead does not break down over time. It does not vaporize, and it never disappears."[4] Sound like any other material we know?

In an article for *The Nation*, journalist Jamie Lincoln Kitman writes that "the leaded gas adventurers have profitably polluted the world on a grand scale and, in the process, have provided a model for the asbestos, tobacco, pesticide and nuclear power industries, and other twentieth-century corporate bad actors, for evading clear evidence that their products are harmful by hiding behind the mantle of scientific uncertainty."

The plastics industry should be on the above list of "corporate bad actors" too, although you could argue that in a way, it already is. Because of course the "leaded gas adventurers" who played fast and loose with the health and well-being of millions of people in using lead as an additive in gas, are in many cases the very same companies, or their descendants, who are emphatically ramping up plastics production, all the while pushing "better recycling," "personal responsibility," and "gee whiz, plastic sure *seems* safe!"

Same playbook. Same players.

But you know what they say: Fool me once, shame on you, fool me twice, now I'm just really pissed. For me the moral of this story is that we can change public health policy, even when powerful economic and political forces are at work, even when a material is so entrenched that it seems we're never going to be able to stop using it.

We did it with lead. We can do it with plastic.

The house is so quiet now. After all the back-and-forth, Greta and Steven returned once again to their apartment in Brooklyn, and Steven has become a bona fide YouTube star. Even as Greta and Steven start out on their journeys in the world, they take this project with them. One day Greta told me she saw a guy finishing a Red Bull who promptly dropped the can on the ground.

"I mean, come *on* dude!" she said, "There was a recycling bin, *literally* like thirteen feet away!" I loved her indignation.

Ilsa meanwhile, after a year of high school relating to the outside world through a screen, is in France as an exchange student. Perhaps it is even made all the sweeter for the contrast, all the more appreciated for the wait.

Of course, travel is another excellent example of activities that are not exactly zero waste friendly, and after the project ended, I'm sure Ilsa was delighted not to have to explain to her gracious French hosts why she can't throw away used Kleenex or empty snack packaging.

Steve still keeps his photography studio trash separate, and from what I can tell he still harbors what I consider to be an overfondness for paper towels. Yet he does talk about things differently. He wonders why film manufacturers can't go back to using spindles made of natural materials, instead of black plastic (once upon a time they used wood). He recalls the days not so long ago when film processing labs collected metal film canisters in large bins to be returned to Kodak. He makes a phone call to find out whether the backing on his 120 film is paper or extruded paper and plastic (of course it's extruded). He asks questions now that he never did before: *Why does it have to be this way? What did we do before?* One morning at breakfast he looked at me with not a little consternation and said, "You're giving me *environmental dreams*, Eve. I thought you should know that."

I'm not gonna lie: there is a tremendous relief in having an actual garbage can again. I feel guilty about the things that go into it, like each item represents a tiny failure, but I also realize that this is the hard-won knowledge we fought for over the course of the project. I'd rather send my plastic cheese wrapper to the landfill than delude myself there is some other wonderful place for it to go when there isn't. It's through delusions like this that impoverished nations around the world are ending up literally swimming in our garbage, and that has got to stop.

A side effect of the project is that I've found I've all but stopped shopping. Aside from groceries, these days I buy very few new things. I'm not going all Marie Kondo minimalist, mind you, because that will never, *ever* happen. I've just realized there are enough things in the world already, so when I do buy I make a very conscious effort to buy used. Whether it's clothes or furniture or items for the kitchen, you can get the most interesting stuff, often cheaper and better made, and without all the problematic packaging. It's also, I think, just more fun.

And despite the presence of an actual trash can in our house, you will not be surprised to hear that I'm still rather impressively stubborn. I'm still trying to find the person who wants my formidable collection of twist ties. I'm still just gonna keep right on trying to find a home for the shattered coffee saucer, the broken pieces of a zipper I replaced, the empty tube of lipstick. Maybe the answers will come to me in one of my highly detailed recycling dreams.

How do we want to live? What kind of people do we want to be? It occurred to me that if we try to find a silver lining in the horror of a pandemic it could be that it was forcing so many of us to stop running headlong through life, believing we don't have time for things. Life *is* time. If we are alive we have time, and no one else should be able to tell you how to spend it. What we, as a culture, need to do is stop ceding *control* of that time, those decisions about how we spend it, to someone or something else—our culture, our job, our technology, our expectations, or someone else's.

One day during the course of the year, when all the kids were still here, I asked Greta to bake some bread for lunch. At the time I marveled at how *un*-modern we were: she didn't use sugar, buy anything new, or make any garbage in the process. I thought to myself, today we've done the best we can do, and that's good enough.

Throughout this time I've learned that we can inhabit two seemingly contradictory worlds at the same time: first, the world where so much has gone horribly wrong and where there is still so, *so* much work to do, and second, the world where I am deeply, profoundly grateful for a family lunch at our table, with everyone here, and a still warm loaf of bread.

TOP TEN TRUE CONFESSIONS FROM A YEAR OF NO GARBAGE

Desperation makes you do strange things.

1. When we disinfected the desks at school, I apologized to the Clorox wipes before throwing them out. (Ilsa)
2. I have put the absorbent pads that come under raw chicken and steak (we have dubbed them: "meat maxi-pads") into the "Health and Safety" garbage. Because, Ew. (Greta)
3. I've flushed used staples down the toilet. (Eve)
4. I made my friend take a bacon wrapper home. (Greta)
5. I've donated ketchup packages to the food cupboard. (Eve)
6. I put an empty bag of potato chips back in the cupboard. Don't tell Greta's mom. (Steven).
7. I don't *always* say, "No receipt, please." First of all, it makes everyone hate you. Second of all, and this is weird, you *do* occasionally need receipts to prove you paid for the things you are removing from the store. *Apparently*. (Eve)
8. There were many things I was willing to do in the name of No Garbage. Washing Saran Wrap? Was not one of them. (Steve)
9. When people ask me what all this is about I reply: "It's this thing . . . garbage . . . can't have . . . year-long . . . NEVER MIND." (Ilsa)
10. So that piece of tinfoil with burned-on fish skin? That I couldn't manage to scrub *entirely* off, and then I tried to save for future recycling anyway?—Because how bad could that little teeny-tiny micron of fish *really* smell? It turns out the answer to that question is REALLY. *REALLY.* BAD. (Eve)

PRODUCTS THAT GET THE YEAR OF NO GARBAGE SEAL OF APPROVAL

···

EVERYDAY PRODUCTS

- 3B bags (reusable nylon produce bags)
- Alpine Provisions conditioner (in aluminum)
- Apiwraps beeswax wraps
- Baggu foldable nylon bags
- Blueland laundry tablets
- Brush with Bamboo toothbrushes
- Clean Planetware Heirloom Mayan Loofah Scrubber (kitchen sponge)
- Dr. Bronner's Pure-Castile Liquid Soap
- Good Juju Normal Hair Shampoo Bar
- Hey Humans deodorant
- Leaf razor
- Nespresso coffee capsules
- New Moon reusable menstrual pads
- Pumice Scouring Stick and Toilet Ring Eraser
- Pyrex
- RADIUS Pure Silk dental floss
- Sheets Laundry Club laundry sheets

- Thinx period panties
- Tiblue (reusable organic cotton produce bags)
- Tshu handmade hankies/hankie holders
- Unpaste Toothpaste Tablets
- Uproot Cleaner lint and pet-hair remover
- VAHDAM Classic Loose Tea Infuser
- Who Gives a Crap bamboo Toilet Paper

BIG-TICKET ITEMS

- Bio Bidet (bidet attachments)
- The Ecowasher (laundry system that eliminates detergent)
- The Vitamix Food Cycler (home composter)

RECOMMENDED VENDORS:

Yes, the most eco-friendly product is the one you don't buy. I encourage you to look in your own home for reusing and repurposing the things you already have before buying *any* product, no matter how eco-friendly its pedigree. But sometimes you really do need to buy something, so here are some good resources for when you do.

The Vermont Country Store
Vermontcountrystore.com
The Vermont Country Store is not what I would call an "environmental vendor" per se, but because they specialize in old-fashioned products that can be hard to find, they do carry some things that predate the plastic revolution, such as 100 percent cotton hankies, flour sack dish towels, aluminum drink cups, and all-glass food storage containers.

EarthHero
EarthHero.com
This is where I get toothpaste tabs, as well as the "heirloom Mayan loofah scrubbers made from giant Egyptian cucumbers." Which is *really* fun to say, by the way.

Life Without Plastic
LifeWithoutPlastic.com
Need beeswrap? Stainless steel food storage? I particularly like
that they don't carry silicone products.

Zero Waste Outlet
Zerowasteoutlet.com
Need deodorant that comes in cardboard, organic cotton bread
bags or laundry detergent strips? Zero Waste Outlet is fami-
ly-owned, and on their website you can read all about owners
Beth and Brian, who have a farm in rural Idaho.

MORE INFO:
FILMS AND BOOKS

WATCH ONLINE

The Plastic Atlas (2021)
A three-minute synopsis of the many, many problems created by plastic. Made by Heinrich Böell Foundation and Break Free From Plastic.

The Plastic Problem, a *PBS NewsHour* Documentary (2019)
The amount of plastic humans have created is equivalent to a billion elephants. This hour-long documentary finds it on the beaches of Easter Island and Costa Rica, in the depths of the Mariana Trench, and in every single fish in the Great Lakes. Notable for an interview with a slightly uncomfortable Unilever executive who vainly tries to argue that disposable plastic bags aren't "single-use."

"Plastic Wars," *Frontline* (2020)
Have efforts to solve the plastic problem actually made it worse? Yup. This hour-long documentary traces how industry strategically shifted the responsibility for plastic waste from industry to consumers, beginning as far back as the 1970s.

Return to Plastics: A Personal Journey Through Time (2019)
By writer and sociologist Dr. Rebecca Altman, this three-minute video describes the journey she and her father take to visit the former Union Carbide plastics manufacturing facility where he worked for a decade. I like that this provides a different, more personal vantage point from which to view the conversation about plastic.

FEATURE FILMS:

(NOTE: As of this writing all of the films listed below are still fairly hard to access. One way is to request to hold a screening, virtual or in person, for your library, environmental group, or classroom.)

Coca-Cola's Plastic Promises (2021)
Coca Cola only started using plastic soda bottles in 1978, and yet today it is the *number one polluter of single-use plastic* in the world, generating two hundred thousand plastic bottles per minute. This film documents the many, many promises Coke has made regarding plastic over the years, clearly never intending to be held accountable to them.

The Recycling Myth (2022)
This film by Why Plastic? not only pulls the veil back on plastic recycling in general, but uses investigative journalism to investigate behind the scenes of Terracycle.

The Story of Plastic (2019)
This is the film Judith Enck showed us as part of our Beyond Plastics class and it will change how you view your garbage *forever*. The scenes of American and European "recycling" strewn about the landscapes and waterways of places like the Philippines, Indonesia, and India. (Not to be confused with the animated short of the same name that came out in 2021, which is also excellent but only four minutes long.)

We the Guinea Pigs (2021)
Now that microplastics are being found in all of our bodies, what does this mean for our health? Chemicals from plastics are linked to

the rise in breast cancer, infertility, early puberty and ADHD, among other things. A scary but riveting short documentary.

BOOKS:

The Story of Stuff by Annie Leonard
When I started to wonder in earnest what was the deal with our wastefulness, this was the book I read first, and it is an excellent place to start. This pointed 2010 critique of consumerism is still deeply relevant today.

Garbology by Edward Humes
An authoritative and engaging guide to the world of our trash, where it ends up, and the fascinating things some people are doing with it, from making art to conducting archaeological digs in our own land-fills, to inventing effective ways to clean up ocean plastics.

Junkyard Planet by Adam Minter
Minter is an excellent guide to the world of what happens to all this stuff when we're done with it, from recycling and trash picking to junk management, from steel and plastic to old Christmas lights. This book puts human faces to the story of our junk, whether it's the guy in Indiana who runs the world's biggest recycling factory or the residents of Wen'an in China who melt and extrude secondhand plastics without safety equipment or shoes.

Eaarth by Bill McKibben
Required reading for anyone currently on the planet. Not to say this is pleasant reading; it's not. It's scary as all get-out, as McKibben expertly makes the case how thoroughly and completely we have screwed up our formerly beautiful and balanced earth, once and for all destroying any illusions we might have been clinging to that things might ever return to a pre-global warming "normal."

Having thoroughly depressed us for the first hundred pages, McKibben at last turns to what-this-means-and-what-we-can-do-about-it, and it's a harsh reality here as well. But not hopeless.

Plastic Free by Rebecca Prince-Ruiz
Can you imagine starting a personal challenge to go plastic-free for a month, and then ending up creating a global movement that one person out of every ten on the planet has participated in? The super-inspiring origin story of Plastic Free July.

The Day the World Stops Shopping by J. B. Mackinnon
How do we solve the dilemma of endless growth? MacKinnon tackles the problem with capitalism—and how it is destroying the planet while not making people noticeably happier. In *The Day the World Stops Shopping* he brings in a wide-range of topics from fast fashion, right-to-repair, planned obsolescence, and climate change, to light pollution, finally saving the whales, and how much is *really* enough. An extended thought experiment on how we got to our culture of "unrelenting busyness," and how we might go about fixing it now that we're here.

101 Ways to Go Zero Waste by Kathryn Kellogg
Want to reduce your personal waste footprint but don't know where to start? Start here. Although personal responsibility isn't the sum-total solution to our waste and plastic problems, that doesn't let us off the hook. This book is the definitive A to Z Guide for making those changes in your life both large and small, from how to make your own hairspray and lip-balm, to how to host a less wasteful party or holiday.

ACKNOWLEDGMENTS

··

Before we began the Year of No Garbage I asked my blog readers to guess what the third and final "Year of No . . ." would be and I promised "something really cool" to whoever guessed it correctly. Do you know who guessed it correctly? Angela Preuss. Angela, I am hoping that having your keen powers of insight recorded here for posterity counts as "something really cool," but if not, may I also offer you a lifetime supply of plastic milk tab jewelry?

Thank you to all of my blog readers, who are a constant source of inspiration: you are smart, you are funny, and you keep me on my toes. Every comment or question over the course of this year let me know I wasn't the only one who wanted answers to these questions, and was like a magic potion giving me the power to keep going.

I made a *lot* of calls during this project. There were folks who, either through a sense of apathy or a sense of real obfuscation sincerely did *not* try to help. For them I employ my Elizabethan-era insult generator: *Away you artless, beslubbering pigeon egg!*

On the other hand, I would very sincerely like to thank the many phone people who sincerely tried to help me along the way to the Answers. People like Alexandra from Trex and Andrea from UltraSource are out there doing their best to answer our questions, and we need to applaud the honestly of their effort, even when we don't always like the answers. We also need to be asking lots, *lots* more questions.

I must especially thank the dear friends who were kind enough to read the earliest version of this book and give me their thoughts: Christopher Byrne, Robin Kadet, Miles Kelly, Tom Rosenbauer, Andrea Sharb, Alex Woodward, Debbi Zukerman, and my environmental friend who prefers to remain anonymous. I am so, so lucky to have you all in my life as my dearest friends and unpaid labor.

Huge thanks to the folks at Beyond Plastics Virtual Group, my partners in activism; in particular Andrea Sharb, David Sayer, Eileen Ryan, Ashley Craig, and Rebekah Creshkoff. I am grateful to plastic for precisely one thing: giving me the opportunity to meet all of you. You inspire me.

Judith Enck, thank you for dedicating your life to telling the world about the horrors of plastic; your class changed my life. To everyone at Beyond Plastics "HQ," especially Megan Wolff and Alexis Goldsmith: thank you for answering my weird questions and helping me track down sources and statistics.

Deep appreciation to my agent Angela Miller. Without your belief in me and my bizarre projects I would never have become the crazy lady in print that I am today. I promise that someday I will probably maybe write a book that isn't a memoir. To my publicist Gail Parenteau, who is so good at her job she deserves a superhero cape. I am extremely grateful to my editor Lilly Golden at Skyhorse for her incredible insight and expertise, and also to copy editor Susan Barnett who exhibited extreme fortitude in the face of my overenthusiastic punctuation.

Thanks to my Mom and Dad for always loving me, no matter how much I wanted to be an artist or a writer. And to Dad for reminding me about the scene from *Airplane!*

Ginormous thanks to Steven He, who is one of the funniest and smartest fellows I know. It's hard to imagine someone being a better sport than you were about this whole endeavor. It has been delightful and inspiring watching your hardworking path to become legit *famous*. I can't wait to see what you do next.

Of course, there are no words to express the love I have for my family members Steve, Greta, and Ilsa, and their willingness to put up with not one, not two, but *three* year-long projects, all of which involved them upending their lives and routines, all in the name of "Gee, what do you think would happen if . . . ?" I could not have done any of it without your love and support. You are the people I want to be hermity with.

And thank you to Anne Corso, for trying to get me a glass. I promise to be more patient next time.

ENDNOTES

TEN STATISTICS TO BE HORRIFIED BY

1. Edward Humes, "Introduction: 102 Tons (Or: Becoming China's Trash Compactor)" in *Garbology* (New York: Penguin Group, 2012), 10.
2. Humes, *Garbology*, 5.
3. Ibid., 114.
4. Sarah Kaplan, "By 2050, There Will Be More Plastic Than Fish in the World's Oceans, Study Says," *Washington Post* (January 20, 2016), https://www.washingtonpost.com/news/morning-mix/wp/2016/01/20/by-2050-there-will-be-more-plastic-than-fish-in-the-worlds-oceans-study-says/
5. "The Role of Plastics in the Climate Crisis," The Climate Reality Project, August 19, 2020, https://www.climaterealityproject.org/blog/role-plastics-climate-crisis#:~:text=Research%20estimates%20that%20across%20its,greenhouse%20gases%20in%20the%20world.
6. Harald Franzen, "There are 8.3 Billion Tons of Plastic in the World," *DW* July 20, 2017, https://www.dw.com/en/there-are-83-billion-tons-of-plastic-in-the-world/a-39765670
7. "How Much Does the Moon Weigh?" Weight of Stuff (last accessed October 6, 2022) https://weightofstuff.com/how-much-does-the-moon-weigh/
8. "Global Plastic Waste Set to Almost Triple by 2060, Says OECD," Organization for Economic Co-operation and Development March 6, 2022, https://www.oecd.org/environment/global-plastic-waste-set-to-almost-triple-by-2060.htm

INTRODUCTION

1. Humes, *Garbology,* 5.
2. Ibid.
3. Humes, *Garbology*, 114.
4. Ibid., 159.
5. Deia Schlosberg, *The Story of Plastic* (2019, The Story of Stuff Project), feature-length documentary film.
6. Doyle Rice, "Oh, Yuck! You're Eating About a Credit Card's Worth of Plastic Every Week," *USA Today*, June 12, 2019, updated June 13, 2019), https://www.usatoday.com/story/news/nation/2019/06/12/plastic -youre-eating-credit-cards-worth-plastic-each-week/1437150001/
7. "Plastic and Human Health: A Lifecycle Approach to Plastic Pollution," *Center for International Environmental Law* (last accessed August 23, 2022, https://www.ciel.org/project-update/plastic-and -human-health-a-lifecycle-approach-to-plastic-pollution/#:~:text =Microplastics%20entering%20the%20human%20body,outcomes %20including%20cancer%2C%20cardiovascular%20diseases%2C
8. Rivka Galchen, "Complete Trash," *New Yorker,* March 9, 2020, 30.

CHAPTER 2: TRASH IS IN THE EYE OF THE BEHOLDER

1. "What Glass Can You Recycle?" Friends of Glass (last accessed October 8, 2022), https://www.friendsofglass.com/ecology/what-glass -can-you-recycle/
2. Merilin Vrachovska, "11 Types of Paper That Cannot Be Recycled," Almost Zero Waste (last accessed October 9, 2022), https://www.almostzero waste.com/non-recyclable-paper/
3. Siobhan Neela-Stock, "How to Recycle Amazon Packaging (Yes, All of It)," *Mashable,* July 10, 2022, https://mashable.com/article/how-to -recycle-amazon-packaging
4. Anne-Marie Bonneau, "Plastic-Free Glue and Homemade Paper Tape," *Zero Waste Chef,* October 7, 2020, https://zerowastechef.com/2020 /10/07/plastic-free-glue-wheat-paste/
5. Kathryn Kellogg, "How to Recycle Metal the Right Way!" *Going Zero Waste,* May 11, 2018, https://www.goingzerowaste.com/blog/how-to -recycle-correctly/
6. https://www.call2recycle.org/locator/
7. Lauren Murphy, "Beverage Container Showdown," *Earth 911,* October 14, 2020, https://earth911.com/living-well-being/recycled -beverage-containers/

8. "4 Tips for Reducing Your Junk Mail," Harvard University: Sustainability (last accessed, October 9, 2022), https://green.harvard .edu/tools-resources/how/4-tips-reducing-your-junk-mail

9. "Prescreened Credit and Insurance Offers," Federal Trade Commission website, May 2021, https://consumer.ftc.gov/articles/prescreened -credit-insurance-offers#other

CHAPTER 4: DID WE PICK AN AWESOME TIME TO DO THIS OR WHAT?

1. Ginny Hogan, "When an Eating Disorder Collides with Climate Activism," *Slate*, February 7, 2022, https://slate.com/technology/2022 /02/eating-disorders-climate-change-plastic.html?via=rss_socialflow _twitter

2. Heather A. Leslie et al., "Discovery and Quantification of Plastic Particle Pollution in Human Blood," *Environment International* 163, May 2022, https://www.sciencedirect.com/science/article/pii/S0160 412022001258

3. Ibid.

4. Antonio Ragusa et al., "Plasticenta: First Evidence of Microplastics in Human Placenta," *Environment International* 146, January 2021, https://pubmed.ncbi.nlm.nih.gov/33395930/

5. Antonio Ragusa et al., "Raman Microspectroscopy Detection and Characterization of Microplastics in Human Breastmilk," *Polymers* (14, no. 13 2700), June 30, 2022, https://www.mdpi.com/2073–4360/14/13 /2700

CHAPTER 5: SECRETS AND FRAUD: WHEN "GREEN" PLASTIC GOES HORRIBLY WRONG

1. Mimi Harrison, "Price-Tag Fasteners, Hanging on Since '64," *Washington Post*, July 10, 2005, https://www.washingtonpost.com /archive/business/2005/07/10/price-tag-fasteners-hanging-on-since -64/1535f5d5-d079-46d4-9f7d-a2b2688e2b08/

2. Joseph Allen, "Stop playing whack-a-mole with hazardous chemicals," *The Washington Post*, December 15, 2016, https://www.washingtonpost .com/opinions/stop-playing-whack-a-mole-with-hazardous-chemicals /2016/12/15/9a357090-bb36-11e6-91ee-1adddfe36cbe_story .html?utm_campaign=Chan-Twitter-General&utm_medium=Social &utm_source=Twitter&utm_term=.719959baa3ab

3. Ed Perratore, "Think Twice About Flushing Wet Wipes," *Consumer Reports*, December 27, 2013, https://www.consumerreports.org/cro/ news/2013/12/think-twice-about-flushing-wet-wipes/index.htm

4. Jeff Kart, "Study Results: Dispose of Your 'Flushable' Wipes in the Garbage," *Forbes*, April 10, 2019, https://www.forbes.com/sites/jeffkart

/2019/04/10/study-results-dispose-of-your-flushable-wipes-in-the -garbage/?sh=779b44e15833

5. Susan Parker Bodine, "COVID-19 Implications for EPA's Enforcement and Compliance Assurance Program," Environmental Protection Agency Memorandum, March 26, 2020, https://www.epa.gov/sites /default/files/2020–03/documents/oecamemooncovid19implications .pdf

6. James Rogers, "How Our Global Battle Against Coronavirus Could Help Us Fight Climate Change," *World Economic Forum*, April 21, 2020, https://www.weforum.org/agenda/2020/04/how-our-global-battle -against-coronavirus-could-help-us-fight-climate-change/

7. Reid Frazier, "This Is Exactly How Natural Gas Gets Turned into Plastics," *The Allegheny Front*, April 7, 2017, https://www.allegheny front.org/this-is-exactly-how-natural-gas-gets-turned-into-plastics/

8. Kathy Hall, "Petrochemicals 101: The In's and Out's of the Ene's," *OPIS*, January 28, 2019, https://blog.opisnet.com/petrochemicals-101

9. Karen McVeigh, "Nurdles: The Worst Toxic Waste You've Probably Never Heard Of," *The Guardian*, November 29, 2021, https://www.theguardian .com/environment/2021/nov/29/nurdles-plastic-pellets-environmental -ocean-spills-toxic-waste-not-classified-hazardous

10. Natalie Wolchover, "Why Doesn't Plastic Biodegrade?," *LiveScience*, March 2, 2011, https://www.livescience.com/33085-petroleum -derived-plastic-non-biodegradable.html

11. Jenny Davies MD MPH JD, "Plastic Packaging and Foodware: Threats to Human Health," (presentation, July 26, 2022), https://vimeo.com /734545516

12. Selina Tisler and Jan H. Christensen, "Non-target Screening for the Identification of Migrating Compounds From Reusable Plastic Bottles into Drinking Water," *Journal of Hazardous Materials* 429, 2022, https://www.sciencedirect.com/science/article/pii/S03043894 22001194?via%3Dihub

CHAPTER 6: "HAS MOM LOST IT?" NO ONE EXPECTS THE GARBAGE INQUISITION

1. Humes, *Garbology*, 5.

2. Yiming Peng et al., "Plastic Waste Release Caused by COVID-19 and Its Fate in the Global Ocean," *PNAS* 118, no. 47, November 8, 2021, https://www.pnas.org/doi/10.1073/pnas.2111530118#:~:- text=The%20recent%20COVID%2D19%20pandemic,tons%20 entering%20the%20global%20ocean.

3. "Fashion's Tiny Hidden Secret," UN Environment Programme, March 13, 2019, https://www.unep.org/news-and-stories/story/fashions -tiny-hidden-secret

4. Marina E. Franco, "Your Old T-Shirt May Be in a Chilean Desert," *Axios*, January 27, 2022, https://www.axios.com/2022/01/27/chile -atacama-desert-clothing-graveyard

5. Owen Mulhern, "The Ten Essential Fast Fashion Statistics," Earth.org, July 24, 2022, https://earth.org/fast-fashion-statistics/

6. Ibid.

7. Bernadette Banner, "Conclusion" in *Make Sew and Mend* (Massachusetts: Page Street Publishing, 2022), 189.

8. Gemma Alexander, "How Landfills Work," *Earth 911*, January 6, 2022, https://earth911.com/business-policy/how-landfills-work/

9. "Understanding Landfill Cover Materials," *Trashcans Unlimited*, May 23, 2018, https://trashcansunlimited.com/blog/understanding -landfill-cover-materials/

10. Peter Montague, et al., "Landfill Failures: The Buried Truth," Center for Health, Environment and Justice FactPack Pub 009, September 2016, 5, https://chej.org/wp-content/uploads/LandfillFailures20191.pdf

11. Ibid., 11.

12. Gemma Alexander, "How Waste Incineration Works," *Earth 911*, February 3, 2022, https://earth911.com/business-policy/how-incineration -works/#:~:text=Materials%20are%20burned%20at%20 extremely,generating%20steam%20through%20heat%20recovery.

13. Dr Wu Dong Qing and Dr Xu Wen Yu, "Feasibility Study for Converting IBA and Marine Clay to Useful Construction Materials," PowerPoint Presentation of Chemilink Zero Waste Engineering, June 27, 2013, http://www.chemilink.com/files/pdf/C-P-SWM04/C-P-SWM04-Presentation.pdf

14. Sanjeev Kumar et al., "Municipal Solid Waste Incineration Bottom Ash: A Competent Raw Material with New Possibilities," *Innovative Infrastructure Solutions*, 6, 201, July 17, 2021, https://link.springer .com/article/10.1007/s41062-021-00567-0

CHAPTER 7: IS TERRACYCLE FOR REAL?

1. Taylor Telford, "U.S. Plastics Recycling Rate Slumps Below 6 Percent, Analysis Finds," *Washington Post*, May 4, 2022, https://www.washington post.com/business/2022/05/04/us-plastics-recycling-rate-drop/

2. "How We Recycle: Zero Waste Box," TerraCycle YouTube video, May 21, 2020, https://www.youtube.com/watch?v=AIeJGEUgyrI&pbj reload=101

CHAPTER 8: TOOTH TABLETS AND PERIOD PANTIES: WE TRY ALL THE WEIRD ZERO WASTE PRODUCTS

1. Kirstin Linnenkoper, "Colgate Leads Toothpaste Tube Recycling Innovation," *Recycling International,* June 28, 2019, https://recycling international.com/plastics/colgate-leads-toothpaste-tube-recycling -innovation/26597/

2. "FDA Warns Consumers Not to Use 'Best Bentonite Clay,'" U.S. Food and Drug Administration, March 23, 2016, https://www.fda .gov/drugs/drug-safety-and-availability/fda-warns-consumers -not-use-best-bentonite-clay

3. "Who Invented the Toothbrush and When Was It Invented?" Library of Congress, Science Reference Section, November 19, 2019, https://www.loc.gov/everyday-mysteries/technology/item/who -invented-the-toothbrush-and-when-was-it-invented/

4. "Frequently Asked Questions About Plastic Recycling and Composting," United States Environmental Protection Agency (last updated September 20, 2021), https://www.epa.gov/trash-free-waters /frequently-asked-questions-about-plastic-recycling-and-composting #resp

5. "Some Dental Floss May Expose People to Harmful Chemicals," *Harvard Chan School of Public Health,* 2019 News (accessed August 23, 2022), https://www.hsph.harvard.edu/news/hsph-in-the-news/dental -floss-harmful-chemicals/

6. Nick Douglas, "Please Don't Use Cloth Toilet Paper," *Lifehacker,* July 24, 2020, https://lifehacker.com/please-don-t-use-cloth-toilet-paper -1823649458

7. "Made in China FAQ,"Who Gives a Crap (last accessed August 24, 2022), https://blog.whogivesacrap.org/home/made-in-china-faq#:~:- text=Our%20products%20are%20responsibly%20made,and%20 our%20planet%20through%20uncertainty.

8. Shelley Vinyard, "The Issue with Tissue 2.0," NRDC, June 24, 2020, https://www.nrdc.org/experts/shelley-vinyard/issue-tissue-20

9. Cara A. M. Bondi et al., "Human and Environmental Toxicity of Sodium Lauryl Sulfate (SLS): Evidence for Safe Use in Household Cleaning Products," National Library of Medicine (published online, November 17, 2015), https://www.ncbi.nlm.nih.gov/pmc/articles/PMC" 4651417/

10. Wan-Lan Chai et al., "Evaluation of the Biodegradability of Polyvinyl Alcohol/Starch Blends: A Methodological Comparison of Environmentally Friendly Materials," *Journal of Polymers and the Environment,* 17, 71, August 29, 2009, https://link.springer.com /article/10.1007/s10924-009-0123-1

11. "What is Silicone?" Life Without Plastic (last accessed August 24, 2022), https://lifewithoutplastic.com/silicone/
12. Tisler and Christensen, "Non-target Screening."
13. "Natural Sponge 10 Pack- Eco Friendly Kitchen Sponge for Sustainable Living, Biodegradable Plant Based Cleaning Dish Sponge," Amazon (Last accessed August 24, 2022), https://www.amazon.com/dp/B08FFGQ717
14. Elizabeth Shogren, "Why Dawn is the Bird Cleaner of Choice in Oil Spills," *NPR,* June 22, 2010, https://www.npr.org/2010/06/22/127999735/why-dawn-is-the-bird-cleaner-of-choice-in-oil-spills
15. "Can Reusable Grocery Bags Make You Sick, or Is That Just Baloney?" *Consumer Reports,* July 22, 2010, https://www.consumerreports.org/cro/news/2010/07/can-reusable-grocery-bags-make-you-sick-or-is-that-just-baloney/index.htm

CHAPTER 9: BUT DO I *HAVE* TO BUY A BIDET? BIG-TICKET ITEMS

1. Maxine von Eye, "Is PVOH a Wash-Out?" *isonomia*, March 31, 2021, https://www.isonomia.co.uk/is-pvoh-a-wash-out/
2. Bob Smith McCollum, "Mastering the Fundamentals of Ozone: Ozone Generation," *Water Quality Products*, October 12, 2020, https://www.wqpmag.com/water-disinfection/ozone-systems/article/10954859/mastering-the-fundamentals-of-ozone-ozone-generation
3. Darrell Weeter, "The Science of Ozone Laundry Systems", *Water Conditioning and Purification International Magazine*, August 15, 2017, https://wcponline.com/2017/08/15/science-ozone-laundry-systems/
4. Grant Gerlock, "To End Food Waste, Change Needs to Begin at Home," *NPR.* November 17, 2014, https://www.npr.org/sections/thesalt/2014/11/17/364172105/to-end-food-waste-change-needs-to-begin-at-home; Kathryn Kellogg, *101 Ways to Go Zero Waste* (New York, The Countryman Press, 2019), 60.

CHAPTER 10: SINGLE STREAM IS A LIE AND OTHER FUN RECYCLING FACTS

1. "Assessing the State of Food Grade Recycled Resin in Canada & the United States," *Environment and Climate Change Canada.* October 2021, 4. https://www.plasticsmarkets.org/jsfcontent/ECCC_Food_Grade_Report_Oct_2021_jsf_1.pdf
2. Clemence Budin et al., "Detection of High PBDD/Fs Levels and Dioxin-Like Activity in Toys Using a Combination of GC-HRMS, Rat-Based and Human-Based DR CALUX Reporter Gene Assays," *Chemosphere* 251, July 2020, https://www.sciencedirect.com/science/article/pii/S0045653520307724

3. Laura Parker, "Fast Facts About Plastic Pollution," *National Geographic,* December 20, 2018, https://www.nationalgeographic.com/science /article/plastics-facts-infographics-ocean-pollution

4. Davies MD MPH JD, "Plastic Packaging and Foodware."

5. Rebecca Altman, "How Bad Are Plastics, Really?" *The Atlantic,* January 3, 2022, https://www.theatlantic.com/science/archive/2022/01/plastic -history-climate-change/621033/

6. "The Real Truth About the U.S. Plastics Recycling Rate," *Beyond Plastics/The Last Beach Cleanup,* May 4, 2022, September 40, 2022 https: //static1.squarespace.com/static/5eda91260bbb7e7a4bf528d8/t/62b 2238152acae761414d698/1655841666913/The-Real-Truth-about -the-US-Plastic-Recycling-Rate-2021-Facts-and-Figures-_5-4-22.pdf

7. Plastics: Material-Specific Data, United States Environmental Protection Agency (last updated September 30, 2021), https://www.epa .gov/facts-and-figures-about-materials-waste-and-recycling/plastics -material-specific-data#:~:text=The%20recycling%20rate%20of%20 PET,was%2029.3%20percent%20in%202018.

8. Davies MD MPH JD, "Plastic Packaging and Foodware."

9. Cole Rosengren, "Some Facilities Stop Accepting Compostable Packaging as Contamination Debate Persists," *WasteDive,* March 8, 2019, https://www.wastedive.com/news/compostable-packaging-rexius -US-Composting-Council-Conference/550012/

10. "A New Industrial Revolution for Plastics," United States Department of Agriculture, August 2, 2021, https://www.usda.gov/media/blog /2018/09/19/new-industrial-revolution-plastics#:~:text=Diversion %20of%20organic%20wastes%20to,biosolids%2C%20and%20 bioplastics%2C%20etc.

11. You can visit the Carton Council Website at: https://www.recyclecartons .com/

12. "How2Recycle Recyclability Insights," *How2Recycle,* (April 23, 2020, last updated August 18, 2020), https://how2recycle.info/insights

13. Katherine Martinko, "Don't Believe the 'Store Drop-Off' Label When it Comes to Plastic Packaging," *Treehugger,* June 15, 2021, https: //www.treehugger.com/plastic-packaging-store-drop-off-label-5188913

14. "Understanding Food and Beverage Carton Recycling!" *Recycle Cartons,* YouTube video, November 14, 2019, https://www.youtube .com/watch?v=JaCLyGYQBvg&t=95s

15. "Fact Sheet: "Recycle By Mail Is a Major Climate Fail," *Beyond Plastics/ The Last Beach Cleanup,* June 28, 2021, https://static1.squarespace.com /static/5eda91260bbb7e7a4bf528d8/t/60d5fe84dce19678 0823fb8f/1624637061907/Recycling+by+Mail+is+a+Major +Climate+Fail_Fact+Sheet+_June+2021.pdf

16. "Plastic Free Foundation Impact Report 2020," *Plastic Free July*, 2020, https://www.plasticfreejuly.org/wp-content/uploads/2020/12/PFF -Impact-Report-2020-screen.pdf

17. Rebecca Prince-Ruiz and Joanna Atherfold Finn, "We're All in This Together" in *Plastic Free* (New York, Columbia University Press, 2020), 199–203.

18. Ibid., 199.

19. Heather Rogers, *Gone Tomorrow: The Hidden Life of Garbage* (New York, The New Press, 9/1/2006)

20. Humes, *Garbology*, 114–15.

21. Macmillan Dictionary, ed. Michael Rundell et al., https://www.macmill andictionary.com/us/dictionary/american/garbage-patch

22. Humes, *Garbology*, 115.

23. "Plastic Bag Found at the Bottom of the World's Deepest Ocean Trench," *National Geographic* (last accessed October 12, 2022) https://education .nationalgeographic.org/resource/plastic-bag-found-bottom-worlds -deepest-ocean-trench

24. Humes, *Garbology*, 131.

25. Ibid., 118.

26. Umair Irfan, "The Alarming Trend of Beached Whales Filled with Plastic, Explained," *Vox*, January 16, 2020, https://www.vox.com /2019/5/24/18635543/plastic-pollution-bags-whale-stomach-beached

27. "Reckoning with the U.S. Role in Global Ocean Plastic Waste," The National Academies of Sciences Engineering and Medicine report (2022), https://nap.nationalacademies.org/read/26132/chapter/1

28. "The New Plastics Economy: Rethinking the Future of Plastics," World Economic Forum report, January 2016, p.7. https://www3.weforum.org /docs/WEF_The_New_Plastics_Economy.pdf

29. Bianca Unger et al., "Large Amounts of Marine Debris Found in Sperm Whales Stranded Along the North Sea Coast in Early 2016," *Marine Pollution Bulletin* 112, issues 1–2, November 15, 2016, 134–41. https://www.sciencedirect.com/science/article/abs/pii/S0025326X16306592 ?via%3Dihub

30. "The New Coal: Plastics and Climate Change," *Beyond Plastics* report, October 2021, 4. p.4. https://static1.squarespace.com/static/5eda91260 bbb7e7a4bf528d8/t/616ef29221985319611a64e0/1634661022294 /REPORT_The_New-Coal_Plastics_and_Climate-Change_10-21-2021 .pdf

31. Wesley James et al., "Uneven Magnitude of Disparities in Cancer Risks from Air Toxics," *International Journal or Environmental Research and Public Health*, December 2012, https://www.ncbi.nlm.nih.gov/pmc /articles/PMC3546767/

32. Ibid.
33. "2014 NATA Summary of Results," United States Environmental Protection Agency (last accessed August 24, 2022), https://www.epa.gov /sites/default/files/2020–07/documents/nata_2014_summary _of_results.pdf
34. Tammy C. Barney, "You Only Have to Smell 'Cancer Alley' to Know How Toxic It Is," *Louisiana Illuminator*, February 10, 2021, https://lailluminator .com/2021/02/10/calling-louisianas-petrochemical-corridor-cancer -alley-cant-be-a-slam-when-its-true/
35. Harriet A. Washington, "Poisoned World: The Racial Gradient of Environmental Neurotoxins" in *A Terrible Thing to Waste* (New York, Little Brown Spark, 2019), 116.
36. Adam Minter, "Plastic Land" in *Junkyard Planet* (New York, Bloomsbury Publishing, 2013), 155.
37. Lourens J. J. Meijer et al., "More than 1,000 River Account for 80% of Global Riverine Plastic Emissions into the Ocean," *Science Advances*, April 30, 2021, https://www.science.org/doi/10.1126/sciadv.aaz5803
38. "Reckoning with the U.S. Role in Global Ocean Plastic Waste."
39. Prince-Ruiz and Finn, *Plastic Free*, 91.
40. Kevin Loria, "How to Eat Less Plastic," *Consumer Reports*, June 2020, 20.
41. "Plastic Ingestion by People Could Be Equating to a Credit Card a Week," University News—The University of Newcastle Australia, June 12, 2019, https://www.newcastle.edu.au/newsroom/featured/plastic -ingestion-by-people-could-be-equating-to-a-credit-card-a-week
42. Gea Oliveri Conti PhD et al., "Micro- and Nano-Plastics in Edible Fruit and Vegetables. The First Diet Risks Assessment for the General Population," *Environmental Research* 187, August 2020, https: //www.sciencedirect.com/science/article/pii/S0013935120305703
43. Laura Parker, "Microplastics Found in 90 Percent of Table Salt," *National Geographic*, October 17, 2018, https://www.nationalgeographic. com/environment/article/microplastics-found-90-percent-table -salt-sea-salt#:~:text=Now%2C%20new%20research%20shows%20 microplastics,Korea%20and%20Greenpeace%20East%20Asia.
44. Graham Readfearn, "WHO Launches Health Review After Microplastics Found in 90% of Bottled Water," *The Guardian*, March 14, 2018, https://www.theguardian.com/environment/2018/mar/15 /microplastics-found-in-more-than-90-of-bottled-water-study-says
45. Max Langridge, "Foods That Contain High Amounts of Microplastics," *DMARGE*, January 2, 2022, https://www.dmarge.com/what-foods -contain-microplastics

46. Davies MD MPH JD, "Plastic Packaging and Foodware."

47. Dennis Thompson, "Is There Plastic in Your Poop? New Study on Microplastics in Stool Raises Concerns," *CBS News*, October 23, 2018, https://www.cbsnews.com/news/plastic-in-poop-study-microplastics-in-stool-raises-concerns/

48. Ed Cara, "Microplastics Are Showing Up in Baby Poop," *Gizmodo*, September 23, 2021, https://gizmodo.com/microplastics-are-showing-up-in-baby-poop-1847734053

49. "Sealants," Mouth Healthy—American Dental Association (last accessed August 24, 2022, https://www.mouthhealthy.org/en/az-topics/s/sealants

50. Steve Allen et al., "Atmospheric Transport and Deposition of Microplastics in a Remote Mountain Catchment," *Nature Geoscience* 12, no. 5) May 1, 2019, https://pureportal.strath.ac.uk/en/publications/atmospheric-transport-and-deposition-of-microplastics-in-a-remote

51. Heather A. Leslie et al., "Discovery and Quantification of Plastic Particle Pollution in Human Blood," *Environment International* 163, May 2022, https://www.sciencedirect.com/science/article/pii/S0160412022001258

52. Ragusa, "Plasticenta: First Evidence of Microplastics."

53. Ragusa, "Raman Microspectroscopy Detection and Characterization of Microplastics."

54. Davies MD MPH JD, "Plastic Packaging and Foodware."

55. Nick Lavars, "Mouse Study Shows Microplastics Infiltrate Blood Brain Barrier," *New Atlas*, November 23, 2021, https://newatlas.com/environment/microplastics-blood-brain-barrier/#:~:text=%E2%80%9CThe%20study%20shows%20that%20microplastics,%2C%22%20says%20study%20author%20Dr.

56. Washington, *A Terrible Thing to Waste*, 9.

57. "Breast Cancer Facts and Figures," National Breast Cancer Coalition (last accessed August 24, 2022), https://www.stopbreastcancer.org/information-center/facts-figures/

58. Louise Kjeldsen, *We the Guinea Pigs* (2021, Why Plastic?), feature-length documentary film.

59. Elizabeth Weil, "Puberty Before Age 10: A New 'Normal'?" *New York Times Magazine*, March 30, 2012, https://www.nytimes.com/2012/04/01/magazine/puberty-before-age-10-a-new-normal.html?campaign_id=9&emc=edit_nn_20220818&instance_id=69609&nl=the-morning&regi_id=63572248&segment_id=101698&te=1&user_id=b04515aa36d46d7deb587aaa7967cb24

60. Maya Salam, "Sperm Count in Western Men Has Dropped Over 50 Percent Since 1973, Paper Finds," *New York Times*, August 16, 2017,

https://www.nytimes.com/2017/08/16/health/male-sperm-count
-problem.html

61. Bijal P. Trivedi, "The Everyday Chemicals That Might Be Leading Us to Our Extinction," *New York Times,* March 5, 2021, https://www.nytimes.com/2021/03/05/books/review/shanna-swan-count-down.html

62. Kjeldsen, *We the Guinea Pigs.*

63. Ibid.

64. Davies MD MPH JD, "Plastic Packaging and Foodware."

65. "The New Plastics Economy: Rethinking the Future."

66. "Global Plastic Production and Future Trends," GRID Arendal, (2018), https://www.grida.no/resources/6923

CHAPTER 11: ALL THE RIDICULOUS TERMS TRANSLATED

1. European Bioplastics (last accessed October 5, 2022), https://www.european-bioplastics.org/market/

2. "Bag Waste Reduction Law," New York State Department of Environmental Conservation (last accessed August 24, 2022), https://www.dec.ny.gov/chemical/50034.html

3. https://www.beyondplastics.org/epr (last accessed October 26, 2022).

4. Beth Gardiner, "Big Oil's Plan B is Already in the Pipeline: More Plastic," *Grist,* January 20, 2020, https://grist.org/climate/big-oils-plan-b-is-already-in-the-pipeline-more-plastic/

5. Isabelle Gerretsen, "Why 'Bio' and 'Green' Don't Mean What You Think," *BBC Future,* March 31, 2022, https://www.bbc.com/future/article/20220330-why-bio-and-green-dont-mean-what-you-think

6. "Report Shows a Third of Consumers Prefer Sustainable Brands," Unilever, April 1, 2017, https://www.unilever.com/news/press-and-media/press-releases/2017/report-shows-a-third-of-consumers-prefer-sustainable-brands/

7. Karen McVeigh, "Nurdles."

CHAPTER 12: IS LIFE WITHOUT PLASTIC EVEN POSSIBLE?

1. You can watch the video I made of this experience on my website here: https://eveschaub.com/2020/12/15/a-day-of-no-plastic/

2. This *Yankee* magazine quote appears on the back cover of my paperback copy of *The Good Life,* which is a combination of two of their previous books, *Living the Good Life* (1954) and *Continuing the Good Life* (1979), published in 1989 with a new introduction by Helen Nearing.

CHAPTER 13: BREAKING UP WITH GARBAGE

1. You can read the filing of the complaint here: http://climateca-sechart.com/climate-change-litigation/wp-content/uploads/sites/16/case-documents/2021/20210304_docket-RG21090702_complaint.pdf, and you can read the Settlement Agreement here: https://www.lastbeachcleanup.org/_files/ugd/dba7d7_ac79b633b9604180b92a035e4d2fdd31.pdf

2. Somini Sengupta, "How Recycling Got So Baffling," *New York Times,* April 22, 2022, https://www.nytimes.com/2022/04/22/climate/plastic-recycling-climate.html

3. Andrew Marantz, "Not Dark Yet: The Sunrise Movement Wants to Revolutionize Climate Politics," *New Yorker,* March 7, 2022, 23–24.

4. The Global Commitment, Ellen MacArthur Foundation (last accessed August 24, 2022), https://ellenmacarthurfoundation.org/global-commitment/overview

5. Sharon Lerner, "Bottled Water Giant Bluetriton Admits Claim of Recycling and Sustainability are 'Puffery,'" *The Intercept,* April 26, 2022, https://theintercept.com/2022/04/26/plastic-recycling-bottled-water-poland-spring/

6. Molly Taft, "Bill Nye, the Sellout Guy," *Gizmodo,* April 7, 2022, https://gizmodo.com/bill-nye-sells-out-shills-for-coca-cola-on-plastic-bot-1848763404

7. Kira Schacht, "European Food Companies Break Their Plastics Promises," *DW,* September 8, 2022, https://www.dw.com/en/european-food-companies-break-their-plastics-promises/a-62622509?utm_source=ActiveCampaign&utm_medium=email&utm_content=Plastic+Pollution%3A&utm_campaign=Plastic+Pollution+Email

8. Katharina Kaiser et al., "Recycling of Polymer-Based Multilayer Packaging: A Review," *Recycling,* December 22, 2017, https://www.mdpi.com/2313-4321/3/1/1/htm

9. Yes, I am going to cite the Star Trek Replicator Wikipedia page right now: https://en.wikipedia.org/wiki/Replicator_(Star_Trek)#:~:text=In%20Star%20Trek%20a%20replicator,larger%20non%2Dfood%20items%20appear.

10. James R. Hagerty, "Free Stuff is All Over Craigslist and Facebook, and It's Getting Weirder," *Wall Street Journal,* February 10, 2021, https://www.wsj.com/articles/free-stuff-is-all-over-craigslist-and-facebook-and-its-getting-weirder-11612974910

11. "8 in 10 American Voters Support National Action to Reduce Single Use Plastic," Oceana Press Release, February 10, 2022, https://usa

.oceana.org/press-releases/8-in-10-american-voters-support-national
-action-to-reduce-single-use-plastic/

12. Emma Newburger, "Canada is Banning Single-Use Plastics, Including
Grocery Bags and Straws," CNBC, June 21, 2022, https://www.cnbc
.com/2022/06/21/canada-is-banning-single-use-plastics-by-the
-end-of-the-year-.html#:~:text=June%2020%2C%202022.&text
=Canada%20is%20banning%20the%20manufacture%20and%20
import%20of%20single%2Duse,waste%20and%20address%20
climate%20change.

13. Angelique Chrisafis, "That's a Wrap: French Plastic Packaging Ban for
Fruits and Veg Begins," *The Guardian*, December 31, 2021, https://www
.theguardian.com/world/2021/dec/31/thats-a-wrap-french-plastic
-packaging-ban-for-fruit-and-veg-begins

14. Axelle Parriaux, "Do Single-Use Plastic Bans Work?" *BBC Future,*
July 12, 2022, https://www.bbc.com/future/article/20220711-do-single
-use-plastic-bans-work

EPILOGUE

1. For more information visit https://www.safehealthyplayingfields.org/
2. Weil, "Puberty Before Age 10."
3. Jamie Lincoln Kitman, "The Secret History of Lead," *The Nation,*
March 20, 2000, https://www.thenation.com/article/archive/secret
-history-lead/
4. Ibid.

INDEX

ABOUT THE AUTHOR

E ve O. Schaub is an internationally published author and humorist who enjoys performing experiments on her family so that she can write about it. She is the author of *Year of No Sugar* (2014) and *Year of No Clutter* (2017). She has been featured on *The Dr. Oz Show* and *Fox & Friends* and in *USA Today* and *The Huffington Post*. Her essay "Our Year of No Sugar: One Family's Grand Adventure" for *Everyday Health* has been viewed over a million times. Her books have been translated into Chinese, Hebrew, and Spanish, and her writing has additionally appeared in *Hyperallergic*, *Bustle*, *The Belladonna Comedy*, *Little Old Lady Comedy*, and *Vermont Life*.

When she is not torturing her family with bizarre, year-long projects, she collaborates with her husband under the name EveNSteve creating monumental artworks and short films.

She holds a BA and BFA from Cornell University and an MFA from the Rochester Institute of Technology.

Eve's life goal is to never to have to jump out of a moving airplane or perform neurosurgery. So far so good. Her favorite word is antidisestablishmentarianism.

www.eveschaub.com
@eveschaub